Dead on a High Hill

Dead on a High Hill

Essays on War, Literature and Living, 2002–2012

W. D. Ehrhart

McFarland & Company, Inc., Publishers
Jefferson, North Carolina, and London

LIBRARY OF CONGRESS CATALOGUING-IN-PUBLICATION DATA

Ehrhart, W. D. (William Daniel), 1948–
    Dead on a high hill : essays on war, literature and living,
2002–2012 / W. D. Ehrhart.
        p.   cm.
    Includes bibliographical references and index.

    ISBN 978-0-7864-7039-6
    softcover : acid free paper ∞

    1. Ehrhart, W. D. (William Daniel), 1948– 2. Poets,
American — 21st century — Biography.   3. Vietnam War,
1961–1975 — Veterans — Biography.   4. United States —
Civilization — 21st century.   I. Title.
PS3555.H67Z46 2012
811'.54 — dc23
[B]   2012015218

BRITISH LIBRARY CATALOGUING DATA ARE AVAILABLE

Front cover photograph: Sgt. Herbert Ohio of Hilo, T.H.,
views the remains of Communist defenders of Hill 268, taken
by 5RCT in their advance on Waegwan, September 21, 1950
(National Archives–photo #FEC-50-9327)

Manufactured in the United States of America

McFarland & Company, Inc., Publishers
  Box 611, Jefferson, North Carolina 28640
    www.mcfarlandpub.com

For Anne and for Leela
forever and always

Contents

Acknowledgments ix

Preface 1

——————— THE ESSAYS ———————

The World Is Watching 8

Batter My Heart with the Liquor Store: or, Teaching Poetry to
    Teenagers 16

Hell's Music: A Neglected Poem from a Neglected War 32

The Power to Declare 40

James Magner, Jr., William Meredith and Reg Saner: Reluctant
    Poets of the Korean War 42

What's the Point of Poetry? 67

Kaleidoscope 70

Carrying the Ghost of Ray Catina 73

Good Fences Make Good Neighbors: A Brief History of National
    Myopia 75

What the Fuss Is All About 80

"I Have to Go Now. Bye!" A Remembrance of Gloria Emerson 83

Concerning Memorial Day 87

"Knock Their Jocks Off, Boys!" 89

The Value of Your Name 93

Words for John Balaban 98

Good Wars, Bad Wars, Forgotten Wars and Poetry 106

"They Want Enough Rice": Reflections on the Late American
War in Vietnam 112

Samuel Exler: The Poet as Historian 125

One, Two, Many Vietnams? 131

The Origins of Passion 133

The Pity of War Poetry 137

"That Damned Bad": Fragments from the Life of Robert
James Elliott 139

Con Thien and Dancin' Jack 143

Dead on a High Hill: Poetry from the Korean War 147

Ken and Bill's Excellent Adventure 163

Military History of W. D. Ehrhart   187

About the Author   189

Index   191

Acknowledgments

Some of these essays first appeared in the following publications:
"The World Is Watching," *Swarthmore College Bulletin*, v.C, #2, 2002;
"*Hell's Music*: A Neglected Poem from a Neglected War," *Proceedings of the Center for the Study of the Korean War*, v.2, #1, 2002; "The Power to Declare," *Seattle Post-Intelligencer*, February 11, 2003; "James Magner, Jr., William Meredith & Reg Saner: Reluctant Poets of the Korean War," *Cycnos*, v.21, #2, 2004; "What's the Point of Poetry?" *VVAW Veteran*, v.34, #1, 2004; "Carrying the Ghost of Ray Catina," *War, Literature & the Arts*, v.16, 2004; "I Have to Go Now. Bye!" *War, Literature & the Arts*, v.18, 2006; "Concerning Memorial Day," *Philadelphia Inquirer*, May 24, 2007; "Knock Their Jocks Off, Boys!" *Swarthmore College Bulletin*, v.CV, #3, 2007; "Words for John Balaban," *War, Literature & the Arts*, v.20, 2008; "Sam Exler: The Poet As Historian," *War, Literature & the Arts*, v.21, 2009; "One, Two, Many Vietnams?" *New Hampshire Gazette*, January 1, 2010; "The Pity of War Poetry," *War, Literature & the Arts*, v.24, 2012; "Dead on a High Hill," *Revisiting 20th Century Wars— Neue Lesarten von Kriegen des 20 Jahrhunderts*, Stuttgart: Ibidem-Vertag, 2012.

"Con Thien & Dancin' Jack" is forthcoming in *We Gotta Get Outta This Place: Music and the Experience of Vietnam Veterans*, Doug Bradley & Craig Werner, eds.

Versions of "Ken & Bill's Excellent Adventure" have been published in the *New Hampshire Gazette* (July 15, 2011), the Veterans for Peace National Newsletter (Fall 2011), the *VVAW Veteran* (v.41, #2, Fall 2011), *Swarthmore College Bulletin* (v.CVIX, # 2, 2011), and *The Haverford School Today* (Fall 2011).

Mac Hammond's "The Liquor Store" is reprinted from *Cold Turkey*, Swallow Press, 1969, by permission of Katka Hammond.

"I Know a Man" is reprinted from *The Collected Poems of Robert Creeley, 1945–1975*, © 1982 by the Regents of the University of California, published by the University of California Press.

Lisa Coffman's "Dog Days" is reprinted from her book *Likely*, Kent State University Press, 1996, and appears by permission of the author and publisher.

"For Anne, Approaching Thirty-five," "Imagine," and "The Origins of Passion" are reprinted from *Beautiful Wreckage*, Adastra Press, 1999, with permission. "What the Fuss Is All About" is reprinted from *The Bodies Beneath the Table*, Adastra Press, 2010, with permission.

Preface

Dead on a High Hill is the sixth book I've published with Robert Franklin's McFarland & Company, Inc., over a span of nearly thirty years. Back in the early 1980s, after I'd spent several frustrating years receiving rejections from publisher after publisher for my Vietnam War memoir, I heard about McFarland — then a fairly new venture — through Merritt Clifton, at the time editor and publisher of the small press journal *Samisdat*. After reading the manuscript, Robbie Franklin bravely offered me a contract for *Vietnam-Perkasie: A Combat Marine Memoir*, and the book was published in 1983. Other editions have since been published by Zebra Books, Orbis, and the University of Massachusetts Press, all under license to McFarland, and the book has been in print continuously since its original publication. My gratitude to McFarland and Robbie Franklin is immeasurable. It's why I keep coming back. Few writers are so lucky to have so loyal a publisher, and I'm acutely aware of just how fortunate I am.[1]

Much of what I've published with McFarland has revolved around my encounter with the Vietnam War, including *Going Back: An Ex-Marine Returns to Vietnam* and *Passing Time: A Vietnam Veteran Against the War*. Even my first essay collection, *In the Shadow of Vietnam*, takes both its title and its tone from the Vietnam War; of its twenty-three essays, eighteen deal directly with the war or its continuing consequences, and most of the others are at least colored by that war.

Certainly the Vietnam War and my encounter with it profoundly altered my life and has influenced me ever since. As I wrote in the preface to my second essay collection, *The Madness of It All*, "That experience has haunted my days. It has troubled my nights. It has shaped my identity and colored the way I see the world and everything in it."

But that is not the whole story. In college, post–Vietnam War, in addition to being a varsity swimmer, I earned a Four-Year Award from the Women's Physical Athletic Department for participating in water ballet. How many

ex–Marine combat veterans can lay claim to that? I published my first book
of poetry when I was 25, and have published multiple collections of poetry
since. How many ex–Marine combat veterans can lay claim to that? (Okay,
Gerald McCarthy can, but not many others.) I've descended Smith Playground's giant sliding board in Philadelphia's Fairmount Park with a dozen
shrieking, laughing 3- and 4-year-olds joyfully clinging to me for dear life.
How many ex–Marine combat veterans can lay claim to that?

More importantly, I've been married for 30 years, my first and only marriage. Anne and I have raised a wonderful daughter, now 24 and an honors
college graduate who has never stopped talking to me, even through those
awkward teen years, and who has been singing with her mother in one per-
forming group or another since she was five, again even through those awkward
teen years. I've voted in every election — primary, general, and special — since
the day I turned 21 (the voting age in those days), lived in the same house for
26 years, never been arrested, and show up for jury duty every time I'm sum-
moned. I have been in and out of classrooms for much of the past 35 years,
and for the past ten years I've taught full-time history and English at the Haverford School in suburban Philadelphia, where I also coach winter track and

**Anne and me congratulating our daughter Leela on her graduation from high
school, 2005 (photograph by Kim Fedchak).**

sponsor the student arts and literature magazine, and where the Class of 2011 honored me with the 2010 Rafael Laserna Outstanding Teacher Award. The essays I've written over the past 35 years, collected in *In the Shadow of Vietnam*, *The Madness of It All*, and in the present work, reflect the depth and breadth of my life.

Of the forty-three essays in the second collection, only fourteen deal directly with the Vietnam War. And that collection, written between 1991 and 2002, also includes essays on Delaware River tugboats and drawbridges, the Internal Revenue Service, the addiction of tobacco, public dishonesty, junk mail, my struggles with technology, growing up in Small Town USA, the American judicial system, doctors and medical care in America, and presidential isolation.

About the time *The Madness of It All* was going to press in 2002, I was offered the opportunity to teach full-time by the headmaster of the Haverford School, Dr. Joe Cox (col., US Army, ret.), who had taught my writing at the United States Military Academy at West Point in the 1990s. I hadn't had a full-time job since January 1984, but my wife had recently been informed that she was going to be laid off from her job of two decades, and it had been her job that had allowed me to avoid regular employment for almost that long. With some reluctance, on the assumption that not many jobs were likely to present themselves unsolicited to a 53-year-old with a work history as spotty as mine, I accepted the offer.

Just as I am grateful to Robbie Franklin for publishing me when no one else would, I am grateful to Joe Cox for realizing something about me that I did not understand about myself. I had taught off and on since my late 20s (more off than on), but had not even considered returning to full-time teaching in a decade or more before Joe offered me the position at Haverford. These past ten years have been the happiest and most rewarding of my life, and I hope to continue teaching for as long as my health and abilities allow it. I don't know what else I could do that would be more fun.

A number of the essays in this collection reflect my new (or perhaps more accurately: renewed) career as a teacher. Three times, a senior class has invited me to be one of their speakers at the Senior Dinner the night before graduation, and those three talks are included here under the titles of "Kaleidoscope," "What the Fuss Is All About," and "The Origins of Passion." At the outset of my Haverford School career, I was invited to give a talk at a conference of high school English teachers, which I titled "Batter My Heart with the Liquor Store" in honor of John Donne and Mac Hammond (two more different poets you are not likely to find if you turn the universe upside down). "The Value of Your Name" is a talk I gave one year at the Haverford School's Honor Assembly.

Also reflected in many of these essays is my gradual transformation from poet and writer to historian and scholar. My doctorate in American poetry of the Korean War, which I earned at the age of 52 from the University of Wales at Swansea, UK (a serendipitous consequence of a fellowship I held in the university's American Studies Department for five years beginning in 1997), is a blend of history and literature, two disciplines I have never been able to separate nor have had any desire to.[2]

So you will find here "They Want Enough Rice," my talk to high school history teachers interested in teaching the Vietnam War, along with "Good Fences Make Good Neighbors," addressed more broadly to history majors at an undergraduate conference. But you will also find "Good Wars, Bad Wars & Forgotten Wars," which looks at overlapping themes in American poetry from three very different wars, along with other essays one would consider more the domain of literature than of history, including essays about the poets John Balaban, Jan Barry, and Sam Exler. "*Hell's Music*," "Reluctant Poets," and "Dead on a High Hill" all reflect my interest in the literature of the Korean War. Sometimes it's literature, sometimes it's history, usually it's both. The requirement to choose is artificially imposed, and seldom beneficial.

I have also included several pieces in tribute to people who were enormously influential in my life: "I Have to Go Now. Bye!" written for National Book Award–winning journalist Gloria Emerson, whose death was noted in the *New York Times* and just about every other major news outlet; "Knock Their Jocks Off, Boys!" written for James J. McAdoo, Jr., whose death was hardly noticed by anyone except the generations of young men who'd been his swimmers over the years; "The Pity of War Poetry," written for Wilfred Owen, who died thirty years before I was born. "The World Is Watching," concerns two of the most fascinating people I have ever known, and living proof that individuals can truly make a difference in this world; my admiration for them is boundless.

All of this notwithstanding, the Vietnam War remains a central fact of my life. Essays you will find here, like "The Power to Declare," "Concerning Memorial Day," and "One, Two, Many Vietnams?" make it clear that the Vietnam War is never far away from my consciousness, especially because we as a people and a nation seem to have learned so little of value from that disaster.

The final essay, however, should make it clear how very far I have traveled since I first enlisted in the U.S. Marine Corps in April 1966 at the age of 17. How very much I have grown and changed since I first wrote and published *Vietnam-Perkasie* in the early 1980s. I don't know how much more I have left to say, or how many more years I have left to get it said. Teaching high school fulltime, especially at my age, is more than a fulltime job that often directly conflicts with writing while in many ways is just as rewarding as putting pen to paper.

But I wrote most of these essays after I returned to the classroom, so who knows what I might accumulate in the next decade (which seems to be the interval for these essay collections)? Meanwhile, if "Ken & Bill's Excellent Adventure" is my last word on the Vietnam War, even if I say so myself, it's a pretty good conclusion to a lifetime of struggling to come to terms with the consequences of the choices I made when I was very young. *Vietnam-Perkasie* ends with me drunk and passed out in the shower in a Marine barracks in North Carolina. "Ken & Bill's Excellent Adventure" ends with ... well, why don't you read it and see for yourself?

Notes

1. I've been equally blessed with my poetry, having had the support of Merritt Clifton early in my career, and for the past thirty years that of Gary Metras at Adastra Press.

2. Incidentally, though a lot of people, upon hearing the topic of my dissertation, quietly pity me for being unable to get away from war, in fact working with the Korean War was like being on vacation: I had no axe to grind, no memories to distract me, no demons to haunt me. I had no dog in that fight. I was not yet five years old when it ended. I have only a single memory of the Korean War — of my older brothers fighting "Commies" with their playmates in our back yard — and that memory may well post-date the war itself.

THE ESSAYS

The World Is Watching

When Henry David Thoreau wrote that most people live lives of quiet desperation, he clearly did not have in mind Bill Weber and Amy Vedder. In the normal course of their professional working lives, one or the other or both of them have been detained by Idi Amin on suspicion of being counterrevolutionary mercenaries; hiked through unfamiliar montane rain forest while suffering from malaria-induced hallucinations; climbed trees to escape Africa's most dangerous animal, the cape buffalo; had their house cut completely in half by a falling Hagenia tree; gone one on one with a 400-pound silverback gorilla; scaled a rugged 12,000-foot mountain while four months pregnant and without climbing gear; assisted in the murder investigation of a world-renowned animal behavioralist; had a $1,000 bounty put on one's head; and set a world record by counting 353 *Colobus angolensis ruwenzorii* monkeys in a single group.

Ok, some of those experiences could be classified as desperate. But "quiet"? Not hardly. And this is only the short list. Even a partial accounting of the couple's adventures over the years would fill a book. In fact, it has filled *In the Kingdom of Gorillas: Fragile Species in a Dangerous Land* (Simon & Schuster, 2001; Touchstone, 2002), co-authored by Weber and Vedder.

The couple, who met and married at Swarthmore College, joined the Peace Corps in 1973, spent two years teaching in what was then Zaire (now the Congo), and fell in love with Africa. Even before their Peace Corps days ended, they knew they wanted to come back. Within a few years, they found their way to Rwanda and the mountain gorillas of the Parc National des Volcans.

Vedder and Weber cover all of this in the book: how they came to work with the famed Dian Fossey and discovered a profoundly disturbed woman who had already outlived her usefulness to the gorillas she loved, how they struggled to save the rapidly dwindling mountain gorilla population in the face of overwhelming odds, and how they watched a country they loved get

Dr. Amy Vedder in Rwanda with a young gorilla she and husband Dr. Bill Weber
rescued from poachers. Despite constant care, the gorilla died of wounds suffered
in the poachers' trap (courtesy Amy Vedder and Bill Weber).

torn apart by civil war and the most intense
genocide of a genocidal century.

It makes for something more than
fascinating reading. Awesome reading is
more like it, made all the more so by their
understated writing. Much about Weber
and Vedder must be found between the
lines because the couple is self-deprecatory
to a fault: Mostly you are left to infer their
physical courage in the face of constant
challenges from both the natural and the
human world; their moral courage in the
face of constant challenges from Rwandan,

Rwandan mountain gorilla named Quince.
Amy and Bill learned to recognize individual gorillas by the pattern of ridges and lines
above their nostrils (courtesy Amy Vedder
and Bill Weber).

US, World Bank, and other officials and fellow conservationists; their single-minded determination to save Rwanda's mountain gorillas no matter what — even if it meant, as it often did, keeping their mouths shut in the face of provocation, obfuscation, and stupidity.

"We had heard that Fossey was difficult," says Weber, "but we decided we were going to go [to Karisoke, Fossey's research center], come hell or high water. We had no idea how high the water would get."

"But the gorillas were amazing," says Vedder, explaining why they stuck it out. "You look into their eyes, and there's a thinking being in there. They couldn't be left alone. They were not going to survive."

"Fossey had won the global battle," Weber adds, "but she was incapable of fighting the local battle. There was no one to do it but us."

"We saw we could make a difference," Vedder says, "And to walk away from that — we just couldn't."

During their first 18 months in Rwanda, Vedder spent much of her time with a single gorilla family, sitting among them day after day in the rain and the cold at 10,000 feet, watching what they ate, studying not just their behavior but their nutritional needs and habitat use patterns. Meanwhile, realizing

Amy and Bill spent long hours over many years in close proximity to the gorillas, gaining their trust to the point of being able to take naps in their midst, as Amy is doing here (courtesy Amy Vedder and Bill Weber).

that "you couldn't save the wildlife without addressing people's needs as well," Weber concentrated on the people side of the equation. "Here were impoverished local people," he says, "who were being told to stay out of their own parks."

Rwanda is the most densely populated country in Africa, and most people depend on farming for a living. Much of the Parc National des Volcans had already been lost to farming in the decade before the couple's arrival in 1978. Weber set out to convince Rwandans that "Rwandan needs couldn't be addressed by destroying the park" but would be better served by turning it into a tourist destination.

Thus was born the Mountain Gorilla Project (MGP), which by 1989 was attracting 7,000 tourists a year willing to pay $200 each to spend an hour with the gorillas as well as providing employment to local Rwandans hired as park rangers and guides, drastically reducing poaching and creating a great deal of indirect spending within Rwanda. It's what has come to be called eco-tourism, though there was no such name for it then. When the concept was finally developed, it drew heavily on Weber and Vedder's pioneering work.

The program has been so successful that the gorilla population is now up to about 360 animals from a low of 260 twenty years ago. Even the terrible civil war did not destroy the program; though it languished for nearly a decade, tourists in the thousands are back again.

Long before the civil war, however, Vedder and Weber had turned to other projects. "I think people find it very hard to understand how we could move on from gorillas," says Vedder. We *were* very attached to them. But MGP was an immediate success. And we felt we were leaving the project in good hands. And finally, there were such big challenges in other areas. The more we learned about the gorillas, the more we realized we had to leave them to save them."

Weber says, "Every moment you spend with the animals, you're not spending with the director of parks. To save the animals, you must deal with the forces that threaten them."

Through the 1980s, the couple worked on a variety of projects in Rwanda while earning doctorates from the University of Wisconsin and raising their sons Noah and Ethan. By 1990, they were both working for the Wildlife Conservation Society (WCS), which, under its old name of the New York Zoological Society, had funded their initial research on mountain gorillas, Weber as director of WCS's Africa programs, Vedder as Biodiversity Program coordinator. When Weber became director of the North America Program in 1993, Vedder took over as director of the Africa Program.

In fact, Weber created the North America Program. "I was very content

Amy crossing a bamboo and vine bridge in Zaire in the early 1980s with younger son Ethan perched on her shoulders (courtesy Amy Vedder and Bill Weber).

to be running the Africa programs," says Weber, "but meanwhile, I'm reading about spotted owls and wolves here in the United States. It seemed odd to me that we're asking the world's poorest people to live with tigers and elephants, but we won't live with wolves. We're asking other countries not to log while we knock down our own forests. I thought we should hold ourselves to the same standards we expect of others. We could be setting a better example for the world.

"This [current Bush] administration is particularly bad," he continues. "They are so in bed with the vested interests, especially oil and energy. They're sticking oil rigs all over the Rockies."

"Bush has lifted the moratorium on building logging roads in our national forests," adds Vedder.

Weber is especially contemptuous of the proposal to drill for oil in the Alaskan National Wildlife Refuge (ANWR). He describes a 10-day rafting trip he recently took with son Noah through ANWR, concluding, "And then to imagine oil rigs there. How do you tell Bolivia and Ecuador not to open their parks?" His tone shifts from incredulity to sarcasm: "All parks should be inviolate," he says, "except ours."

"I just came back from meetings in Bolivia," says Vedder, "and I can tell you that the world is watching what we do. Ecuador. Congo. Gabon. Are we going to drill in the most pristine wilderness left in our country?"

Two years ago, Vedder left the Africa Program herself to become a WCS vice president as well as director of the newly created Living Landscapes Program. "I was really torn," she says. "I hated to leave Africa, but the Living Landscapes Program sounded neat intellectually, and I wanted to help it work and make sure it was linked to on-the-ground programs."

She hasn't had to leave Africa entirely, however. The Living Landscapes Program has projects all over the world, and despite dealing with much larger geographic areas and many more species of animals, it isn't much different from those early efforts of Vedder and Weber to balance the needs of gorillas with those of people.

One Living Landscapes project in Congo-Brazzaville, for instance, involves the million-acre Nouabale-Ndoki National Park, which is abutted by multiple logging concessions, the Lac Tele Community Wildlife Reserve, and a legal trophy-hunter zone as well as the borders of Cameroon and the Central African Republic. The project is studying five key species of animals known as "landscape species" because if you can protect these, you can protect just about every other species in the area.

"If you don't know how these animals behave," says Vedder, "you'd think: 'a million acres [the size of the park], that's huge.' But the animals have ranges even larger than the park's boundaries. Bongos [large antelopes] travel up to 75 miles, elephants 100. Dwarf crocodiles move back and forth between the park and the reserve. Chimpanzees disappear from areas that are logged. Nobody knows why. But you can't just say to people, 'No hunting. No logging.' People need to eat; they need to make a living. What is sustainable?"

Another Living Landscapes project involves Madidi National Park in Bolivia, and, of course, the lands and animals and people all around the park. Here, however, the primary conflict is not over hunting or logging but between the indigenous Tacana people of the lowland forests and developers backed by the provincial government, with additional conflict in the mountains between farmers and spectacled bears.

Two of Vedder's Living Landscape projects involve Weber's North America Program: Greater Yellowstone and the Adirondacks, both just now in the process of selecting landscape species, "People ask us, 'How can you work with each other day in and day out?' But it's all we've ever done," says Vedder. From all appearances, they're about as durable and compatible a couple as ever was, even commuting together daily from their home in Yorktown, N.Y., to WCS headquarters at the Bronx Zoo.

Nevertheless, over the years, they have spent a great deal of time apart — on a few occasions, as much as six months but much more often for shorter periods, ranging from days to weeks. Vedder recently missed the couple's 30th wedding anniversary because of a trip to Bolivia and followed that almost immediately with another to Alaska.

Through it all, however, one or the other parent has always been home with the boys. Weber say: "One thing about WCS if that they let us kill ourselves at our own pace." Vedder translates, "We have incredible flexibility in shaping our schedules."

Weber adds, "We don't have a life outside of work, family, and sports." The boys — Noah is now a senior at Washington & Lee, and Ethan is a senior at Yorktown High — have always taken after their athletic parents, who between them won varsity letters at Swarthmore in football, lacrosse, softball, and swimming.

For many years, both parents coached community youth soccer and lacrosse, and Vedder still coaches the girls' lacrosse team she founded ten years ago. She missed two games in June because of her trip to Bolivia, but Weber covered for her.

"Sometimes one of the girls or a parent will ask, 'Where's Amy?' I'll say, 'She's in Bolivia. She'll be back for Saturday's game.' I'm not sure that fully registers."

It probably doesn't. To all outward appearances, Vedder and Weber look

To all outward appearances, Amy and Bill, posing here with sons Ethan (far left) and Noah, look like ordinary suburbanites, not like people who have dodged rampaging elephants and challenged poachers armed with machetes and axes (courtesy Amy Vedder and Bill Weber).

like just another middle-class couple from the 'burbs, not like folks who have dodged rampaging elephants or confronted poachers armed with machetes and axes — though Vedder still wonders what impression she made on neighbors when the couple first moved to Yorktown Heights, and she immediately began hacking away at an old tree stump in the front yard with a wicked-looking machete, whose Rwandan name translates roughly into "the peacemaker."

Whatever the neighbors may think, this is decidedly not an ordinary couple. Though you are not likely to get them to say as much themselves, together they have helped to revolutionize the way the world thinks about and deals with conservation issues. But the myriad forces arrayed against conservation success seem at times overwhelming.

"There's never been a rate of extermination like we've seen since the turn of the last century," Vedder says. "There has to be something of higher value than consumption. The world cannot survive at the level that we [in the United States] are living. This is just not sustainable."

Weber adds: "We're just totally dependent on our addiction to oil — on sticking that hypodermic needle into the ground, on this thing that is killing us. And we're losing the population battle."

"And the corruption battle," Vedder interjects. "You've got to have your eyes wide open."

Yet Vedder and Weber remain positive. "The great success of the Mountain Gorilla Project made us optimistic really for all of our lives," says Vedder. "It showed us what you could do. There was a lot of doom and gloom around, but we made it work. We came away feeling that we really could make a difference."

Weber says, "You have to fight the fight. I don't know what the alternative is. And there *are* good things happening. Moose are coming back to our national forests. Beaver, martens, fishers. It looked like wolves were finished in the lower Forty-Eight, but now they're represented in eight different states."

"We do win battles," says Vedder. "You can make a difference. It's just really important to have wilderness in our lives. We need that. To remember that this world is more than just ours. Just be aware. That's the first step."

❖   ❖   ❖

"Batter My Heart with the Liquor Store: or, Teaching Poetry to Teenagers"

Keynote Address
Margins Conference of Independent
Secondary School Teachers of English
April 20, 2002

Last autumn, through a complicated sequence of events involving the now-no-more Downtown Detroit YMCA, a visiting friend from St. Clair Shores, Chubby's chicken cheese steaks over on Philadelphia's Henry Avenue, and several teenaged girls infinitely more attuned to American popular culture than I ever was or ever hope to be, I learned that a former 10th grade English student of mine had, over the course of the dozen years since I'd last seen him, managed to transform himself into G. Love, a successful blues-rock musician whose star is even now still rising.

My standing with the girls instantly skyrocketed at their discovery that I had actually taught G. Love and could produce a high school yearbook containing both his photograph and mine. Never mind that I had not seen or heard from Garrett Dutton even once in all the intervening years and had never until that very day heard of G. Love. To Shelby Liebler and her friend Lisa, I was definitely way cool, gray hair or not, especially after I was able to show them the very house in which G. Love had grown up.

Shortly thereafter, I tracked Garrett down and wrote him a letter congratulating him on his musical success and telling him the story of how I had come to make a pilgrimage to his former house.

By the time Garrett wrote back to me, the events of September 11th had occurred, and in his letter he told me that the troubling times we were living through reminded him of a Stephen Crane poem I had taught him and his classmates. He then proceeded to offer a pretty fair paraphrase of this poem:

> Should the wide world roll away,
> Leaving black terror,
> Limitless night,
> Nor God, nor man, nor place to stand
> Would be to me essential,
> If thou and thy white arms were there,
> And the fall to doom a long way.

In the horror of the moment, he had forgotten that Crane's poem is a love poem, but he remembered the wide world rolling away, and the black terror, and the limitless night, and the fall to doom. In the wake of that bleak day, he had turned back to a half-forgotten memory of poetry for some kind of comfort and stability and sense-making.

As a teacher, I could hardly have asked for a sweeter return on my labor than G. Love's affirmation that I had taught him something he remembered and could find applicable to the world in which we live. But it was doubly sweet for me because I come to the teaching of poetry from a somewhat different perspective than perhaps most of you. I myself am a poet — of modest reputation, alas, but not for lack of trying — and I was engaged actively in the art of poetry for almost fifteen years before I even considered becoming a teacher.

That so few people buy, read, or care about poetry is therefore not for me just an odd quirk of our culture, but a sorrow in my soul, a rejection of my very identity — not to mention the bane of my sad little bank account. Fond as I am of teaching, I would much rather write poems than grade compositions, but there is money in grading compositions while the independent school my daughter attends will not accept poems in lieu of cash. What disturbs me even more is that most people are actively antipathetic to poetry found anywhere other than on Hallmark Greeting Cards and in books by Rod McKuen, believing that it is dull and boring, requires a special component in one's brain with which ordinary humans are not equipped, and bears no relevance to anything that matters.

These feelings are deeply imbedded in most people's heads at a frighteningly early age. By the time most students reach the age G. Love was when I introduced him to Stephen Crane, they are already jaded and jaundiced and convinced that poetry is not for them. A year ago, I had occasion to teach a unit on the English Romantic poets to a group of high school seniors. While the circumstances were perhaps a bit more challenging than usual, I found the experience the pedagogical equivalent of trying to persuade my cat to jump into a bathtub filled with cold water. But it's not just boys and it's not just seniors. Years ago, at a different school in very different circumstances, I had a very bright junior girl blurt out, "Do we *have* to do poetry?!"

In Vietnam, poets are revered. Stop anyone on the street — absolutely anyone of any age — and ask them to recite a poem. They will immediately reel off half a dozen *ca dao* folk poems or a verse by Ho Xuan Huong or a hundred lines of *The Tale of Kieu*. In my lifetime, poets in Nicaragua, El Salvador, Chile, and South Korea have been jailed or shot by their own governments because people were paying too much attention to them. Even in this country, as recently as fifty years ago, you could regularly find good poems by good poets on the pages of *Ladies Home Journal*, and folks took Allen Ginsberg's *Howl* seriously enough to make a federal case out of it.

What happened to poetry in America? A lot of things, of course, many of them well beyond the control of any high school classroom. There has been a gradual erosion of reliance on literature of any kind, beginning with silent movies and radio, and then television at the dawning of my own lifetime. Since then, our culture has evolved into something based on the constant bombardment of our senses by high speed visual and auditory stimuli.

Take a good hard look, for instance, at the much acclaimed and beloved children's program *Sesame Street*. Notice how rapidly the show moves, how quickly the subject changes, how the screen is constantly filled with sharp sounds and bright colors moving rapidly and changing constantly. There is no time for reflection or contemplation or digestion. It is all agitation based apparently on the erroneous assumption that the attention span of children is something close to zero.

Is it any wonder that children who grew up on *Sesame Street* and similar fare now flock to movies and advertisements and television shows that flash by in a blur of perpetual motion? Compare the pace of the old *Dragnet* Show or a Cary Grant movie with *NYPD Blue* or a Mel Gibson movie. How can a good poem, let alone a 400-page novel, compete with Nintendo and Gameboy, MTV and the World Wrestling Federation? Completely surrounded by a culture that seems deliberately designed to avoid reflection or contemplation, real thought of any kind, high school teachers have what appears to be the impossible task of convincing teenagers that words on paper are worth some small amount of time and trouble and effort.

But as difficult as that task may seem, it is not impossible, and some things are still in our control as teachers. If the world has conspired against literature in general and poetry in particular, teachers as a group have consistently made some bad choices about what to teach and how to teach it. Here I am likely to step on some toes and gore some sacred cows and otherwise upset some or all of you, for which I apologize, but Dan Slack [the conference organizer] told me that part of my job today is to get people thinking and talking.

He may shortly wish he hadn't told me that. I know, for instance, that my once and future colleagues here at the Haverford School teach a survey course of British literature in their VI Form. I'm not exactly sure what they cover, but the massive anthology they use includes all the heavyweights like Geoffrey Chaucer, Edmund Spenser, John Donne, John Milton, Alexander Pope, William Blake, William Wordsworth and the rest. I know that back in January, the seniors here did a healthy chunk of *Paradise Lost*.

Now *Paradise Lost* is a masterpiece, of course, one of the great works of literature, a monumental achievement. I took a whole semester's course on it when I was a 24-year-old senior in college. But masterpiece or not, I found it very hard going even then. I cannot imagine what sense I might have made of it as a 17-year-old high school student. I consider it a mercy that none of my teachers ever made me try. Now there may be a high school teacher out there, and more than one, who can make Milton come alive for teenagers, but I doubt that I am one of them. If I am tasked with teaching Milton in the future — and I very well may be — I'll do the best I can, but I keep thinking about my cat in the bathtub, and I'm not looking forward to trying.

Or consider another classic, T. S. Eliot's "The Waste Land." I've heard it called the greatest English-language poem of the 20th century. Again, I first tried to read the poem not in my teens but in my twenties. I had no idea what Eliot was trying to say. I still don't. Before I even get to the first line of the poem, Eliot subjects me to Latin, Greek, and Italian, and a dozen lines into the poem he hurls German at me, too. And he offers no translations — like I'm just supposed to know all these languages and my tough luck if I don't. At least the editors of my *Norton Anthology of Modern Poetry* were kind enough to include footnotes.

Indeed, of the twelve pages Eliot's poem occupies, almost 50 percent of the space is taken up by footnotes in a typeface smaller than the text itself. Printed in the same typeface, the footnotes would be considerably longer than the poem. I like to think I'm not a stupid man. True, I enlisted in the U.S. Marine Corps in 1966, which is about as dumb as it gets, but I also hold degrees from Swarthmore College, the University of Illinois, and the University of Wales. I don't know who Eliot was writing for, but he wasn't writing for me. And if we give "The Waste Land" to high school kids and tell them this is great poetry, I think we can hardly blame them when they conclude that poetry isn't for them.

But how can you teach British literature without Milton or Eliot or Pope or John Dryden or name your literary giant? I remember once — I must have been in my twenties — my father said to me that he didn't see how anyone could be truly educated unless he had read all the classics in their original languages, and by this he meant Euripides and Aeschylus, Ovid and Catullus, and all those other fellows from antiquity. But what we think of as essential changes over time, as well it must and should. Though undoubtedly I might enrich my life by knowing Greek and Latin, I have read all sorts of fine literature that my father did not. Has anyone in this room not read Denise Levertov or Toni Morrison or Athol Fugard, let alone Eugene O'Neill or William Faulkner or William Butler Yeats? Yet none of these was a part of my father's education in the 1930s.

Moreover, we would do well to remember that we are teaching high school students, not graduate students. Unless maybe you teach AP English and there are certain writers and works you simply must familiarize your students with, I think the two questions you must constantly ask yourself are: (1) Do I like what I'm teaching? (2) Are my students going to like what I'm teaching? Obviously, you can't please all of your students all of the time, but just as obviously the goal is to engage as many of them as possible.

This doesn't mean you can't teach some of the truly great literary giants of British and American literature. Andrew Marvell's "To His Coy Mistress" is a terrific poem for high school kids because it jumps right into the middle of something they are just coming to grips with in their lives. You can really have fun with this poem, and so can they. You can acknowledge their awkwardness and energy and thereby validate their struggle to understand themselves and their urges. You can raise issues like the similarities and differences between what women in Marvell's day and women today have to fear from such liaisons. You can deal at once with both the humor and the seriousness of the poem.

Or try Donne's "Song," especially if you are teaching coed classes. The poem is likely to insult and enrage the girls, as well it should, especially when all the boys sit there smirking and saying, "Yeh, yeh, right on, go John Donne," which is almost invariably most boys' initial reaction. But the girls won't stand for it, and I've witnessed some pretty amazing classroom exchanges growing out of this poem.

Because many teenagers are much preoccupied with death and mortality, they often find resonance in Percy Shelley's "Ozymandias" and John Keats's "When I Have Fears" and Emily Dickinson's "I heard a Fly buzz — when I died." Because they are discovering love, and the heart's pain of love, you can give them Yeats's "Adam's Curse" or William Shakespeare's "Let me not to the marriage of true minds" or Elizabeth Browning's "When our two souls stand up erect and strong."

Try reading Robert Browning's "My Last Duchess" with your students, and then pose this question for an essay: "If the duke were in your hands, and you had liberty to do with him whatever you wished, what would you do?" Don't be surprised — or worried — if your students write about hanging, drawing and quartering or other suitably gruesome fates. After all, doesn't the duke pretty much deserve whatever he gets? Try reading Thomas Hardy's "Channel Firing" and see if your students find any parallels between the dawn of the 20th century and the dawn of the 21st. And I can still remember, now 38 years ago, when I first read Matthew Arnold's "Dover Beach"; I had never then seen a pebble beach, but when I finally did, I already knew what it would sound like, and it did.

So you don't have to discard the giants of literature, but you do need to choose the poems you give your students with an eye to what will engage them in the world they inhabit, and what seems great to you and me may well and with good reason strike most teenagers as utterly opaque, unfathomable, cruel and unusual punishment. I would suggest that the touchstone ought to be, not "What does this poem mean?" but rather "What is this poet trying to say?" And if you need an annotated guide to help you begin to formulate an answer, you are probably making a mistake asking most high school students to read such a poem.

Such poems, of course, the ones that mean rather than say, are the stuff of erudite scholars and tenured professors and literary critics. I had a very kindly old professor years ago in graduate school with whom I took a course in modern American poetry. He was in Hog Heaven week after week over Robert Frost and Wallace Stevens, Ezra Pound and Eliot. He could and did joyfully dismantle poem after poem, revealing every moving part: the similes and metaphors, metonymy, heroic couplets, terza rima, blank verse, hexameter and pentameter and trimeter, spondees and caesuras, allusions of every imaginable kind, all those wonderful elements of poetry he had spent so many years mastering.

When we got to Carl Sandburg, however, all he said as he gave out the assignment was, "Well, this is Chicago. I guess we should read some of Sandburg." At the next class meeting, Professor Hardy squirmed and fidgeted for nearly an hour. There aren't a whole lot of literary pyrotechnics in Sandburg's poetry. Maybe a few historical allusions, but no rhyme or meter, certainly no references to Chinese poetry or Sanskrit or Epictetus. Poor Professor Hardy didn't know what to do with Sandburg because it never occurred to him to ask the most obvious question of all: "What is Carl Sandburg trying to say?"

Here's one of Sandburg's poems that I like a lot. It's called "Child of the Romans":

> The dago shovelman sits by the railroad track
> Eating a noon meal of bread and bologna.
>> A train whirls by, and men and women at tables
>> Alive with red roses and yellow jonquils
>> Eat steaks running with brown gravy,
>> Strawberries and cream, eclairs and coffee.
> The dago shovelman finishes the dry bread and bologna,
> Washes it down with a dipper from the water-boy,
> And goes back to the second half of a ten-hour day's work
> Keeping the road-bed so the roses and jonquils
> Shake hardly at all in the cut glass vases
> Standing slender on the tables in dining cars.

Imagine a teacher with nothing to say in the face of a poem like that. I've seen sadder things, but mostly not in a classroom.

Sandburg has fallen from favor since I was a schoolboy, and even when he was taught, all we learned was that the fog comes on little cat feet and Chicago used to be hog butcher to the world, tool maker, stacker of wheat, player with railroads and the nation's freight handler, nothing disturbing like the poem about the dago shovelman or the one that ends "I wish to God I never saw you, Mag. / I wish to God the kids had never come." Or the one that insists "There are men who can't be bought." What a line to discuss in an age where the counterculture protest songs of my youth now regularly show up on television in car commercials and ads for $100 sneakers made in Indonesia by teenaged girls earning fifty cents a day. Indeed, especially in the schools where most of us teach, it might be a very good exercise to have your students spend some time with a poet who often sounds like a cross between Jesus of Nazareth and Karl Marx.

It's not enough, however, for poems to be understandable. They have to be interesting, too. Engaging. In some way relevant to the lives your students live, or at least to the world in which they live. It's why I love to teach Stephen Crane. Though recognized as a master of the short story, perhaps the first modern realist, Crane isn't taken very seriously as a poet. Like Sandburg, he's not a poetic virtuoso, not a master of rhyme and meter and all those other things so dear to old Professor Hardy's heart. But he's got lots to say, and much of what he has to say resonates very deeply with teenagers. He asks questions about God and justice, honesty and hypocrisy, what is the difference between wisdom and foolishness, illusion and reality, truth and lies, why does life seem so futile, what's the point?

The very questions, in fact, that most teenagers are grappling with. Crane, after all, wasn't much more than a teenager when he was writing his poems. He certainly spoke to me as no other poet had done before and few have done since. Crane is why, I think, I became a poet. He made it okay for a teenaged boy to aspire to poetry. And he said things that I wanted to say. He raised questions to which I wanted answers, and he offered the possibility of finding them. I loved his poetry, and I still do.

Earlier this year, my daughter and her 9th grade classmates read and discussed Henry Wadsworth Longfellow's "Paul Revere's Ride." If my daughter's English teacher is here today (and I do believe she is), I hasten to point out that my daughter is not her father's keeper—though at times I suspect she would like to keep me in a cage in the basement, and this is probably one of those times. Be that as it may, as I watched my daughter struggle through Longfellow, I couldn't understand why a bunch of 14- and 15-year-old girls should have to spend a week on something only a cut above doggerel. Longfellow couldn't even get the story right. More to the point, however, my daughter couldn't understand why she had to study a poem that taught her only that poetry is dull and boring. When I asked her if she'd enjoyed any of the poems she's studied this year, she said that she'd liked "The Highwayman," but only because, in her words, "It was kind of morbid." Remember the bit I said earlier about teenagers and death. There it is.

Meanwhile, I think my daughter and her classmates might have had a more lively time with Sylvia Plath's "Daddy." You want morbid? So what if it doesn't all make sense. They'll certainly get the part about the stake through the fat black heart, and what teenaged girl hasn't felt like doing that to her father from time to time?

As for the boys, well, try Mac Hammond's poem "The Liquor Store." Here it is:

When I am old, shivering, and confined,
At last, to a wheelchair, by the fire,
I will want whiskey, even as now,
Run out on a New Year's Eve, alone, I dream
Of the shut-down place where they sell it:
Rows of bottles brim full of the South —
Kentucky Tavern, Virginia Gentleman, straight
And sour mash, aged eight full years in oak.
I wonder what I would do, when old,
If broke, I could not buy whiskey?
Would I be sober and go, laughing
To the grave? Whiskey, spare me,
Think of all the truth I have told
Drunk on Barleycorn, think of all
The poems I wrote half-stoned,
Half out of my mind, and the dances
I danced around the thyrsus. Dionysus,
When I am old and crying for whiskey,
Bless all places where whiskey is sold.
O, pickle me stiff against the stiffening cold.

You can actually do more with Hammond's poem than at first you might think. How can an obvious bourbon drinker like the poem's persona not mention Jack Daniel's or Maker's Mark or Wild Turkey? Oh, wait, Kentucky Tavern and Virginia Gentleman are the cheap stuff, aren't they? What does that tell us about the poem's speaker? Who is Dionysus and what's a thyrsus? One might even ask who is John Barleycorn and why must he die? Is this a humorous poem or a sad poem, or maybe both? Is this a poem about alcoholism or perhaps a poem about the fear of death?

Here's a poem of my own that I once read in an assembly at a Catholic girls' high school. It's called "For Anne, Approaching Thirty-five":

Alone in the basement, sorting clothes,
I found that pair of panties I like
(the beige ones with the lacy waist).

I meant to put them in the washer —
but they felt so smooth, so soft, I
just stood there getting hard. Woman,

never mind the crows' feet and creeping slack.
For me, you'll always be sultry,
mysterious, ready for anything.

In the instant I said "panties," you could hear gasps coming from the stricken faces of the nuns, and by the time I got to the part about me getting hard, I was the only adult in the auditorium who wasn't on the verge of a heart attack. But the girls were all grinning and elbowing each other and casting furtive glances at their teachers.

I know my poem doesn't hold a candle to William Carlos Williams's "The Red Wheel Barrow." But I once spent the better part of a week trying to figure out what depended upon a red wheel barrow glazed with rain water beside the white chickens, and why, but I never did come up with an answer. Meanwhile, though I was never invited back to the Country Day School of the Sacred Heart, I'll bet somewhere down the road more than one of those girls will be telling her granddaughter about that afternoon, and there'll be a twinkle in Granny's eye as she talks.

As a poet, that's what I want a poem to do. Shake things up. Get under people's skin. Get into their heads and stay there. Irritate adults and make teenagers cheer. Irritate teenagers and make adults cheer. Who cares, so long as nobody falls asleep. I want to make my readers laugh and cry and ache and gasp and see the world in ways they never thought of made suddenly familiar by my words. And when they put down a poem of mine, I want them to say to themselves, "Wow."

Come to think of it, that's not much different from what I want as a teacher. And there are hundreds and hundreds of poems, maybe thousands of poems, that can do that for students. Where does one even begin? How about with Robert Creeley's "I Know a Man":

> As I sd to my
> friend, because I am
> always talking,—John, I
>
> sd, which was not his
> name, the darkness sur-
> rounds us, what
>
> can we do against
> it, or else, shall we &
> why not, buy a goddamn big car,
>
> drive, he sd, for
> christ's sake, look
> out where yr going.

What could be more American than driving around in a big car spiritually at loose ends? And what could be more poignant, more heartbreaking, than Jon Silkin's "Death of a Son"? Students may not relate as easily to this one as you and I do, especially if you're a parent, but I can't even read it without choking up, and so I have deliberately read it to students on occasion because I think it's good for them to see what a good poem can do to an ex–Marine sergeant.

I remember a night many years ago when Don Cassidy and Kathy Gamble and I, all young teachers, me in my first year of high school teaching, sat in my apartment for hours, pulling book after book off my shelf and reading our favorite poems to each other: James Dickey's "The Heaven of Animals," Philip Appleman's "Waiting for the Fire," Elizabeth Bishop's "The Fish," Allen Ginsberg's "A Supermarket in California." Twenty-three years later, there is even more to choose from. Who had heard of Seamus Heaney in 1979? Some of you, perhaps, but not me. How about Yusef Komunyakaa? Or John Balaban? Have any of you ever heard of Lisa Coffman? Here is "Dog Days" from her book *Likely*:

> I mind I've been an hour beside shut books,
> or more. The wind moves almost nothing
> in trees that move like a heavy woman
> I once saw blowing kisses. All work
> suspends: tomatoes shine on the wiped table
> from noon gardens. Grain stands in the fields.
>
> Summer was a dream that broke. Memory's fields
> mark this a time of loss. I've lived off books
> while locusts husk a last call and the table
> piles with clothes to store. Nothing
> ends easily as this season, work
> of the round year. When I was not a woman,
>
> quite, my sixteenth year, like a woman,
> I swam alone once in a river. The fields
> touched into August evening in its work
> toward September. The moon came out. In books
> a moon required lovers. I wanted nothing
> but to give a woman's love, sturdy, like a table,
>
> weight-bearing. We sat across a table,
> drank and forgot the hour, spoke woman-
> to-woman about an anger. She said, "nothing
> tires me like the old boys: men teaching men fields
> of knowledge. Xanthippe sent off crying." Books
> to come, we toasted those, an audience, our work.
>
> Drink deceives, but so does work:
> at best it passes time. Idling at the table
> I've known what the Preacher set in books
> as a truth: for child of woman

(I paraphrase), what labor, in actual fields,
or of the mind, satisfies? We come to nothing.

I stare at trees in wind and finish nothing
but hours. I think of two who work,
dear to me, shut in, as sick for fields,
perhaps, as I for work. Along a table
sun whitens a lax arm. The woman
admires the tiny hairs, forgets books.

She forgets the fields and laden table
that soon hold nothing, while birds work
south across a woman and shut books.

I could spend all day reading you my favorite poems, but we haven't got time for that. Suffice it to say that if a student (or anyone else, for that matter) says he or she doesn't like poetry, he or she has simply been reading the wrong poems. If you can read the English language, you can find poems that will speak to you, that will move you, that will touch you, that will ease your troubled soul, that will address whatever condition you happen to be in, that will do just about anything you need and be just about anything you want.

The hard part, of course, is finding those good poems among the even greater number of bad poems and dull poems and incomprehensible poems and stupid poems. The trouble with what I'm suggesting is that there aren't really any anthologies organized along the lines I've staked out here: say, a poem of Marvell's, a poem of Donne's, a poem of Sandburg's, a poem of Plath's, a poem of Hammond's, a poem of Coffman's — and they have to be the right poems, too. So much of Marvell's poetry is so deeply rooted in events contemporary to him that it is almost meaningless to anyone but a scholar of 17th century English political

Poet Lisa Coffman, 1993 Pew Fellow in the Arts and author of the poem "Dog Days" from her book *Likely*, which won the Wick Poetry Prize from Kent State University in 1996 (courtesy Lisa Coffman).

history. Not too many high schoolers are going to find the same passion in Donne's "Batter My Heart" that the poet brought to it.

Moreover, what works for you as a teacher might not work for me, and turnabout as well. I had great success teaching Stephen Crane to Garrett Dutton and his classmates, but the woman who taught the other half of the 10th grade hated Crane's poetry and could hardly bear to teach it. I don't suppose her students got much out of the exercise, and after two years with Crane, my colleague politely demanded that we drop Crane from the 10th grade curriculum. We settled on Sandburg instead. She wasn't all that wild about Sandburg either, but I wasn't going to try teaching Ezra Pound to 10th graders.

My point is that I can't go out and create the perfect poetry anthology for high school English teachers. Would that I could. I'd make a bundle. But the best I can do is only to create the perfect poetry anthology for me. For all I know, some of you might well be able to make Donne's divine poems come alive, or even *Paradise Lost* or "The Waste Land." Like I said, it's a two-step process: what will engage you and what will engage your students?

That's just what you need to hear, isn't it? Each of you has to go out and read through the corpus of English-language poetry and create your own personal anthology for use in your classroom. Like you haven't got enough to do already. But I know those poems are out there just waiting for you to find them and give them to your students. And as a poet, I can honestly say that I'd be really grateful to you if you would. Every student who gets away from each of you believing that poetry is not for him or her is one less person who might buy

Robert F. Hollenbach, my junior year English teacher at Pennridge High School, Perkasie, Pennsylvania, 1964-65. Together with John Diehl, he taught me that it was okay for a teenaged boy to love poetry (courtesy Robert Hollenbach).

a book of my poems. Meanwhile, I am going to be grading compositions until I drop dead or go blind.

But I want to come back to something I said earlier, which is that for most high school students, it really isn't important that they grasp the whole grand sweep of poetic tradition in the English language any more than it is absolutely essential for them to remember all their lives the exact date of the Peace of Augsburg or how Bolivia got its name. I did trigonometry and quadratic equations and imaginary numbers in high school math class, forgot it all during the three years I spent in the Marines before I got to college, and have never missed any of it. I know enough to balance my check book, which is all I need to know. I learned in high school that I don't particularly enjoy higher mathematics, but I do enjoy history, so I took no math in college, but I took a lot of history, and I still read history all the time. It is a lifetime habit.

And I learned in high school to love poetry, thanks in large part to two wonderful English teachers who were able to give to me their love of literature, and to the wonderful poetry they shared with me. If as a poet I have always wanted to be like Stephen Crane, as a teacher I have always wanted to be like Robert Hollenbach and John Diehl. They taught me to love poetry. I want to do that for my students.

I am certain that each of you wants the same thing. Of course, even the best of us aren't going to reach every student, no matter what we try. But if you show them what poetry can be — that it can be almost anything and come in almost any guise and deal with almost any subject and speak with almost any voice — if you show your students that poetry is indeed for them, at least some of them will keep that habit for a lifetime.

Having said that I think poetry is for everyone, however, I am now going to say something that may sound contradictory, but isn't. Just as I think it a mistake to teach *Paradise Lost* and "The Waste Land" in high school, so do I think it a mistake to teach creative writing. When I first started teaching high school,

John B. Diehl, my senior year English teacher, 1965-66 (courtesy John Diehl).

Bob Hollenbach and me in the fall of 2011. I had not seen him since the mid–1970s, but writing and delivering my talk to the Margins Conference prompted me to locate and reconnect with him. Now retired from teaching, he remains an avid reader and writer of literature (photograph by Anne Ehrhart).

I used to teach creative writing. But I eventually came to realize that my students had read so little poetry in their young lives that they really had no idea what poetry is or should be or can be. They didn't know Robert Herrick from Robert Burns from Robert Bly from Robert's Rules of Order. Half my students took the class because they wanted to write poetry, but they didn't know where to begin; the other half took my class because they figured creative writing would be easier than reading a book.

Meanwhile, here were students graduating from an elite private school and going off to college never having read a word of Samuel Taylor Coleridge or Herman Melville or Joseph Conrad or Eugene O'Neill or a whole host of other really good poets and writers, which is the downside of our otherwise laudable efforts to broaden and make more inclusive the canon of English literature. So I stopped teaching creative writing and started teaching what my students quickly dubbed "Ehrhart's Dead White Guys Course."

I don't think I could ever be persuaded to teach creative writing again. Certainly not to high schoolers. Maybe not to undergrads either. It amazes me that one can actually reach one's late 20s, holding bachelor's, master's, master of fine arts, and doctoral degrees, all in creative writing, while never having done anything in one's whole life except be a student. Remember those puzzles we used to do when we were all in kindergarten: What's Wrong with This Picture? I don't care to add to what's wrong by trying to teach creative writing to kids who should be reading.

It's fine, of course, and a good thing, actually, to give your students exercises in poetry writing from time to time. When my students read "The Rime of the Ancient Mariner," I have them write ballads of at least eight stanzas. It's a nice break from the usual literature assignment, and it teaches them that what they are reading is a lot harder than it looks. It's a good thing, too, to offer poetry clubs and literary magazines and other informal opportunities for kids to write if they want to. I had a journalism teacher who took a particular interest in my poetry in high school, and her encouragement meant a great deal to me.

But it does well to remember that the best way to learn how to write, especially when one is young, is to read. If any of your students have the urge to write poetry, they will write poetry whether you make it part of your formal curriculum or not. And the sooner they realize that the writing of poetry is not like a job that you go to, not like doing your physics homework or going to wrestling practice, but rather something you squeeze into your life in the middle of the night when you are totally exhausted or early in the morning with the sleepers still in your eyes, something that requires sacrifice and commitment while offering in return nothing our culture values, the better off your students will be. What a terrible shock it must be to all those 27-year-old doctors of creative writing who suddenly discover for the first time in their lives that the world beyond the ivy walls doesn't care about their fancy degrees and won't pay them a dime for their poetry. There are only so many places in academia for teachers of creative writing to create more teachers of creative writing.

Moreover, as a poet, I would like to know how the idea came about that anyone can write a poem. I see that notion everywhere — in creative writing workshops for kindergartners and old age pensioners, prison inmates and AIDS sufferers, gay stockbrokers and left-handed albino Puerto Ricans. Poetry as therapy. The pen is mightier than post-traumatic stress disorder. We would never think of offering workshops at the local library for nuclear physics or structural engineering or heart bypass surgery, open to whoever cares to show up and plunk down $25. Why do we imagine that anyone can write a poem? Having spent the past 38 years laboring to master the art of writing poetry, I am nonplussed at the idea that anyone can do it. Anyone can't. Most people can't. Even a lot of the ones who are publishing can't.

And you don't have to worry about the ones who can because they will. The obstacles they must overcome in order to do so are part of the winnowing process, the way the world has devised to find out if you are really a poet. Imagine poor William Shakespeare, who never had a creative writing course in all his life. Or John Keats. Or Emily Dickinson or Alfred Tennyson or Robinson Jeffers. I wonder how any of them ever managed to learn how to write without some well-meaning English teacher like you or me to point them in the right direction, pat them on the bottom, and send them on their way toward immortality. Yet somehow they did. There is, I think, a lesson in that.

And there is a huge difference between appreciating poetry and writing it. Or perhaps I should put that the other way around: we can't all write poetry, but most of us can appreciate it. You don't need to be a carpenter to know a good table. You don't have to be a musician to love Mozart or Piaff or Hendrix. Few of us can do the mechanical work on our cars, but most of us can drive them. You don't have to teach your students to write poetry; you only have to teach them to love it. Okay, maybe "only" is a bit misleading, and maybe you'll have to settle for getting most of them not to dislike it, but even that would be a huge improvement from where we are now. And if you can get most of them not to dislike it, you will in fact get some of them to love it. Meanwhile, the ones who have it in them to write will write sooner or later. And the ones who want to read *Paradise Lost* and "The Waste Land" and *The Faerie Queene*, well, I say that's what college is for.

❖   ❖   ❖

Hell's Music: *A Neglected Poem from a Neglected War*

Though the Korean War did not produce a body of poetry comparable in size to either World War Two or the Vietnam War, contrary to both popular and scholarly perceptions[1] it has served as a source of poetic inspiration for a number of writers, veterans and non-veterans alike. The list of Korean War veterans-turned-poets includes Premio Casa de las Americas winner Rolando Hinojosa, Devins Award winner William Childress, the prolific Southwestern poet Keith Wilson, Walt Whitman Prize winner Reg Saner, the fabulously unruly William Wantling, and the profoundly devout James Magner, Jr. Foremost among non–Korean War veterans who wrote about the Korean War are Thomas McGrath, Hayden Carruth, and Howard Fast.[2]

In subsequent essays included here, I will discuss the poetry of most of these men.[3] Here I would like to focus on one of the earliest, least known, and most ambitious attempts to address the Korean War in verse. *Hell's Music: A Verse Narrative of the Korean War* appeared even before the Chinese entered the fighting in the fall of 1950 and must have been written within the first three months of the war.[4] Co-authored by Paal Ramberg and Jerome Miller, it is one continuous work of 56 pages comprised of a short prologue and three sections titled "Sunset," "Midnight," and "Sunrise." Long, loping lines of free verse, almost indistinguishable from prose, are interspersed with more formal passages in a variety of fixed forms ranging from couplets and quatrains to Shakespearean and Petrarchan sonnets.

Aside from the three-page prologue, titled "For the Fallen Men, 1950" and providing a context for what is to follow, the whole poem takes place from dusk to dawn of a single night in the lives of two American soldiers during the summer of 1950 when American and South Korean forces were still in retreat. At the outset, Tom Larson, a boy from "Minnesota. Just a small town there," has his legs crushed by a North Korean tank and cannot flee with the rest of his shattered unit. But a medic we will come to know only as Bill, from "a farm about twenty miles from Buffalo," refuses to abandon Tom, instead treating his injuries and remaining by his side through the night.

Sometimes the men talk to each other. At other times, each is lost in his own thoughts. We learn that Bill is an older man, a veteran of World War Two, and that he had married a woman named Lila only to discover:

Front cover of *Hell's Music* by Paal Ramberg and Jerome Miller, 1950 (photograph by Anne Ehrhart).

All you wanted was sensation, and I had to rediscover that I was
a farmer with simple wants.
What you demanded of me, you demanded of others while I was away,
believing in you.[5]

In contrast to the adulterous and shallow Lila, Tom's girlfriend Elise is virginal and chaste, "pure love and innocent." Though Tom cannot help wondering, "would she marry a cripple," Ramberg and Miller clearly want us to know that she would.

She will not get the chance, however, because Tom's wounds are too grievous and help is too long in coming and finally he succumbs in spite of Bill's best efforts to keep him alive:

O leaf, I am so tired now, it seems,
The wind calls ...
And I shall dream, they will be lovely dreams,
The leaf falls.

Almost immediately thereafter, as "the cringing hills grew green and yellow in the morning," North Korean soldiers with "callous, almond eyes" storm the shell-hole in which Bill and Tom have been lying and capture Bill. When he resists having his hands tied behind his back, he is "stunned by a booted foot in the groin" and then shot to death.

Less than a page later, only two and a half pages after Tom's death, the poem ends with an American tank battalion commander shouting, "COUNTER-ATTACK!" But the relief comes too late to save either Tom or Bill.

Throughout the poem, Ramberg and Miller set up a number of other comparisons and contrasts in addition to Lila and Elise. The "sapling young-ster" Tom with his faith in "God's hand" vs. the world-weary Bill who reasons, "if God is really merciful,/He wouldn't stand for this hellish/bloodshed, this strangulation of/mankind." The horrors of war where bayoneted men flop and struggle like "speared fish" vs. the beauty of nature where "every perfect bud, pink, delicate [trembles] in the springtime." "This extraneous peninsula" of Korea vs. "those wooded hills outside of [a Minnesota village with] its white houses with porch swings." The decency and courage of American sol-diers "willing to be there" fighting because it is their duty vs. "the haggling fishwives of Washington" who believe that "Korea was nowhere and/they could save money by skimping." The poets even liken Tom to "The Nazarene," and Bill to a "mother coming into the/room late at night" and tucking Tom in.

It is difficult at times to tell where Ramberg and Miller are coming from and whether or not they support or condemn the war. Certainly they are on the side of the common soldier who is "glad to be from the United States" and "almost too willing to die" for "this thing called freedom." (They are on the side of chastity, too: Bill remembers that "Ma was never like Lila" while Tom recalls proudly "what magic there was in waiting for the culmination of our/love, what strength, what purity.") They have grave doubts, however, about the leaders into whose hands the common soldiers have entrusted their lives, questioning "was the government as ready, as willing" as those soldiers, chastising the politicians as "all you whores of war." And their portrayal of General of the Army Douglas MacArthur is surprisingly unreverential for the summer and fall of 1950[6]:

> "I am here now," said the General, posing in front of the plane
> call BATAAN. "We will hold them
> at the Kum."
> And some said, "God the man is great."
> Bulletin, July 15: RED TANKS PIERCE KUM RIVER DEFENSE LINE.
> Said a Chief of Staff, "He's the greatest man alive."
> Taejon? A short holding action. Abandoned.
> And another said, "He's the greatest man in history."
> Korea. What then?

Certainly war is portrayed as an ugly and inglorious business, with "muttering tanks" and mangled men "with tenantless eyes," and this war in particular seems "useless," Korea itself "extraneous." In the prologue, Ramberg and Miller write:

> In the land of superlative riches, the President arose and said,
> "We are not at war."
> But the Goodwins, the Hardings, and the Shadricks got telegrams.
> In Skin Fork, West Virginia, Shadrick's father said, "He was
> fighting for some kind of
> government."

The implication is clearly that American boys are dying for reasons the parents of the dead cannot explain or understand in something Harry Truman refuses to call a war.

Antiwar sentiments are laced through the poem, and even undertones of outright pacifism. After Bill bayonets a North Korean soldier to death, he spits out, "We're animals ... filthy animals." And after throwing up, Tom tells Bill:

> "It wasn't the killing that got me sick, not entirely anyway. I
> had an awful dream, as if all this
> couldn't be real, as if God didn't
> want to have anything to do with me
> for being here."

Tom also recognizes the humanity of the enemy, acknowledging that "every boy, / even those against whom he / was raging," has fond remembrances of his childhood and his home, while Bill reflects:

> We are brothers and yet not brothers.
> The most simple thing is the most beautiful, but is not simple.
> The simple and beautiful thing is brotherly-love, but it is
>   preached and not absorbed; that
>   which was given by One has been
>   rejected by many.

Yet Ramberg and Miller, while suggesting that Communism may have had idealistic beginnings, describe it now as "a changed star, poisoned, puffed up. ... A beast ... in the land of the white-robed people,/in the land of the morning calm." The North Korean invaders, "the Warriors of the North," in the end are callous-eyed, "tiger-like," and do not hesitate to crush the testicles of an unarmed and helpless man before shooting him in cold blood.

And if the poets have little faith in politicians or generals, nevertheless the dying Tom reflects, "despite the old griping, that he was glad to be from the United States."

> And in those States, he knew there was a village that was
>   sleeping in safety through the
>   night and in that village there
>   were people whom he loved.

People who "knew there was this thing called freedom beating in them, true as their own blood." Though the poets lament "ungrateful souls" too "submerged in the murk of greed" to heed God's "wondrous work," whatever their reservations and doubts about the efficacy of war in the abstract, they finally accept and argue that this war is necessary, however sad and tragic. They do not criticize their government for waging war in Korea, but rather for not providing adequate support and leadership to the Toms and Bills who have been sent in America's name to wage it. Or so it would seem. Nevertheless, Miller considers the "message" of *Hell's Music* to be "anti-war," and believes that it "is as relevant today as it was then."[7]

Aside from a 1990 history of New London, Minnesota, that Ramberg co-authored with Eric W. Leaf,[8] *Hell's Music* is the only book either Miller or Ramberg ever published.[9] According to Miller, he and Ramberg (born in 1925 and 1927 respectively) had known each other in childhood, then renewed their friendship in college after World War Two. Though Ramberg dropped out after a year, the two men often saw each other on Miller's visits to New London, where both men were from.

Says Miller of *Hell's Music*:

> It was a true collaboration, rare at any time. Each of us had a store of
> poems from which we selected those appropriate to the narrative. Of
> course we discussed and deliberated, but easily agreed. If I remember, it
> couldn't have taken more than a month to complete the book. Neither of
> us was in Korea, but I was a Marine veteran of World War II, and I was
> in on the invasion of Saipan, June, 1944.... In a sense the two of us were
> the protagonists we imagined. I was Bill and Paal was Tom. I was the vet-
> eran, older, bitter, cynical; Paal was the boy, the innocent dreamer.... I
> can't truly explain why we felt compelled to write about Korea except that
> it was, of course, much in the news.

Indeed, the few factual details contained in the poem — quotes by and about
MacArthur, bazooka shells bouncing off tanks "like ping-pong balls," that
Tom and Bill belong to the 24th Division, the atrocities committed by North
Korean soldiers — would easily have been gleaned from accounts of the fighting
carried in daily newspapers.[10]

At times, in fact, the poem seems as much a paean to rural and small
town life in America, or a discourse on the nature of romantic love, as it does
"a verse narrative of the Korean War." In a Shakespearean sonnet, Bill recalls:

> Brief furlough in the country, it was good
> To see again vast spaces, breathe fresh air,
> Herd restless cows to straw and evening food,
> Renew acquaintance with a friendly mare[,]

while Tom, in a sonnet written in tetrameter, reflects on his relationship with
Elise:

> So holy are the laws that bind
> The Champion sacrament of love.
> White snow must not be stained by wine
> Nor gates of chastity should move.

Long sections of the poem are also devoted to monologues on humanity,
divinity, and the relationship between the two. "O God who made us in Your
stamp," Bill demands,

> To live in harmony,
> Regard with me the mortal lamp,
> An oily flicker in Your damp
> And dark creation.

To a large degree, the Korean War seems more like an excuse for *Hell's Music*
than its subject.

And at times the writing is very bad indeed, one might say very youthful. As Bill imagines how Mary must have felt watching Jesus dying on the cross, Ramberg and Miller write:

> Dear Son, my hands were helpless in Your woe,
> These pale and trembling hands that wanted so
> To touch Your face or stop the blood to flow.

"Woe" is a miserable cliché, and "stop the blood to flow" is as fine an example of forced rhyme as any writing teacher should ever need. Or consider yet another reverie of Tom's on the woods near his village:

> Cedars crowded round me. A blue crane
> Croaked and fanned the darkness on the pond,
> (Cedars and cranes of which I am so fond).

The first two lines are not bad — the image of the crane fanning the darkness is in fact very interesting — but the third line is atrocious. Elsewhere they write of the retreating Americans (there is no acknowledgement in the poem that South Korea had forces in the field): "The defenders had receded into the night, and their snarls were/growing feeble in the South." And the poem's conclusion is cheaply ironic and uninspired.

Still, parts of the poem are more skillfully rendered. The range of closed forms Ramberg and Miller attempt is admirable: pairs of five-line stanzas with a rhyme scheme of *abcbd efgfd*, for example; three stanzas consisting of nine lines each and each with a metric scheme of *434314442* and a rhyme scheme of *abcbdeeef*; seven stanzas of free verse except that all but the first and last stanzas close with a couplet; these among many other variations. Their choice of words is as good in some places as it is bad in others. Tanks are likened to "snakes with fangs of flame," and the song of war is "the stomping heel and the lisping/of yellow dust from the engines of war." If Ramberg and Miller can get absolutely sappy about young love ("love in youth is golden"), there is great power in the observation that among aging couples who have been together for a long time, "love lies/Deep in old hearts, and there it never dies." And has anyone ever written an image more powerfully sensual than "the lure of a certain pair of legs in the dusty Manhattan sunlight"?

Taken altogether, *Hell's Music* is a fascinating if flawed poem. It's ambivalent message — even at the very end of the poem, Tom says of his own death, "I feel like a fool because this/was so useless" — perhaps reflects the ambivalence of many Americans about having to fight another war so soon after the end of World War Two in a country few Americans had ever heard of for reasons that weren't entirely convincing. The image of American life as both pastoral and ideal — the only city even mentioned in the poem is Washington, where the haggling fishwife politicians are — is straight out of a Norman Rockwell *Saturday Evening Post* cover. And the portrait of Douglas MacArthur in the poem's prologue rises to the level of grand farce.

While the poem is, finally, of only peripheral literary value, it has great value as a cultural and historical artifact. It offers a window into America just at the point when the nation seemed quite literally to bestride the world but was about to enter into a darkness of doubt and uncertainty that would stay with us for the rest of the 20th century.

Notes

1. See, for instance: "The Korean War and American Memory" by James R. Kerin, Jr., unpublished doctoral dissertation, University of Pennsylvania, 1994, pp. 42 & 182, or "Death's Aesthetic Proliferation in Works of Hinojosa" by Donald A. Randolph in *Confluencia*, v.1, #2, Spring 1986, p. 42.

2. The Korean War poems of Hinojosa, Childress, Wilson, Saner, Wantling and Magner are most readily available in *Retrieving Bones: Stories and Poems of the Korean War*, W. D. Ehrhart and Philip K. Jason, eds., Rutgers University Press, 1999. McGrath's most important Korean War poem, "Ode for the American Dead in Korea" can also be found in *Retrieving Bones*. Carruth's "On a Certain Engagement South of Seoul" first appeared in *The Crow and the Heart* (1959) and is also included in his *Selected Poems* (1985) and *Collected Shorter Poems* (1992). Howard Fast's seven-poem sequence "Korean Litany" was reprinted in *War, Literature, and the Arts* 12/1, Spring/Summer 2000.

3. See "James Magner, Jr., William Meredith & Reg Saner: Reluctant Poets of the Korean War," "Good Wars, Bad Wars, Forgotten Wars & Poetry," and "Dead on a High Hill." For the poetry of Howard Fast, see *The Madness of It All: Essays on War, Literature & American Life*, McFarland & Co., Inc., 2002.

4. The book's foreword is dated October 8, 1950, and the copy housed in the library at St. Cloud State College in Minnesota is inscribed by the authors and dated "November 1950." See also Note 9.

5. *Hell's Music* was published without page numbering of any kind, so it is not possible to give page references for quotes.

6. "At the time," writes General Paik Sun Yup in *From Pusan to Panmunjom* (pp. 20–21), MacArthur was regarded as "almost a god. He was the hero of World War II and accepted the surrender of the emperor of Japan. People today can't imagine the extent of his prestige."

7. Except as noted, all biographical information concerning Miller and Ramberg, and all the quoted material from Miller, are taken from two letters Miller wrote to WDE dated January 3 and January 11, 2000.

8. E-mail from Leaf to WDE dated December 30, 1999.

9. It was published in an edition of 500 copies by The American Yearbook Company (now Josten's) at Ramberg and Miller's expense, and carries the imprimatur of Green Spires Press of New London, Minnesota, the town both men are from. The book's foreword was written by Agnes Louise Hovde, whom Miller describes as "a good friend" from Glenwood, Minnesota, about 40 miles from New London, and "an excellent poet." (The Library of Congress lists two books of poetry under Hovde's name: *Song Before Sleep*, Chicago: Dierkes Press, 1948, and *Prelude to a Journey: A Story of the Ukraine*, New York: Vantage Press, 1954. Vantage is a "vanity press," and according to Georgina Murphy of La Salle University's Connelly Library, e-mail to WDE dated December 10, 1999, Dierkes, which operated from 1932 to 1971, publishing books of poetry under 70 pages in length, may have been as well.) *Hell's*

Music also contains a number of illustrations, but Miller says, "I don't know anything about the illustrator, Kendall Wolfe, except his generous contribution."

   10. See John Toland, *In Mortal Combat*, pp. 59–63; T. R. Fehrenbach, *This Kind of War*, p. 67; Richard Whelan, *Drawing the Line*, p. 169 & 173; and Fehrenbach, *This Kind of War*, p. 55, respectively.

❖   ❖   ❖

The Power to Declare

I was talking the other day with the Walrus and Mogerdy, two old Marine Corps buddies of mine from the Vietnam War. We had all served together in 1st Battalion, 1st Marine Regiment in the Battle for Hue City during the Tet Offensive in 1968.

All three of us had friends among the 58,000 Americans killed in that long and sorry war. We call the Vietnam War a war, of course, because it was. But it was never a declared war.

Only Congress has the power to declare war. The Founding Fathers thought war so grave a matter that they chose not to give the power to declare war to a single individual, not even the Commander in Chief, but instead placed that gravest of responsibilities in the collective hands of the people's representatives (you may recall from high school history that back in 1789 only the House of Representatives was directly elected by the people).

Congress, however, seems to have forgotten its Constitutional responsibility. Or given it away. Or run away from it. Or something. Since I was born, this country has fought the Korean War, the Vietnam War, a war in Grenada, the Gulf War, a war in Serbia, and the Afghan War, along with costly deployments in Lebanon, Panama, and Somalia, without Congress ever once declaring war.

The outcomes of those wars are a pretty mixed bag. Korea was at best a draw. By any reasonable measure, we lost the Vietnam War. We thought we'd won the Gulf War, but more than a decade later, it seems we actually didn't. The Taliban are gone from Afghanistan, but life there remains pretty grim, and most of Al Qaeda has apparently eluded our forces.

Our record in Lebanon and Somalia wasn't that hot, either. And as for Grenada and Panama, the National Hockey League could have handled either of those. Meanwhile, a lot of Americans have been killed in the last 50 years, more than a few of them friends of mine and Mogerdy and the Walrus.

And now it looks like we're about to do it again. President Bush has already said that with or without United Nations backing, he's going to wage war against Iraq. An interesting method of coalition building, to say the least, but even with UN approval, that still leaves Congress out of the loop.

Oh, you'll say, but back in — when was it, October, November? — Congress passed a resolution giving the President the authority to wage war at his discretion.

I've got a copy of the Constitution in front of me as I write this, and it doesn't say anything about Congressional resolutions delegating war-making powers to the President. It says, "The Congress shall have the power to declare war," which is pretty unambiguous.

Meanwhile, the last time Congress decided to give the President authority to wage war at his discretion, it was called the Gulf of Tonkin Resolution. Anyone my age or older knows how well that turned out.

Which brings me back to my conversation with the Walrus and Mogerdy, two honorably discharged combat veterans who have put their lives on the line for this country and who are not all that happy about the current situation.

The Walrus had what seems to me a really good idea. He suggested that any time an American serviceman or woman is killed in action, that person's Congressional Representative should have to be the one to break the news to the family of the deceased. In person.

Those duly elected representatives of the people should have to look into the people's eyes and see the shock and the grief and the forever unfillable emptiness. They should have to come face to face with the consequences of war.

The Walrus thought this might make our Congressional Representatives a bit more careful about how and to whom they give the power to make war. It might make them a little less eager to shirk the responsibility our Founding Fathers entrusted specifically and only to them.

James Magner, Jr., William Meredith and Reg Saner: Reluctant Poets of the Korean War

The Korean War (1950–53) is the least remembered and least acknowledged of all of America's wars. Even as it was being fought, ordinary Americans were aghast to find the country at war again so soon after World War Two; they found it profoundly embarrassing to be put to rout not once but twice in six months by what they perceived to be a rabble of Asian peasants; and they did not understand a war in which total victory was not and could not be the goal. And once it was over, the Korean War all but vanished from the American landscape.

Just as the war has vanished, so too has its poetry. Indeed, the very notion of Korean War poetry is all but unheard of, even among scholars of war poetry. Yet there is very much a body of work that can be called Korean War poetry, and while it is much smaller than the bodies of poetry from the American wars that came immediately before and after the Korean War, it ought not to be dismissed out of hand.

Among the most prominent of the Korean War soldier-poets are the Chicano writer Rolando Hinojosa, author of the novel-in-verse *Korean Love Songs*; New Mexico poet Keith Wilson, author of *Graves Registry*; poet and journalist William Childress, whose two collections *Burning the Years* and *Lobo* contain numerous poems based on the Korean War; and the hard-living, early-dying William Wantling, who scattered a handful of Korean War poems through his many small press publications.

Elsewhere, I have written about each of these poets at length.[1] In this essay, I would like to devote my attention to the Korean War poetry of three men who have each devoted a lifetime of creative energy to poetry, yet who have written startlingly little about their experiences in the Korean War. What these poets wrote — and didn't write — is worth examining.

In the course of ten books published over a span of more than three decades, James Magner, Jr.,[2] has written fewer than a dozen poems that seem in any way related to the war. The chronological distribution of the poems, however, is interesting: three appear in his first book in 1965, one in 1968, two in 1973. Three subsequent books in 1976, 1978, and 1981 contain none, but another appears in a 1985 book. A 1992 book contains none, but his latest book, published in 1996, contains four. It is almost as if, throughout his life, he cannot make up his mind to confront the war or not. That ambivalence is inadvertently made apparent in a 1997 letter of Magner's.[3] At one point he writes, "How much shall you write about the horrific Knives of War that froze, wounded and killed so many of my brothers?" But on the next page he mentions his desire to publish "an elegy for *all* who have died in war, that they will not be lost but remembered in our hearts and souls."[4]

One might make the case that Magner is too insubstantial a poet to warrant more than cursory attention. Though he has published multiple books;[5] received an Ohio Poet of the Year award, a Hart Crane Memorial Award, and a special commendation for poetic achievement from the Ohio House of Representatives; and published in *College English, Hiram Poetry Review*, and *New England Review*, the closer one looks, the less impressive these achievements seem.

Of his ten books, five were published by the Golden Quill Press, which describes itself as a "subsidy publisher"[6] but is commonly referred to — perhaps more accurately — as a "vanity press." Two more were published by Ryder Press, of which Magner was, at the time of publication, editor and publisher.[7] Still another was published by Blue Flamingo Productions, founded and operated (apparently as a one-man operation) by a former student of Magner's.[8] Most of the poems in Magner's books have either never been previously published, or appeared in religious-oriented periodicals such as *America* and *Christian Century*, various campus publications of John Carroll University (where Magner has taught since 1962), and the littlest of little magazines. Though the body of secondary literature on most of the Korean War poets is slender, for Magner it is all-but-nonexistent.[9]

None of this, in and of itself, is reason to dismiss Magner. William Wantling spent his entire brief career publishing in the littlest of the little magazines, and if Wantling did not resort to "subsidy publishing," he certainly published with the smallest of the small presses. Moreover, Richard Eberhart has said of Magner that "his poems attest to timeless realities, invite us to contemplate imponderables, and incite us to pleasures in his findings, soundings, and adorations."

But this same quote of Eberhart's, which first appeared on the jacket of *Till No Light Leaps* in 1981, appears again on the jacket of *Rose of My Flowering Night* in 1985, and again on the jacket of *The Temple of the Bell of Silence* in 1992. Only this quote, again and again, and with no indication of when it was made or under what circumstances, leaving the impression that this is the only testimonial Magner ever got from a poet or critic of recognizable stature, which seems to be the case. Other collections of Magner's include testimonials that liken him to Emily Dickinson and Walt Whitman,[10] or call him "a major poet"[11] and "a poetic genius,"[12] but these come from people whose names are not likely to be recognized by anyone other than their friends and families, and Magner's poetry, taken as a whole, simply does not justify such encomiums.

Every once in awhile, he does come up with an arresting (if not Dickinsonian or Whitmanesque) poem, such as "The Cocktail Party," a sharp commentary on social vacuity:

> This place is like a mortuary,
> dead men embalming themselves
> that they may, later, two-step to oblivion
> in a jiggle of smiling desperation.
> Pallid face clicks smiling teeth
> at smiling teeth of pallid face
> powdered for an evening that moves unnoticed
> to eternity.
> I do not abhor the Boar's Head
> but there are too many dead men here.
>   [*Till No Light Leaps*, p. 24]

Or a touching poem, such as "Where Did You Go?"

> (On the Death of Kevin Hurley)
> Boy, where did you go
> out of this class and world?
> Where the electric, the life, the talk,
> the auburn dutch-boy hair
> that in its going
> leaves your mentor
> the constant student
> of your loss?
>   [*The Dark Is Closest to the Moon*, p. 40]

Or an amusing poem, such as this untitled piece:

> Ya wanna be my wife,
> ya wanna?
> I'll play your favorite games
> and bring you milk and cookies in your bed
> and take you to the park
> of pastel frisbies
> and make love to you
> in outrageous places,
> ya wanna?
>   [*Rose of My Flowering Night*, p. 36]

But while each of these poems has its moments ("pallid face clicks smiling teeth" wonderfully evoking a skull, the sad reversal of expected roles between student and teacher, the playfulness of the diction in "Ya wanna be my wife"), they are moments only. Most of Magner's work lurches from archaic romanticism:

> When I am with you
> I allow myself my weakness.
> The warrior, come home to arms,
> sheds the arms of war
> and bares the satin flesh
> that exercised an iron arm to foes
> *Women of the Golden Horn*, p. 14)

through overburdened mysticism:

> It was a sin as all sin is
> against the Heart of Being:
> A falling of love back into
> the opiate den of self,
> for self is made complete
> when self becomes the Other
> and burgeons fruit in marriage
> with the Other, the sacredness
> of all that is not me
> (*Till No Light Leaps*, p. 67)

to something verging on the ridiculous:

> Kiss me into day,
> still Thy singing child,
> and I will be Thy emptied,
> Thy lucid,
> Thy tenderest samurai;
> Samurai with breasts
> who gives the milk of Being
> to Thy Presences, Thy children[.]
> (*The Temple of the Bell of Silence*, p. 9)

Along the way, he turns Ezekiel and Delilah into verbs;[13] falls back too often upon clichés such as "virgin arms," "woman's mildness" and "stallion-sinewed;"[14] and repeatedly invokes the names of Borges, Melville, Jeffers, and other great writers, as if putting their names into his poems will somehow infuse his poems with their greatness.[15] His language is often pompous and stilted, and is laced with references to God, Christ-God, Human-God and the like, which is off-putting for anyone who does not share Magner's religious fervor.

And yet for all that, his few poems about the Korean War stay in one's head, lines repeating themselves over and over again, remaining in the memory long after they should be forgotten. His Korean War poems may well be his best work, for all that there are so few of them, and whatever Magner's weaknesses, there is a sweetness to his Korean War poems, a love for his fellow sufferers, a sense of bewildered innocence, that touches the heart. And touching the heart, finally, is what good poetry does.

Born in 1928 in New York City, Magner grew up on Long Island and in New Rochelle, New York. He enlisted in the army in 1948, arriving in Korea at just about the same time as the arrival of Chinese Communist Forces turned what appeared to be an American victory into stunning disaster for the second time in less than six months. Magner served less than three months in Korea, but between the bitter retreat in the face of the Chinese divisions and the bitter Korean winter, they were three of the toughest months of the war. While fighting as an infantry sergeant with Headquarters Company, 1st Battalion, 7th Regiment, 3rd Division,[16] he was badly wounded by machinegun fire in North Suwon in February 1951 and evacuated to a hospital in Japan.

Because his wounds were too severe for him to be returned to active duty, he was discharged from the army in September 1951. But his experiences in the war had had a profound impact on him. "The war made me 'The Soldier of the Night,'" he writes, referring to the poem of that title, "It took all but the life of God from me."[17] While in the hospital in Japan, Magner had struck up a correspondence with a monk of the Passionist Order from a Catholic monastery in Dunkirk, New York, and upon his return to the United States, he entered the monastery as a novice, where he remained for five years.

Thereafter, Magner earned a Bachelor of Arts degree in philosophy from Duquesne University, and Master's and Doctor's degrees from the University of Pittsburgh. While in graduate school, he began teaching at South Hills Catholic High School and the Allegheny County Workhouse, and in 1962 he was hired by the English Department of John Carroll, where he has been ever since, teaching modern poetry, American literature, literary criticism, and creative writing.

Though Magner never took the vows of a monk, and eventually left monastic life to return to the secular world, the body of his poetry — whatever its flaws — overtly reflects his deeply spiritual concerns, and his lifelong quest to bridge the gulf between human imperfection and divine perfection. Though his two most recent books reveal a marked change in certain elements of his style, including a more minimalist use of language, through most of his work the language often has a Biblical feel to it — the tone, the diction, the choice of words — almost a kind of grandeur that often falls flat in many of his poems but seems to work in several of the Korean War poems.

What becomes clear in reading his Korean War poetry is that Magner cannot bear the madness of the war, the unspeakable misery, the destruction of bodies and minds and hearts, without the hope and possibility of divine grace and human redemption. Thus, in "Elegy for the Valiant Dead," he pleads "that those who've gone before/may be wrapped in the quilt of Thy arms of night." And in "Christ of Battle," he prays, "Christ-God carry me!/give hope in storm-mud and grave-bed."

These two poems (both from Magner's first book, *Toiler of the Sea*, pp. 34 & 49 respectively) most overtly reflect Magner's religious preoccupations. Beginning "Glory ends in night" (which could well be taken as a succinct commentary on the futility of war), "Elegy for the Valiant Dead" pays homage to the "dust/of brothers" who "struggled in the night;/whose folly and whose glory/was their slaughter in the night[.]" The poem includes such phrases as "brooding piety," "Thy arms," and "the lamp of God," and concludes:

> therefore do I grieve in hope
> that their outward dooms
> light lamps of inward victory
> in a kingdom of no swords
> and the kingly kiss of peace.

The progression of movement in "Christ of Battle" is especially fascinating. It begins with a generalized plea, rather like that in "Elegy for the Valiant Dead," for Christ to have pity on the dead:

> Christ of the battle-field
> Take them in your sinewed arms,
> Press their bloodied death-dent brows
> with God's human cheek.

A few lines later, Magner shifts from the general to the specific:

> I remember deep my friend, my burly Marsh,
>   his head cleaved through.
> Did you speak silent-soft to him
> Just before they blazed him to somewhere
>   away from here?

Marsh's death is particularly poignant, troubles Magner especially, because Marsh was his friend and because Marsh was "burly," strong and healthy, and therefore seemingly invulnerable — yet dead in an instant, "his head cleaved through." Still without a stanza break — there are none in the poem — Magner next shifts his attention from the dead to the living, whom he describes as "alert in their graves" (a reference to the soldiers' fighting holes or foxholes, which resemble graves and too often become them). "Speak softly to us," Magner pleads, "no one so much as we/ — soldier-sinners —/need gentleness." What follows a few lines later seems to be a reference to Magner's own wounding:

> Across rigid seas of froze-stung ridges
> Was I borne upon invisible shoulders
> While I sigh-groaned Your name[,]

the "invisible shoulders" being both the medics who would have carried Magner from the battlefield and the Christ who spared Magner's life. The last third of the poem shifts to what is clearly post-war present time, and is Magner's prayer to Christ to help Magner himself live with the continuing aftermath of war, with survivor's guilt, and with the terrible knowledge of what humanity is capable of:

> Christ-God carry me over the froze-vast bleakness
> of long life's plain
>   — so vast, so frozen — so unending.
>   * * *
> And in the end, look not for bravery
> for there is none
> But only have mercy, my Christ, my God
> carry me
>   — I will bend the shot-stiff knee.[18]

In the third Korean War poem in his first book, Magner effectively conveys the lonely anonymity of the battlefield. "The Man Without a Face"[19] is "gutted, tangled — sprawled like a broken crab" on barbed wire, "dead and alone in his body." The poem does not indicate if the dead man is Chinese, Korean, or American, nor does Magner care. That he is "one of those who fought," a fellow sufferer, is all that matters.

Accounts of that first winter of fighting in Korea constantly stress the horrible, debilitating cold that was an enemy in and of itself, almost as deadly as the Chinese. The historian Richard Whelan, in *Drawing the Line*, describes Americans "not only battling through a gauntlet of Chinese hordes but also struggling with 'General Winter's' relentless subzero winds."[20] And the cold runs through Magner's poems from the "rigid seas of froze-stung ridges" in "Christ of Battle" to the "rock-white silent day" of "To a Chinaman, in a Hole, Long Ago" (*The Dark Is Closest to the Moon*, p. 21) to the "Soldier of the Night" (see above, p. 15) moving "on stumping unfelt feet" through "fields of white[.]" But the cold, bleak, unforgiving moonscape of Korea in winter in war could not be better rendered than in "Zero Minus One Minute" (*Although There Is the Night*, p. 27):

> The dawn has come
> to sleepless night
> again
> and it is time for us to answer
> from the gray, crystal holes
> that seem to womb
> just northern night and nothingness;
> but we are there;
> our eyes electric,
> our bodies splinters
> in bundled rags[.]

It is this poem, more than any other, that keeps drawing one back to Magner, and this image: "our bodies splinters/in bundled rags." The cold, the pain, the fear, the loneliness are palpable, as is a dogged perseverance in the face of every reason to give up and give in. And if, as Magner says, "the world doubts/that we exist," nevertheless "we are there," Magner says for a second time, insistent, refusing to allow himself and his comrades to be dismissed,

> and we shall creak
> our frozen bones
> upon that crystal mount
> that looms in silence
> and amaze the world.

That Magner sees himself not as a soldier, but as a "soldier-sinner" (a phrase he uses in "Christ of Battle") is made evident in "To a Chinaman, in a Hole, Long Ago," a poem that exhibits — like William Childress's "Letter Home" and Keith Wilson's "Commentary" — a remarkable sensitivity toward "the Other" (be it Koreans, northern or southern, or in this case Chinese). It is also a poem not about survivor guilt (a major element of "Christ of Battle"), but about the guilt of soldier-sins, in this case Magner's guilt for the life he has taken. Speaking directly to the dead Chinese soldier he has killed, Magner writes:

> I, your ordered searcher
> with a killer on my sling,
> do bequeath my life to you
> that you might fly the Yellow Sea
> to your startled matron's arms
> and curl beholden
> amid the pygmies of your loins.[21]

It is as if Magner is trying to apologize, wishing to trade his own life for the life he has taken, though he knows this cannot be done: "But marbled you lie," he concludes, dead and cold as stone, while the dead man's wife sleeps "self-graved, ice-wombed" and Magner is left to "the rock-white silent day/of our demagogue damnation" (another brief commentary on the war, no doubt).

Thus, Magner is much in need of God's mercy to give meaning and comfort to him and to all "soldier-sinners," but this need is matched by his insistence that those who fought and died be remembered. For Magner, to forget is to render utterly meaningless the suffering, the sorrow, the irreplaceable losses. "The Man Without a Face" may have no name nor even a nationality, but he is nevertheless "entombed in the heart of our mind." And in "Repository" (*Rose of My Flowering Night*, p. 117), the epigraph for which is a telling Henry James quote: "*Be one on whom nothing is lost*,"[22] Magner begins by relating the story of the Sportsline reader who asked "what college/quarterback/named Adam/died/in the Korean War" and received the reply that there was "no record" of such a person, not "even from the army and alma mater." Magner's reply is outraged disbelief:

> Impossible to mind, impossible to heart
> that one so quick,
> who stepped so quick
> in pocket
> and rifled passes forty yards
> for alma mater and the infantry
> could die and be forgotten...
> by all except me[.]

Magner struggles through four stanzas to remember the name of the man, whom he met once briefly "before we sailed from Sasebo," Japan to Korea. And when he finally succeeds, in the fifth and final stanza — "Vanesca!" — he shouts the name over and over again "so someone will remember."

The four poems in Magner's most recent book, *Only the Shadow of the Great Fool*,[23] are indicative of the sharp change in Magner's style after the mid-1980s. The spare language, the matter-of-fact diction, the short often one-word lines are all in marked contrast to earlier poems such as "Christ of Battle" or even "Repository." One example, "The Prayer of the Former Infantryman," should suffice:

> One
> thing
> I
> know.
> The

Ground

Is

My

Friend.

These later poems are all single thoughts, one to a poem, straightforward and lean. But however different they may be, the later poems, by their mere being, quietly testify to the fact that if Magner is a reluctant Korean War poet, the Korean War is never far from his thoughts. Half a century after he left Korea on a stretcher, he remains a "Soldier of the Night" wherein there is "no house, no lamp, no chimneyed curl/but only life outstepping night."

William Meredith could hardly be more different from James Magner. They were both born in New York City (Meredith on January 9, 1919).[24] They both served in the Korean War. They are both poets who spent their professional careers in academia (the bulk of Meredith's at Connecticut College in New London). But there the similarities stop.

Meredith's credentials as a first-rate poet, one of the most important poets of his generation, are truly impressive. The author of nine books of poetry,[25] he received the prestigious Yale Series of Younger Poets Prize in 1943 for *Love Letter from an Impossible Land,* the Pulitzer Prize for Poetry in 1987 for *Partial Accounts,* and the National Book Award for Poetry in 1997 for *Effort at Speech.* His lesser awards — most of which would be considered major for most poets — are almost literally too numerous to list.[26] He has received grants and fellowships from the Rockefeller Foundation, the National Endowment for the Arts, the Guggenheim Foundation, the Ford Foundation, and the National Institute of Arts and Letters (of which he is also a member), and has served as a chancellor of the Academy of American poets and as Poetry Consultant to the Library of Congress (a post now designated Poet Laureate of the United States).[27]

Also unlike Magner — or Reg Saner, or indeed any of the other "soldier-poets" of the Korean War — Meredith's Korean War experience seems to have had virtually no impact on him at all, certainly not as it is reflected — or rather not reflected — in his writing. This is all the more odd since Meredith, a 1940 graduate of Princeton who flew combat missions in the Pacific Theater of World War Two as a U.S. Navy aviator and carrier pilot, included nearly a dozen World War Two poems in his first book, published with the war still raging. Of these war poems, Archibald MacLeish writes:

> They are not only poems written by a Navy flyer about the air war in an "impossible land": they are poems written from within that experience. They have an accent, a tone, of participation. They give a sense of having *seen,* of having been present, which a man's face sometimes gives, returning.[28]

A handful of additional World War Two poems appear in Meredith's second book, published in 1948.[29]

After the war, Meredith returned to Princeton as an English instructor and Woodrow Wilson fellow in writing, then moved on to the University of Hawaii as an associate professor. But in 1952, according to Susan Trosky, "he re-enlisted to fly missions in the Korean War as well."[30]

What came out of his Korean War service, however, literarily speaking at least, is as close to nothing at all as one can get without its literally being nothing at all. In his third book, *The Open Sea and Other Poems*, the first book he published after the Korean War, there are two poems (on p. 36) under the heading *Two Korean Poems*. The first is "Full Circle":

> The farmer in the round hat
> Who treads the waterwheel
> In the dust of the jeep road
> At the turn of summer,
> Wants a philosophy
> Older than wheels.

Except for the reference to "the jeep road," the poem has nothing to do with war and could as easily be set in 1933 or 1983 as 1953. The second poem, "Old Ones," is not much different in that regard:

> The old woman and the old man
> Who came a day's journey to see the airfield,
> Having nothing to keep them at home,
> Slide down the embankment of rubble
> Like frisky children
> Under the starboard wing as we taxi by.
> They are afraid of the roar. Also they know
> Better than we that anything can happen.

Again, this can hardly be considered a war poem at all except for the slightly ominous suggestion in the last line and the fact that we know Meredith was an aviator during the Korean War. The poem could just as easily be set in peacetime as in wartime. Neither of these two poems, moreover, appears again in any of Meredith's subsequent books.

A third poem in *The Open Sea and Other Poems*, "A Korean Woman Seated by a Wall" (p. 46), while much longer (four stanzas totaling 38 lines), is only slightly more obviously informed by the war. "Suffering has settled like a sly disguise/On her cheerful old face," Meredith begins,

> If she dreams beyond
> Rice and a roof, now toward the end of winter,
> Is it of four sons gone, the cries she has heard,
> A square of farm in the south, soured by tents?

Because we know this woman is Korean, and we can surmise from the date of the book in which the poem first appears that the poem is probably from the time of the Korean War, and we know Meredith is a Korean War veteran (though no reader of the book would know this from anything in the book itself), we can speculate that perhaps her four sons are in the army — or dead — and perhaps the tents are those of soldiers bivouacked where once the old woman's farm was.

There is another reference to the war, clear if oblique, indeed quite clever, in these lines:

> Hunger and pain and death, the sorts of loss,
> Dispute our comforts like peninsulas
> Of no particular value, places to fight.

But the poem itself is about "the capriciousness with which [suffering] is dispensed," and "the unflinching way we see it borne," and how Meredith's "guilt" at a brief reverie he has in the third stanza combines with the old woman's "grace" to "alter the coins I tender cowardly[.]" It is a poem about haves and have nots and there-but-for-the-grace-of-God. Meredith is obviously fond of the poem because he includes it in all three of his subsequent new & selected volumes.

But these few poems are the only poetic evidence — slim as it is — that he ever served in the Korean War. Why this should be so, we will probably never know. Meredith seems never to have talked about the Korean War on the record, nor written about it except for these few poems. In poor health since a stroke in 1983, he is not likely to add much to the record at this point in his life.[31]

In *Babel to Byzantium*, James Dickey characterizes Meredith's poetry as often "muffled and distant, a kind of thin, organized, slightly academic murmur."[32] Archibald MacLeish's comments notwithstanding, this is certainly a fair assessment of Meredith's World War Two poems. With a few exceptions — "Navy Field" perhaps, or brief flashes in "June, Dutch Harbor" (both in *Love Letter*, pp. 46 and 41 respectively) — the poems lack visceral power, emotional drive. In "Airman's Virtue" (*Love Letter*, p. 48) for instance, he writes of a fellow flier:

> High cloud whose proud and angry stuff
> Rose up in heat against earth's thrall,

> The nodding law has time enough
> To wait your fall.

Through four stanzas of "Airman's Virtue," we are not even sure if this pilot has been shot down, or been downed by mechanical failure, or what — or even if the poem is about a specific pilot or is merely a generic paean to the possible fate of airmen in general. It is hard to imagine how carrier duty in the Pacific against the Japanese Imperial Navy could have produced such restrained, bloodless, almost vapid poetry from someone so highly acclaimed.

Considering this, and looking at the few poems Meredith wrote about the Korean War — none of which convey anything like the power of Magner's "Zero Minus One Minute" or "Repository," let alone the poems of William Childress or Keith Wilson or any of the other Korean War soldier-poets — one must uncomfortably admit to feeling no real sense of loss for what Meredith did not write about the Korean War.

The same cannot be said of Reg Saner, the third of the reluctant Korean War poets, and the poet whose lack of writing about the war creates the greatest sense of literary loss. Among the few poems Saner has written that touch at all on his war experience are some of the very best poems to come out of the war, offering tantalizing hints of what he might have said and how skillfully he might have said it had he chosen to make the war a focus of his literary attention. But he chose instead to do the opposite. "I've tried to put [the war] behind me," he writes, "I have not really tried to write about Korea. Wanted to forget it."[33]

Saner was born Reginald Anthony Saner in Jacksonville, Illinois, in 1929.[34] He grew up in a flat land where there were "no hills whatever," in winter "walk[ing] happily home through snowfall," or building skis that wanted "his backyard to be a hill," and in summer dancing to Boots Brennan's band playing "Blue Rain" in Nichols Park pavilion with the Second World War as a backdrop. [35]

In 1946, Saner went off to St. Norbert College in Wisconsin, graduating in 1950 — only weeks before the outbreak of the Korean War — with a Bachelor of Arts degree and a Reserve Officers Training Corps commission as a second lieutenant in the army. Called to active duty in January 1951, he was sent to the army's arctic survival school in Alaska, where he learned mountaineering and skiing, before being deployed to Korea in April 1952. He served with the 14th Infantry Regiment, 25th Infantry Division, until January 1953, six months of that time as an infantry platoon leader, earning a Bronze Star and promotion to first lieutenant.[36]

Getting out of the army in April 1953, Saner earned a Master of Arts degree from the University of Illinois in 1954, and a Doctor of Philosophy degree from the same institution in 1962, writing a dissertation on Shakespeare and Italian Renaissance Drama. That same year, 1962, he was hired by the English Department of the University of Colorado, and has been there ever since. "If I had a dozen lives to live," he writes, "I'd live every one of them in Colorado."[37]

As an academic, Saner has received a Fullbright scholarship to the Universita di Firenze in Italy, a resident scholarship to the Centro Culturale della Fondazione Rockefeller in Italy, and multiple awards from the University of Colorado.[38]

As a poet, Saner has been equally successful. His first collection of poems, *Climbing into the Roots* (Harper & Row, 1976), was chosen by — of all people —

1st Lieutenant Reginald Saner, 25th Infantry Division, U.S. Army, Korea, 1953 (courtesy Reg Saner).

William Meredith to receive the first Walt Whitman Award. His second collection, *So This Is the Map* (Random House, 1981), was chosen by Derek Walcott as a National Poetry Series winner. He has two additional collections, *Essay on Air* (Ohio Review Books, 1984) and *Red letters* (Quarterly Review of Literature, 1989). Along the way, his poems have also earned him a National Endowment for the Arts fellowship, a Colorado Governor's Award for Excellence in the Arts, and numerous other awards,[39] and have been published in over 140 periodicals and 30 anthologies including *The Atlantic Monthly*, *The Yale Review*, *Poetry*, *The Paris Review*, and *The Pushcart Prize Anthology*.[40]

Poet, essayist, professor, and Korean War veteran Reg Saner (courtesy Reg Saner).

In addition, since the late 1980s, Saner has increasingly turned to the nonfiction essay as a form of creative expression, publishing in such journals as *The Georgia Review, Western Humanities Review, Nimrod, Ascent* and others. His two collections of essays to date are *The Four-Cornered Falcon: Essays on the Interior West and the Natural Scene* (Johns Hopkins University Press, 1993) and *Reaching Keet Seel: Ruin's Echo and the Anasazi* (University of Utah Press, 1998), the first of which earned him a Colorado Center for the Book Award, nomination for the John Burroughs Medal, and the Wallace Stegner Award from the Center of the American West.[41]

In both poetry and prose, the American West has become Saner's all-but-exclusive subject. "Every line, every page I write," he says, "takes place outdoors — mountains, deserts, canyons, dunes, mesas — explored by ski or by snowshoe, as well as by boot sole and backpack. Whether I hike to write, or use writing as a pretext for being outside, I've never known. Only know that it's there I'm happiest, most at home."[42] A native Easterner who did not see his first mountain until after he graduated from college, Saner took to the American West with the zeal of a convert, turning himself into an expert mountaineer in the process, as well as a first-rate amateur naturalist, botanist, archeologist, anthropologist, and geologist, his poems and essays packed with observations ranging from asides to fullblown discussions on everything from

> moss
> crannies lush as a thumbnail
> hothouse — their blossoms
> purple and white, pincushioning
> tufts with calyxes not even
> a raindrop across[43]

to "the development of photosynthesis in anaerobic bacteria" some 3,000 million years ago.[44]

Richard Gustafson, in *Poet and Critic*, describes Saner as "a voice from the Rockies, distinct and personal,"[45] while J. D. McClatchy, writing in *Poetry*, says that Saner's writing is "about the process of knowing the world, about its mysterious reflection of depth within us."[46] Louis Martz, writing in *The Yale Review*, observes that while Saner writes about "Florence and New York City, memories of friends and relatives in various regions, poems inspired by Quasimodo and Borges, and love poems for Anne" [Saner's wife], his work is still grounded in "the Rocky Mountain West" and "the indestructible strength of nature."[47] Writes Peter Stith in *The Georgia Review*: "At the center of [Saner's] work lies a powerful strain of praise which *seems* to be directed entirely at the 'glories of the world' but actually is concentrated upon man's ability to perceive, understand, and 'aria' those glories."[48] And Ursula LeGuin, in the *New York Times Book Review*, applauds Saner's "plain sense of responsibility" toward nature and the natural world, calling this "the great ethical and practical issue of our lifetime."[49]

Reviews of Saner's writing have varied enormously — one might even say wildly, radically. D. H. Williams writes of *Climbing into the Roots*, in *Library Journal*, that "most of these poems are dismal attempts to convey a sense of nature"[50] while Alfred Corn, in *Poetry*, says of the same poems that "Saner has a good eye. The book abounds with sharp-focus diapositives of a clarity and perfection I associate with stereopticons."[51] Of *So This Is the Map*, J. F. Cotter writes in *America*, "Saner looks unblinkingly into the heart of darkness, into the caverns and burnt-out woods, and, with an Emersonian eye, sees the map of Being in strata and stream" while *Library Journal*'s Michael Williamson says of the same poems that "we are left with a disturbing, disjointed vision of virgin nature seen through cynical eyes that strain after Blakean innocence."[52] While R. W. Flint, writing in the *New York Times*, accuses Saner's *Essay on Air* of "the debased existentialism of the travel brochure or the pop school of alpine metaphysics," *Choice*'s B. Galvin calls the same book "important and superb."[53]

Even, most of those who find fault with Saner, however, also find qualities worthy of praise. Hayden Carruth, for instance, writes in the *New York Times* about *Climbing into the Roots*, "I don't suggest that Saner has nothing to say, only that he has very little to say," but also adds that Saner is "talented, perhaps very talented."[54] Not so of Mary Kinzie, writing in *American Poetry Review*.[55] Her assessment of Saner's *So This Is the Map* is unrelentingly hostile, beginning with "Reg Saner's poetry is as badly served by his diction and his logic as by his prosody" and ending with "it is less than second-rate poetry: it is genuinely bad." In between, among the poems she savages is "Leaving These Woods to the Hunters," about which she writes: "Or consider this example of macho self-congratulation: 'Yet I'll slog downtrail/leaving these woods to the hunters,/having never myself/killed anything/more beautiful than a man.' Are deer more beautiful than men? Has the speaker committed homicide?"

"Her presumptive arrogance still bugs me," Saner writes even fifteen years later of that reviewer and that particular passage in her review.[56] But in fairness to Kinzie — if fairness she deserves — there is nothing in any of the poems in *So This Is the Map*, and next to nothing in any of his other three poetry collections, to warn Kinzie to choose her words with more care and thoughtfulness, nothing to indicate that between Saner and homicide is little more than a uniform and a flag. Not even the books' brief biographical notes on the author mention that Saner is a combat veteran of the Korean War.

From the first book, only "One War Is All Wars" (p. 41) deals with war at all, and Saner's description of the white crosses on soldiers' graves, "line after line after/line regular as/domino theory," echoes the "crosses, row on row" of the Great War and Canadian poet John McCrae's "In Flanders Fields" while use of the phrase "domino theory" quite deliberately invokes the Vietnam War at least as much as it does the Korean War — which, one assumes, is Saner's point, as the title implies. "Nuisance Caller" (p. 78) includes the lines, "I recall shrapnel flecks/that glanced and rang for somebody else,/now ringing for me," but the same stanza also speaks of "patriot/mothers still shelling Viet Nam/with their wombs." Thus, even when one knows that Saner is a Korean War veteran, the reference to Saner's own wartime experience is gone before it even registers; without that knowledge, the reference is almost no reference at all.[57]

From his second book, Saner himself says that "From Chief Joseph I Turn the Page" (p. 19) and "Doc Holliday's Grave" (p. 29) may be related to residual anger about the Korean War, and that "Talking Back: A Dream" is perhaps prompted "at least partly by survivor guilt,"[58] but the connections, such as they may be, exist only for Saner, not for the reader. Only "Leaving These Woods to the Hunters" makes anything like an identifiable reference to Saner's Korean War service, and that too, as has already been noted, really depends on information to be found beyond the poem in order to give those closing lines —"having never myself/killed anything/more beautiful than a man"— the power they ought to have.

The poems in Saner's third book travel from Colorado to Egypt to Italy, but they don't go anywhere near Korea. Of the poems in his fourth book, "Little Rituals" (p. 50), with its "men wearing guns, belted jackets" riding in trucks that "jolt and sway through long tunnels of dust, ... each truckload of troops in the convoy/lurch[ing] and loll[ing], passive as drunks," is, like "One War Is All Wars," entirely nonspecific. As Saner himself says, the poem "distances the war stuff."[59] Another poem, "Straw Gold" (p. 51), which is not about war, nevertheless includes the lines, "Oh, once upon a time of dodging hot metal/aimed at the rest of my years/years ago, I hadn't time to consider[.]" But again the reference is there and gone.

"Re-Runs" (p. 49), however, another poem in *Red Letters*, is a bit different. It seems to suggest that if Saner has "wanted to forget" his wartime experiences, what he has managed to do is merely to repress them, and not entirely successfully. The poem begins:

> All that flying iron was bound to hit something.
> His odd nights re-visit a stare, let a torn head

> trade looks with him, though the incoming whine
> was only a power saw,

and concludes with these lines:

> Odd nights, a clay pit or two may waken him
> still, alone inside a nameless grief holding
> nothing: their faces, grass shrapnel — which some field
> on the world's other side bothers with. Like seed,
> the shapes that won't go away without tears.
> They just lie where they fell, and keep going.

Though the poem is in the third person, the "he" is almost certainly Saner himself, "alone inside a nameless grief" where "what's buried won't cry/and won't go away." What troubles Saner, however, he will not say beyond "flying iron," "a torn head," and "crossfire tracers," all "on the world's other side" (a phrase he uses twice in this short poem) where Korea is to be found. He tells us only that sometimes there are "odd nights" in which he trades looks with "a torn head."[60]

And that poem is as specific and graphic as Saner gets about the Korean War in any of his four collections. One has to go past the poetry collections entirely, all the way to 1993 and *The Four-Cornered Falcon*, before one even encounters the word "Korea," let alone the admission that Saner is a Korean War veteran.

Curiously enough, however, Saner has written two much more personal and particular poems about the Korean War — published fifteen years apart — that do not appear in any of his four collections. That "Flag Memoir," published in *Ontario Review* in 1991, does not appear in book form may or may not be as simple as the fact that it was possibly not written until after his most recent collection was published in 1989.[61] But "They Said" has been around since at least 1976, when it appeared in the anthology *Demilitarized Zones: Veterans After Vietnam*,[62] predating the publication of three of Saner's four books of poetry.

Both poems are quite unlike anything else in Saner's repertoire. "They Said" is bitter and cynical and angry. The first stanza shows us young school children sorting blocks according to instructions delivered by some higher authority identified only as "They." The second stanza has children coloring in a manger scene:

> They said, "Now color Holy Manger brown
> and Virgin Mary blue the Christ child pink
> and St. Joseph anything you like." So this one boy
> colored him polka-dot but was allowed to try again
>   * * * *
> ... he colored him pink a suitable color.

The emphasis of "They" is clearly on conformity, and the poem concludes:

> They said, "Democracy is at the crossroads everyone
> will be given a gun and a map in cases like this
> there is no need to vote." Our group scored quite
> well getting each of its villages right except
> one but was allowed to try again on a fresh village
> we colored it black and then wore our brass
> stars of unit citation almost all the way home.

When it comes down to it, the poem could well be about some other war than Korea — certainly the editors of *Demilitarized Zones* thought it applied to the Vietnam War quite readily — but the vehemence of the sarcasm bespeaks something very personal here: an old grudge, a raw nerve, an unhealed wound. The repetition of the unnamed "They"; the Big Brother authoritarianism masquerading as benign paternalism; the smiling insistence upon conformity; the use of bland modifiers like "nicely," "suitable," and "quite," taken altogether, powerfully convey the poet's disapproval of, even revulsion at, what he describes. The latent hypocrisy of power becomes overt in the second stanza, where the children are told they can color St. Joseph "anything you like," but in fact cannot, which can and should be read as a commentary on the narrow range of opinion and debate permitted in American public discourse, First Amendment or not.[63]

Most striking, perhaps, is Saner's implication that the wholesale destruction in the last stanza, where under the guise of supporting democracy "there is no need to vote," is made possible by the years of conditioning that preceded it. And if there's any doubt that Saner rejects the end result, if only in retrospect and too late, there is that fascinating use of the word "almost" in the final line. Like Siegfried Sassoon before him and the Vietnam veterans of Dewey Canyon III after him, Saner rejects the decorations given for actions in which he can take no pride.[64]

In "Re-Runs," Saner mentions "a torn head" among the things he revisits on "odd nights." In his stunning prose poem "Flag Memoir," we learn that the torn head belongs to the first man killed in action from Lieutenant Saner's infantry platoon: "the country boy," Barnett. At Graves Registration, "with almost a flourish, [two clerks] unzipper a dark rubber bag to show a slashed head." Saner must identify the body, and he can "face the remains of his face [only] by saying inwardly, again and again, 'This isn't him, he's not here. He's elsewhere.'"

In ten stanzas of tight, hard writing, Saner seems to try to get down all that he has kept inside, out of the public eye, for nearly forty years. Though one war may be all wars, it turns out Saner may have had a particular war in mind when he wrote "One War Is All Wars," for this is how he begins "Flag Memoir":

> The white crosses alter whenever I move. Row on row, they realign pre-
> cisely, geometrically: perfect as close-order drill. While I look for the
> friend I don't find, the arms on the crosses shift, so as always to focus and
> open toward me. They do it by night too; faces and places I start awake
> from, as if hitting a trip wire. Back where the past is mined.

These are not generic crosses, suitable for any war, but the crosses Saner will later describe in *The Four-Cornered Falcon*:

> At the U.N. graveyard outside — was it Pusan? — I remember wandering
> among thousands of soldiers my age, tucked under white crosses aligned
> with the greatest precision. Name, rank, serial number. As I kept looking
> for one name in particular, I remember feeling, "Him. Him. Him. And
> him. And not me?"

If one has to take Saner's word for it that "Talking Back" is at least partly about survivor's guilt, that emotion fairly leaps off the page in the opening stanza of "Flag Memoir."

The poem goes on to offer a series of vignettes, very specific, very graphic: this is Korea; this is Saner's war. He describes learning to fire single shots from a .50 caliber machinegun, waiting until his target "sets down his ammo load; half standing, looking my way," before giving the gun's butterfly switch "one quick, accurate tap. " After identifying Barnett's body, Saner and one of the Graves Registration clerks, a private first class, "suck [beer] lather-warm from cans, talking of Red Sox and Yankees under summer shreds of something once like an orchard." He shows us the skull hanging "from commo wire looped between tent poles," someone's idea of a joke, "green crabapples plugged into each socket." He prepares for a Chinese assault in which the "third and fourth waves may carry scythes, hooks, farm tools, sticks" instead of rifles. Soldiers are warned to stop shooting rats because "the fever spreads when vermin desert the carcass," and to stop shooting themselves because "self-inflicted wounds equal refusal to serve."

And all of this is "memoir," memory, called back by 4th of July municipal fireworks that, for Saner,

> report to the eye as muzzle flash and sheared jaw, red teeth, clay dirt on
> the brains. Or maybe with one long zipper-pull some corporal exactly my
> age throws open a dark rubber bag, there yet, in any such zipper I hear: a
> metallic hiss taking my breath, taking it back through tanks gutted and
> rusting like fire, through cratering in fields and roads, through stump
> forests reseeded in shoe mines that end legs at the ankle.

A stadium anthem can do it, or flag at a ballpark; its vague sidle, stirring in breeze over one or two rows of empty seats. The flag slowly dipping, lifting, over nobody there. Explaining. Trying to explain.

But failing, Saner implies, the flag and all it stands for incapable of offering any reason good enough to justify the death of a single Barnett, the fields and fields of dead Barnetts, or the memories those who live must live with. If Saner has not really tried to write about Korea, "Flag Memoir" suggests that he has forgotten nothing, and likely never will.

Why, except for these few exceptions, has Saner chosen not to write about the Korean War? Perhaps without meaning to do so, he offers a few clues in several of his essays in *The Four-Cornered Falcon*, as has been noted already the first book in which he clearly states that he is a Korean War combat veteran. In "Glacier Gorge" (p. 13), he writes:

> In war, a body of men is your address. Mine: Twenty-fifth Division, Fourteenth Infantry Regiment, First Battalion, Company D, ... the Iron Triangle, the Punchbowl, Heartbreak Ridge, Sandbag Castle — gathering, every blue moon, into one somber wave that wants to be tears; the irrational tide we call sorrow.

Or in "Magpie Scapular" (pp. 35–36), after describing his visit to the cemetery in Pusan (quoted above):

> I never mention those men or that place in conversation. Merely to go near its image brings on waves of sorrow that mount like a warning; like waves of nausea telling a seasick person he's about to throw up ... an incoherence of tears and fury that wants to indict somebody, blame someone, wants to *scream* at someone, make somebody *pay* ... and can't. So it has to swallow its tears and its rage. It has to subside humiliated by its own irrelevance. It knows, despite the sincere feigning of others, there aren't any listeners. The only ones who could speak with and answer that grief, and be understood by it, are young men living ten thousand miles off, underground; in a dark beyond sympathy or flags; in disturbed earth my spoken words never go near.

And finally, in "Technically Sweet" (p. 85), while giving a speech before hundreds of demonstrators protesting the Rocky Flats Nuclear Weapons Plant in 1983,[65] he recounts that

> when I mention 1,200,000 Chinese estimated killed in "my" war, the Korean War, something deep in me overflows. I choke up, can't talk. Then the upwelling subsides. As if giving myself confidential advice, I murmur into the microphones, "That's a minefield. Better stay away from there."

Elsewhere Saner has written, "To be completely honest, writing about [the war] would make me cry, and I was raised to *know* that men don't cry. Therapeutic grief can go to hell."[66]

It is clear that Saner has avoided writing about the Korean War because he fears opening a Pandora's Box he will never again be able to close, and to no good end. Whether therapeutic grief can go to hell or not, whether it is better for Saner to live his life struggling to keep the lid on that box or to open it and deal with what comes out, is not for anyone but Saner to judge. And while one can look at "They Said" and "Flag Memoir" and think wistfully — in a literary and historical sense — of what Saner might have written had he chosen to address his war head-on, there is little to be gained by imagining what might have been. Better to be grateful that Saner chose to write — or perhaps could not help writing[67] — what few poems he has given us, for they include among them some of the finest poems to come out of the Korean War.

Notes

1. See "Soldier-Poets of the Korean War" in *War, Literature & the Arts*, v.9, #2, Fall/Winter, 1997; "'I Want to Try It All Before I Go': The Life and Poetry of William Wantling" in *American Poetry Review*, November/December 1998; *Retrieving Bones: Stories and Poems of the Korean War* (with Philip K. Jason), Rutgers University Press, 1999; "Setting the Record Straight," *Poetry Wales*, v. 37, #1, July 2001; "Burning the Years: The Korean War Poetry of William Childress" in *Revista de Estudios Norteamericanos* #8, 2001, and "A Dirty and Murderous Joke: The Korean War Poetry of Keith Wilson," in *Revista de Estudios Norteamericanos* #9, 2003.

2. Magner's first few books were published under the name of James Edmund Magner, Jr. In the 1970s, he published several books under the name James Magner. Since the early 1980s, he has consistently used James Magner, Jr.

Unless otherwise noted, biographical and bibliographical information about Magner comes from an author's questionnaire provided by Magner to WDE in October 1997, an accompanying biographical & bibliographical statement provided by Magner, and a bibliographical addendum provided by Magner in February 1999.

3. Letter to WDE dated June 10, 1997.

4. Magner has written such an elegy, a 141-page fictional work called *That None Be Lost*, but it has yet to be published. Probably first written in 1982 (since a 1981 *Carroll News* article mentions that Magner had been granted a university fellowship for the spring of 1982 and "plans to find the 'quiet moments' for a longer work"), it purports to be the journal of a soldier killed in early 1951. The circumstances of the soldier's life and death — including his New York childhood, his love of jazz and boxing, his assignment with a headquarters company, and other particulars — suggest that the piece, while fiction, is highly autobiographical. Even the particulars of the dead soldier's father, who wishes to get the journal published decades after his son's death, match the man Magner describes as his own father in a poem in *Rose of My Flowering Night*, p. 114. A number of Magner's poems are incorporated into the manuscript, as though they are the work of the soldier, whose name is John Mannix (J.M.

being Magner's initials as well). Magner has apparently attempted for years to get *That None Be Lost* published, but without success. His letters to WDE dated June 10, 1997, and February 23, 1999, ask for help in finding a publisher. The latter letter also included a manuscript of short stories titled *So Bright the Day, So Dark the Night*; five of these stories are taken verbatim from episodes in *That None Be Lost*.

5. His books of poetry are:

Toiler of the Sea, Golden Quill Press, 1965;
Although There Is the Night, Golden Quill Press, 1968;
Gethsemane, Poetry Seminar Press, 1969;
The Dark Is Closest to the Moon, Ryder Press, 1973;
The Women of the Golden Quill, Ryder Press, 1976;
To Whom You Shall Go, Golden Quill Press, 1978;
Till No Light Leaps, Golden Quill Press, 1981;
Rose of My Flowering Night, Golden Quill Press, 1985;
The Temple of the Bell of Silence, Fred Press, 1992;
Only the Shadow of the Great Fool, Blue Flamingo Productions, 1996.

Magner has also written a scholarly work, *John Crowe Ransom: Critical Principles and Preoccupations*, published by Mouton & Company in 1971.

6. E-mail dated September 20, 1999, to WDE from Georgina Murphy, Collection Development Librarian, La Salle University, Philadelphia, Pennsylvania.

7. According to the jacket of *The Dark Is Closest to the Moon*.

8. See Publisher's Preface to *Only the Shadow of the Great Fool*.

9. Two articles appear in *The Carroll News*, the campus newspaper of John Carroll University; the first in 1981 when Magner was named Ohio Poet of the Year by the Ohio Verse Writers Guild and the Ohio Poetry Day Association for *Till No Light Leaps*, the second in 1992 when *The Carroll News* named him Person of the Year. Magner sent another short newspaper article with photograph to WDE that was also about his being named Poet of the Year; though the photocopy sent does not indicate the publication, it seems to be from a local or neighborhood paper called the *Sun*. A short review of Magner's first book appears in *Fine Arts*, where Magner served as poetry editor. And according to Magner's bibliographic addendum, a review of *Till No Light Leaps* appeared in an issue of *Mickle Street Review*. Whatever else may have been written about Magner and his poetry over the years — and one would have to speculate that it is not very much — has already vanished. The first and only serious critical attention Magner seems to have received is in WDE's essay "Soldier-Poets of the Korean War" in a 1997 issue of *War, Literature and the Arts*, a condensed version of which also appears in Ehrhart and Jason's *Retrieving Bones: Stories and Poems of the Korean War*.

10. James E. Miller, Jr., quoted on the jacket of *Although There Is the Night*.

11. Owen Herman, quoted on the jacket of *The Dark Is Closest to the Moon*.

12. This phrase appears in "About the Author" in *Only the Shadow of the Great Fool* and is presumably the judgement of the publisher, Magner's former student, Vicque Vassinger.

13. See *Rose of My Flowering Night*, p. 84, and *Although There Is the Night*, p. 16, respectively.

14. All three of which appear in a single poem, "Something Stupid," in *The Women of the Golden Horn*, p. 9.

15. See, for instance, his untitled poem *Today, somehow, reading Borges*, in *Rose of My Flowering Night*, p. 34.

16. Magner's author's questionnaire says that he served with both 1st Bn. and 3rd Bn. of the 7th Regt., and does not specify a company, but the biographical note on Magner included in Paul M. Edwards's *The Hermit Kingdom*, p. 42, indicates HQ Co., 1st Bn., 7th Regt.

17. Letter from Magner to WDE dated June 10, 1997.

18. In an undated hand-written note attached to the manuscript of *So Bright the Day, So Dark the Night*, Magner mentions that he was hit in the tibia by machinegun fire, which undoubtedly would have shattered the bone and left, among other damage, probably permanent, a "shot-stiff knee."

19. This poem is reprinted in *Till No Light Leaps*, p. 18. The other two appear only in *Toiler of the Sea.*

20. Whelan, *Drawing the Line*, p. 263.

21. One might mistake Magner's description of the Chinese children as "pygmies" for a racist comment on Chinese physical stature, but in fact, in "Booze, Fort Devins, and Angels" (*The Dark Is Closest to the Moon*, p. 27), Magner describes his own children as "pygmied curling gods."

22. According to Magner's letter of June 10, 1997, the quote comes from James's "The Art of Fiction."

23. "March 15th, 1987 (1950)," p. 42; "The Prayer of the Former Infantryman," p. 50; "Instruction," p. 51; and "Recruit & Sgt. 1st Class," p. 108.

24. Biographical information in this paragraph comes from Trosky, *Contemporary Authors*, v.40, pp. 301–302.

25. His books of poetry are:
Love letter from an Impossible Land, Yale University Press, 1944;
Ships and Other Figures, Princeton University Press, 1948;
The Open Sea and Other Poems, Knopf, 1958;
The Wreck of the Thresher and Other Poems, Knopf, 1964;
Earth Walk: New & Selected Poems, Knopf, 1970;
Hazard, the Painter, Knopf, 1975;
The Cheer, Knopf, 1980;
Partial Accounts: New & Selected Poems, Knopf, 1987;
Effort at Speech, TriQuarterly Books, 1997.
Meredith has also edited *Shelley: Poems* (Dell, 1962), translated Guillaume Apollinaire's *Alcools: Poems 1898–1913* (Doubleday, 1964), and published a collection of essays, *Poems Are Hard to Read* (University of Michigan Press, 1991).

26. Among them are the Harriet Monroe Memorial Prize, the Oscar Blumenthal Prize, the Loines Prize, the Van Wyck Brooks Award, the Brandeis Medal, and the International Vaptsarov Prize.

27. Information in this paragraph comes from Trosky, *Contemporary Authors*, v.40, and from Michael Collier's foreword to *Effort at Speech*, pp. xiii–xvi.

28. From MacLeish's foreword to *Love Letter from an Impossible Land*, p. 9.

29. Roger Matuz, in *Contemporary Literary Criticism*, v.55, p. 190, states that in *Love Letter from an Impossible Land*, "Meredith employs imagery and themes drawn from his experiences as a naval aviator during World War II *and the Korean conflict*" (emphases added), but this is incorrect — indeed an absurdity — since the book was published six years before the Korean War began.

30. *Contemporary Authors*, v.40, p. 302. In an August 13, 1999 letter to WDE, Paul Fussell, who taught at Connecticut College with Meredith in the mid-1950s, writes of Meredith's decision to return to active duty during the Korean War: "I do recall a strident argument he and I had about returning to the military after what we'd learned in World War II. He thought I was deplorably unpatriotic. I thought he was a boy."

31. Four letters written by WDE to Meredith and his long-time companion Richard Harteis (who has handled much of Meredith's correspondence since Meredith's severe stroke in 1983) between February and July 1997 all went unanswered.

32. *From Babel to Byzantium*, New York: Farrar, Straus & Giroux, 1968, pp. 197 198. Quoted in Riley, *Contemporary Literary Criticism*, #4, p. 348.

33. Letter from Saner to WDE dated January 23, 1997.

34. Jane Bowden, ed., *Contemporary Authors*, v.65–68, p. 515 (hereafter Bowden), says Saner was born in 1931, but Saner himself, in a questionaire he sent WDE in September 1997, says 1929.

35. Saner, *The Four-Cornered Falcon*, pp. 190, 192, 190 & 78–80.

36. Information in this paragraph comes from author's questionnaire and accompanying "Brief Biography" and *Curriculum Vitae* provided to WDE by Saner in September 1997.

37. Information in this paragraph comes from Bowden, and a letter from Saner to WDE dated September 2, 1999. The quote is from Saner's "Brief Biography."

38. University awards include Distinguished Research Lecturer, a Hazel Barnes Award, two Van Ek Awards, and five faculty fellowships. Information in this paragraph comes from Saner's "Brief Biography" and *CV*.

39. These include a Borestone Mountain Poetry Award, the Creede Repertory Theatre Poetry Prize, and a creative fellowship from the Colorado Council on the Arts & Humanities.

40. Information in this paragraph comes from Saner's "Brief Biography" and *CV*, Bowden, and the cover of *Climbing into the Roots*.

41. Information comes from Saner's *CV* and letter to WDE dated September 2, 1999.

42. Saner's "Brief Biography."

43. "Long's Peak Trail," *Climbing into the Roots*, p. 76.

44. "The Ideal Particle and the Great Unconformity," *The Four-Cornered Falcon*, p. 152.

45. Quoted in Bryfonski, *Contemporary Literary Criticism*, v.9, 1978, p. 469.

46. *Poetry*, v.140, #6, September 1982, p. 351.

47. *The Yale Review*, v.72, #1, October 1982, pp. 70–71.

48. *The Georgia Review*, v.38, #1, Spring 1984, p. 171.

49. Quoted in Mooney, *Book Review Digest 1994*, p. 1820.

50. Quoted in Samudio, *Book Review Digest 1976*, p. 1055.

51. Quoted in Bryfonski, *Contemporary Literary Criticism*, p. 469.

52. Both quoted in Mooney, *Book Review Digest 1981*, p. 1260.

53. Both quoted in Mooney, *Book Review Digest 1985*, p. 1391.

54. Quoted in Samudio, *Book Review Digest 1976*, p. 1055.

55. Kinzie, *American Poetry Review*, March/April 1982, p. 16.

56. Letter from Saner to WDE dated January 23, 1997.

57. In his letter to WDE of September 2, 1999, Saner writes: "I was lightly wounded by rock bits when a rocket exploded close to me. No shrapnel, not much blood, and my medic dug out what particles he could without much ado."

58. Letter from Saner to WDE dated January 23, 1997.

59. Letter from Saner to WDE dated January 23, 1997.

60. In his letter to WDE, January 23, 1997, Saner says, "'Re-Runs' refers to the dreams that haunted me for a long time. They weren't just 'bad dreams.' They brought with them the power of afterimages that I couldn't dispell merely by waking, because their effects persisted for ten, twenty minutes, even a half hour while I sat up in the living room, trying to get clear of their fumes or spirits. The poem doesn't go into that at all, but it derives from such."

61. See *Ontario Review #34*, Spring/Summer 1991, pp. 65–67.

62. Barry & Ehrhart, eds., *Demilitarized Zones*, p. 22.

63. One wonders, also, if there is not in that stanza an implicit condemnation of the enforced conformity of religion in general and Catholicism in particular. In *The Four-Cornered Falcon*, p. 26, we learn that Saner was educated by Dominican nuns during twelve years of parochial school, yet in *Contemporary Authors*, v.65–68, p. 515, under the heading "religion," he lists himself as an atheist.

64. Both Sassoon's protests and the protests of Vietnam Veterans Against the War are well documented. See, for instance, Giddings's *The War Poets*, pp. 111–112, for an account of Sassoon's July 6, 1917, letter to his commanding officer, and Stacewicz's *Winter Soldiers*, pp. 241–251, for an account of the Dewey Canyon III action in mid–April 1971.

65. The essay itself does not date the demonstration, but in a February 15, 1999, letter to WDE, Saner says it took place in 1983.

66. From an unpublished essay titled "Why So Little Korean War Poetry?" accompanying a letter to WDE dated June 4, 1997.

67. In that same unpublished essay, Saner says that he has written "a few poems [about the Korean War] out of images that molested me."

What's the Point of Poetry?

"I joined the army and went to Vietnam to become a soldier," Jan Barry writes in his preface to *Earth Songs: New & Selected Poems* (iUniverse, 2003). "Vietnam turned me into a poet and peace activist." In his poem "Peace Time," he adds, "It was all so / easy to go off to war.... What's been hardest / in life has been to risk / my neck for peace."

Yet risking his neck for peace is exactly what Barry has been doing for forty years now. A Republican farm boy from upstate New York who'd grown up idolizing his dead uncle killed in the Pacific in 1944, he dropped out of college and joined the army with grand visions of one day becoming "a battle general," as he says in "The Struggle."

Sent to Vietnam in 1962, when the war was still a small and almost casual affair, Barry soon began to understand that Vietnam "was no great crusade, which the generals think they lead" ("Duty"), but rather a heartbreakingly "green land" rapidly being "reduced to smoke" ("Long Before") by American arrogance and stupidity.

Awarded a coveted appointment from the ranks to West Point, Barry could not dismiss what he'd seen and learned in Vietnam. In "Duty, Honor, Country," he writes of the irony of "impeccable cadets [who] will assault villages, / turn rice fields into killing zones / and farmers into corpses," and concludes: "Time to stop soldiering, / turn from weapons / to words —"

Barry resigned his appointment, got out of the army, and set off in search of a different future, one that has included founding Vietnam Veterans Against the War, editing *Winning Hearts and Minds: War Poems by Vietnam Veterans* (one of the most influential and remarkable poetry anthologies ever published), becoming a major force in the 1980s Nuclear Freeze Movement, and authoring books on grass roots organizing, all while simultaneously maintaining a life as a working journalist, husband and father.

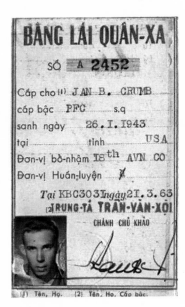

Vietnamese driver's license of PFC Jan B. Crumb (aka Jan Barry), 18th Aviation Company, U.S. Army, Republic of Vietnam, 1963 (courtesy Jan Barry).

But at the heart of his life lies poetry. As he writes in his preface, "I've never made a living from poetry, but poetry is what has gotten me through life.... *Earth Songs* is a tribute to the world I discovered beyond battlefields ... a true tale — the hardest there is to tell — of a teenage soldier growing into a world citizen." Though he is far too self-effacing to say so, it is also a tribute to Barry himself, and to the remarkable and admirable life he has lived.

Fans and aficionados of Vietnam War poetry will find many familiar poems of Barry's in *Earth Songs*, poems first appearing in *Winning Hearts and Minds* and its companion anthology *Demilitarized Zones: Veterans After Vietnam*: "In the Footsteps of Genghis Khan," "Nights in Nha Trang," "Floating Petals," "Thap Ba," "Memorial for Man in Black Pajamas," "The Colonel's Daughter," "Harvest Moon," "The Struggle," and others. But along with these older and more familiar poems are scores of other poems previously available only in very limited circulation anthologies and limited edition chapbooks, or published here for the first time.

Poems like "Sparrow" and "A Childhood Tale," "Young Soldiers, Old War" and "Saturday Night" add depth and breadth to Barry's experiences as a young soldier in Vietnam. But the war is only the book's starting point, from which Barry journeys forward and backward, weaving a life in poems: his West Point experience, the death of his Uncle Ted in the Battle of Leyte Gulf, discovering New York City, falling in love with the woman who would be his wife for more than thirty years, reading the names of the Vietnam War dead at Riverside Church and marching with VVAW comrades to Valley Forge, a whole section of poems about a trip Barry took to the Soviet Union at the height of the Cold War Reagan years.

Barry's experiences as a journalist are reflected directly in poems such as "Choosing the News," in which he writes, "Inside the editors' eyrie, / eyes that never saw a body fall / decide how many words a life was worth / or not worth mentioning at all," and indirectly in poems such as "Bitter Fruit" and "March Madness," poems dealing with AIDS and urban violence respectively. An assortment of elegies for the famous (Allen Ginsberg), the beloved (old VVAW member Sheldon Ramsdell), and the all-but-anonymous (Cindy Villalba) is complemented by Barry's irrepressible optimism in poems like "Down Town" and "Magnolia Morning."

Most moving of all, I think, are Barry's poems to his wife, Paula Kay Pierce, from the early love poem "Paula Kay" to "Us," in which he writes, "After so many battles / we are a pair of ruffled swans / who have survived / a great many storms / together[,]" to "Death in America," where he writes of Paula's losing battle with cancer, "There are no words to express what it's like to watch / your lover and best friend die," to her return to him in dreams:

Jan Barry at Taughannock, New York, 2011 (photograph by Paula Rogovin).

"'Time to get up!' she snaps / in an impatient mood, / rousting me from the dead."

So Barry rousts himself from the dead, from his sorrow and grief, and goes on with his life, acknowledging in "Listen, Death" that "Death will catch me / in due time," but insisting that "until then / the time is mine." *Earth Songs*, dedicated "To Paula — for love and life," is proof of that insistence.

And over the years, few voices have been as insistent, as cogent, as compelling, or as thoughtful as Barry's. In "In the Footsteps of Genghis Khan," Barry writes of American soldiers "unencumbered by history in a foreign land." In "Lessons," to his son's question "What's a patriot, Dad?" Barry replies, "Well, I guess a person / who loves the land. / Although some people act as though / a patriot's a man / who hates another land." In "The Peace Monument," Barry asks, "Where are the statues to those brave souls / Who kept the peace[?]"

Such questions and observations are surely as relevant today — as vital — as when they were written ten, twenty, and thirty years ago. Likewise for one of Barry's newest poems, "What's the Point": "What's the point of poetry? / Might's well ask what's the point of spring, / what's the point of a flower opening."

❖   ❖   ❖

Kaleidoscope

Senior Dinner Talk
The Haverford School
June 10th, 2004

Thank you very much for inviting me to speak to you tonight. I've spent a lot of time in the past week thinking about what I could say that would not be the same banal stuff that gets said to every group of high school graduates at every school in America and probably the entire world year after year after year. What I've finally decided upon is to read you a poem I wrote for, and gave as a speech at, my own commencement ceremony from Pennridge High School in Perkasie, Pennsylvania, in 1966. Perhaps you will hear something in it that resonates with you. Perhaps not. But this is what was going through my mind when I was sitting where you now are:

> I stand, silently watching
> The kaleidoscope of ideas race through my mind.
> A thousand images pass in front of my eyes —
> All of them vague and transient,
> Not one clear enough to grasp.
> I see a babe, a child, a youth, a man.
> Yesterday I was a child;
> And there were no dark thoughts to cause this
> Heavy emptiness I now feel.
> No — no dark thoughts.
> There were ice cream cones and brown puppy dogs,
> Kaptain Kangaroos and red fire engines.
> I had to decide whether jelly beans or gum drops —
> It was difficult;
> I stood for many hours, my nose to the glass,
> Searching for the answer that would not come.
> At last, sorry because I had not two pennies but only one,
> I chose gum drops;
> They tasted good, but not so good as jelly beans.
> I spent all afternoon chasing a butterfly,
> How it jumped from flower to flower!
> I cried because I could not catch it.
> And the cool water from the stream flowing around my ankles —
> I watched the tadpoles and water gremlins,

Once — when there was time to sit by the bank;
And the wind scattered the seeds of the dandelion
To the far and mystic corners of the earth.
There were thoughts of Christmas; I was anxious
For it seemed that it would never come.
The day the lightning crashed across the heavens,
I thought the clouds would surely break and I was afraid;
I ran to the comforting strength of my mother's arms.
I woke up one morning and the ground was covered with snow;
My brothers took me sledding and I was happy.
I spent a whole summer thinking of how it would be;
School — I had to go in September, summer flew.
But that was a long time ago in another land;
How I wish for just one day to sit by the stream —
And still the images race across my mind.
Dreams, bright hopes for the future, deep forebodings.
Yesterday I was a child;
Today I am a youth not ready to be a man,
But with no choice.
Today there is no candy to choose, no butterflies;
Today I must decide, shall I heal men or destroy them.
I see, somewhere back in the dark caverns of my mind,
A youth in conference at the dinner table;
Asking for more privileges, more freedom.
How I wish I could warn him, tell him what I have learned:
Independence is a loadstone which hangs about the neck,
Breaking the back of all who wear it.
It was so easy when father, teachers decided for me;
And yet I hated them for not realizing that I was old enough
To decide for myself.
But I can not warn him,
And there was no one to warn me;
And what good would it have done?
I am unready to be a man, nor will I be ready
Until I learn to wear the loadstone.
And still the colors whirl,
Clouding my mind until I cannot sleep at night.
I think of the endless days —
Rise and off to school — and sleep was only false relief,
It began again each day.
I cursed the books and classrooms and associations —
The very things that were so vital —
And it seemed as though twelve years were all eternity;

Yet today they are gone forever.
And the images race on into the obscure future —
They are misty and shrouded in doubt.
Lindbergh felt what I now feel
As he coaxed his frail plane into the early morning air,
Its nose pointed toward the unknown;
Also Columbus as he sailed toward the uncharted west.
Can I ever find the same strength which they had
Deep within the marrow of their bones?
Fleetingly it runs through my head;
I feel it now and then within my blood but cannot hold it to me:
It appears now on a crude wooden cross,
Now in the face of a young woman;
There, rising in the sky,
Here in my hand.
I close my hand but it has fled.
And tomorrow, what will tomorrow bring?
I see a student crossing a sunny campus;
I see long nights spent sweating over a thesis on the Ages of Man;
Pulling at the hairs of my head
Are the hands of a worker building machines,
Throwing structures upward toward the sky,
Remolding the very earth I stand on;
And through the cries of pain and the moans of the dying
Walks a merciful angel, easing the misery
Of the sick, the lame, the dying;
And now I am standing on the low rolling hills,
And all about me grow the yellow shoots of wheat;
I see a man behind a desk,
Teaching those who were once me.
The loadstone hangs heavy and there are none to tell me
What is in my mind.
Many hands reach toward me,
But as I grasp they melt before my eyes;
For I alone must choose.
So I stand, silently watching
The kaleidoscope of ideas race through my mind.
A thousand images pass in front of my eyes
Of things gone by and things to come —
All of them vague and transient,
Not one clear enough to grasp.
Today I am a youth not ready to be a man,
But with no choice.

I think one last sighing thought of days gone by
And reach out for the morning sun.

❖   ❖   ❖

Carrying the Ghost of Ray Catina

Carrying the Darkness: The Poetry of the Vietnam War has had a long and successful life for an anthology of poetry. It has been in print almost continuously since 1985, first with Avon Books and since 1989 with Texas Tech University Press. It has reached thousands of readers, and still sells several hundred copies each year.

Inevitably, the book has some glaring omissions. No female veterans are represented, though as Lynda Van Devanter said to me when she and Joan Furey were preparing *Visions of War, Dreams of Peace,* "Of course they wouldn't send you their poems. You're a man." David Connolly and Doug Anderson had not yet published their first books, and thus are not represented. And of course, it doesn't contain a number of wonderful poems written since 1985 by contributors such as John Balaban, D. F. Brown, Dale Ritterbusch, and others who have continued to produce new work.

If I had the book to do again, I would therefore do a number of things differently, but the only actual errors I've ever come upon in all these years were some egregious proofreading mistakes in the Avon edition that I was able to correct in the Texas Tech edition. I've mostly been satisfied that I did the best I could do with what I had available at the time.

Not long ago, however, I stumbled upon yet another egregious error, this time not of proofreading but of fact. The discovery began with a July 2004 e-mail from a long-time friend, the poet Linda Lerner of New York City. Linda is a great supporter of Vietnam War literature and knows the field well. "I thought of you," she wrote, "when I got a book by Alan Catlin called *Ghost Road.* On the back cover it says: 'He has been anthologized extensively, most prominently in *Carrying the Darkness,* edited by W. D. Ehrhart,' but I have your book and he's not in there."

I'd never heard of Alan Catlin, and he's certainly not in my anthology, so I wrote to Scott Douglass at Main Street Rag, publisher of Catlin's 2000 *Ghost Road.* Douglass replied that the jacket information was supplied by

Catlin and he had taken Catlin at his word. "If it helps," he added, Catlin "lives in upstate New York. Any two-poem contributors in the Albany/Schenectady area?"

With this information, I went through the book looking for two-poem contributors from Schenectady. Only one name fit both criteria: Ray Catina.

Readers familiar with *Carrying the Darkness* may remember Catina as the author of "Negotiations" and "Philosophy." In the Notes on Contributors section, compiled from information provided directly by the poets, one finds that Catina was born in 1948 and served as a U.S. Army infantryman in Vietnam, 1969–70.

I checked and re-checked my paperwork. Neither the author's biographical notes, handwritten by Catina, nor the permission form signed by Catina make any mention of an Alan Catlin, and the check for the permissions fee was made out to Ray Catina and sent to Ray Catina. But the address was Schenectady, New York. Moreover, Catina wrote in 1985 that he "occasionally tends bar in upstate New York," while the back jacket of *Ghost Road* says that Catlin "has been working as a bartender in Albany, New York" for the last twenty years.

Armed with this information, I checked my *Poets & Writers* directory, found an address for Catlin — in Schenectady — and wrote to him, presenting the information I had found. Confronted with the evidence, Catlin readily admitted he himself is not a veteran and that he had invented "Ray Catina," adding that "it was a strange time in my life."

Maybe it was. I've had strange times in my life, too. And I've got no problem with pseudonyms. Consider Elia or Mark Twain or Ellis Peters. Nor have I a problem with poetic personas. Consider Bryan Alec Floyd's *The Long War Dead* or William Childress's "The Soldiers." But I do have a problem with someone who invents a fictitious person with a fictitious military history, publishes under that name, receives mail under that name, cashes checks under that name, and never mentions that it's a pseudonym, allowing me to propagate false information in two different editions of *Carrying the Darkness*, and never admitting to the falsehood until nearly two decades later when he's found out. As I told Catlin, "Not cool."

So, for the record, those of you with copies of *Carrying the Darkness*, please amend your Credits, Table of Contents, the author's name on page 69, and the Notes on Contributors, striking out the name of Ray Catina and replacing it with Alan Catlin. And please accept my apology for allowing, however inadvertently, so many readers for so many years to think that Ray Catina was a real person who had fought in Vietnam.

Good Fences Make Good Neighbors: A Brief History of National Myopia

Phi Alpha Theta History Honor
Society Regional Conference & Undergraduate History Forum
Clarion University, April 2nd, 2005

About a month ago, Dr. Todd Pfannestiel asked me what the title of this talk would be. I had no idea. I'm a full-time high school English and history teacher, and it's all I can do to be ready each day to face a classroom full of 16- and 17-year-olds. I hadn't had time even to think about this talk, let alone do anything about it. At the time Todd asked me, however, we happened to be reading Robert Frost's "Mending Wall" in my English classes, and my history class was studying the rise of American Imperialism. With very little thought as to the consequences, I told Todd my talk would be titled "Good Fences Make Good Neighbors: A Brief History of National Myopia."

Then I promptly forgot about it again. Only when the Haverford School let out for spring break last week did I fully realize the corner I'd painted myself into: clever title, but no talk to go with it. So if what I have to say today doesn't really relate to my title, don't be surprised.

As I've thought about it, however, I do think there is some connection between Frost's poem and the way in which we Americans see ourselves — or don't see ourselves. When the narrator in "Mending Wall" observes,

> There where it is we do not need the wall:
> He is all pine and I am apple orchard.
> My apple trees will never get across
> And eat the cones under his pines,

his neighbor only replies, "Good fences make good neighbors." Frost goes on to present a chilling image of the neighbor with a stone

> In each hand, like an old-stone savage armed.
> He moves in darkness as it seems to me,
> Not of woods only and the shade of trees.
> He will not go beyond his father's saying,
> And he likes having thought of it so well
> He says again, "Good fences make good neighbors."

What Frost is getting at here are the ways in which so many of us simply accept all sorts of ideas, beliefs, truisms, and perceptions at face value without ever wondering where they came from or how we acquired them or whether they actually pertain. Indeed, they seem to fit us so well that we imagine we invented them rather than merely and thoughtlessly inheriting them from the equally thoughtless generations who preceded us.

Let me give you a very personal example. In 1966, when I was 17 years old, I turned down four colleges to enlist in the United States Marine Corps. I believed absolutely that I was following in the footsteps of my forebears who at every generation in our nation's history had fought and died for freedom and democracy. As the saying goes, "Freedom isn't free." All of my rights and liberties were secured only at terrible cost to others who were willing to sacrifice for me. Now it was my turn to prove my devotion to liberty.

What I found in Vietnam, however, was nothing at all like what I had been prepared for by my teachers and the other adults of Perkasie, Pennsylvania, by the Philadelphia *Evening Bulletin* and *Time* Magazine, by President Lyndon Johnson.

I found a military dictatorship rife with corruption and venality and repression, and clearly devoid of the support of the vast majority of Vietnamese. I found the wholesale forced removal of hundreds of thousands of people from their ancestral homelands to poverty-stricken, misery-laden shantytowns where men had no work and women rooted through American garbage trying to find food for their children. I witnessed and participated in the destruction of civilian homes and sometimes whole villages, the brutal interrogation of civilians, and the killing of unarmed men, women, and children along with their crops and livestock. I saw the terrible consequences of sending tens of thousands of young Americans, armed to the teeth and scared to death, into the midst of an alien world we had no chance of ever understanding or mastering. I found that the people we were supposedly defending hated us because we destroyed their forests with chemical defoliants, and burned their fields with napalm, and called the people of Vietnam gooks, chinks, slopes and zipperheads, turning their sons into shoeshine boys and their daughters into whores.

What any of this had to do with protecting American liberties and freedoms was exactly nothing. Make no mistake about it: there were Viet Cong in Vietnam, and they tried very hard to kill me. But they had better reasons for killing me than I had for killing them. I had come ten thousand miles to make war on them in their own country. They were the Minutemen; I and my comrades were the Redcoats.

Yet in 1980, when then-candidate Ronald Reagan declared that it was "time to admit that ours was, in truth, a noble cause" in Vietnam, millions of Americans sent up a collective sigh of relief and proceeded to transform the ugly truth of the Vietnam War into something more palatable to American tastes, complete with welcome home parades, monuments, *Rambo* and "I Ain't Fonda Hanoi Jane" bumper stickers. We really were fighting for truth, justice, and the American Way after all.

Never mind that the resurrection of the Vietnam War as noble cause cannot be squared with the facts of what actually happened and why. Who cares about the facts anyway? We love to imagine that our Pilgrim forebears eked out a place in the wilderness by sheer dint of hard work and the grace of God. Never mind that Plimoth offered them a readymade village complete with housing, fresh water, plowed and planted fields, and a good harbor, all conveniently vacated by a tribe that had been wiped out by disease contracted from European fishermen several years earlier. Indeed, we love to imagine that North America was a howling wilderness inhabited by a smattering of nomadic Indians when in fact most tribes were already agriculturalists who migrated, if they migrated at all, only between summer and winter quarters, and not one of the probably millions of Indians inhabiting North America ever imagined they were living in a wilderness.

We love to think of George Washington and his battered troops huddled at Valley Forge, determined against all odds to defeat the mightiest army on earth, and we conveniently forget — or do not know — that we fought our war for independence with French money, French guns, French powder and ball, French uniforms and boots, and ultimately with French ships and French soldiers, all secured not by the courage of Washington, courageous though he was, but by the wily and patient diplomatic skills of Benjamin Franklin.

We love to remember the Alamo, most of us unaware that the freedom those Texans were fighting for was the freedom to keep their slaves in the wake of the Mexican government's decision to abolish slavery. We love our Statue of Liberty with Emma Lazarus's stirring lines, "Give me your tired, your poor, your huddled masses yearning to breathe free," and we don't want to hear about the Chinese Exclusion Act of 1888 or the Immigration Act of 1924.

I could go on for hours — for days, actually — but I said this would be a brief history, didn't I? A few moments ago, I posed the question, "Who cares about the facts?" It doesn't take a rocket scientist to figure out that most Americans certainly don't. Fifteen of the nineteen 9/11 hijackers were Saudi Arabians. None of them was Iraqi. But the U.S. remains a staunch ally of Saudi Arabia while invading Iraq. We had to invade Iraq because Saddam Hussein posed an imminent threat to the U.S., but we don't have to invade North Korea any time soon, even though Kim Jong Il has nuclear weapons and the missiles with which to deliver them. Meanwhile, the massive new Department of Homeland Security that was supposed to solve the communications problems between the FBI and the CIA includes neither the FBI nor the CIA.

As if that weren't shame enough, most Americans not only don't seem to care about the facts; they actually get very upset whenever someone tries to give them the facts. Ask former U.S. Attorney General Ramsey Clark. Ask former U.S. Ambassador to El Salvador Robert White. Ask former Marine and former U.N. weapons inspector Scott Ritter.

But at least one group of Americans should and must care about the facts, and that group is us: the historians. I'd like to be able to report that we are doing our best to battle the relentless tide of ignorance and shortsightedness that blights our fellow citizens. But alas, large numbers of historians seem to care no more about the facts than anyone else. Let me give you a few examples:

In the high school history textbook I used last year, *The American Pageant*, my students read that Americans of the 1890s supported the Cuban insurrection against Spain because our sympathies are "ever on the side of patriots fighting for freedom." Do the authors know anything about U.S. policy toward Haiti from the 1790s onward? Or the struggle between the Cherokee Nation and the state of Georgia? How about the misnamed Philippine Insurrection? Have they ever heard of Major General Smedley Butler, or read his famous speech, "War Is a Racket"? Do they know anything about the Reagan Wars in Central America and the Caribbean?

My own students know nothing at all about any of this stuff, and so they are perfectly happy to believe that Americans have always been on the side of patriots fighting for freedom. They stare at me goggle-eyed when I explain to them what a "gugu" is, or the water cure, or what it means to "civilize 'em with a Krag," or where the term "deadline" comes from. They had no idea, until just the other day, how the United States managed to acquire a naval base at Guantanamo Bay right in the heart of Communist Castro's Cuba.

I am not here to badmouth the United States of America, but the truth is that much of what we imagine about ourselves as a people and a nation simply does not square with the facts. And more often than not, when our beliefs don't match the facts, it is the facts that suffer, not our beliefs. Even historians, who ought to know better, seem prone to this phenomenon.

Consider this: that same U.S. history textbook I cited above carries a chart of U.S. battle deaths in major American wars. It lists all the biggies, including the War of 1812, the Mexican War, and the Spanish-American War. Nowhere, either in the text or in the chart, is there mention of the Philippine War for Independence, either by that name or by the much less embarrassing misnomer of the Philippine Insurrection (as if those unruly Filipinos had to be disciplined for their own good). This is an amazing oversight when you consider that the Philippine War cost the U.S. more battle deaths than the

War of 1812, the Mexican War, and the Spanish-American War combined. Why would a war that cost us so dearly not even merit a mention among major American wars? For that matter, why aren't the Indian Wars ever mentioned among America's major wars? After all, they went on intermittently for more than 250 years, and cost thousands of lives. In a single battle against the Wabash Indian Confederacy in 1791, the U.S. lost more than twice as many dead as were killed in the entire Spanish-American War.

How can we reasonably assess what is done in our name, with our dollars, and often with our lives, if we don't even know who we are or how we came to be who we are? If we don't even know our own history? Thomas Jefferson wrote: "People who expect to be ignorant and free expect what never was and never will be." And when it comes to history, most Americans are profoundly ignorant and willfully so.

Let me come back to my war, an experience that first made me question what I'd been taught and what I thought I knew. The American people were told in the summer of 1964 that North Vietnamese torpedo boats had attacked U.S. destroyers without provocation in international waters. In response, Congress passed the Gulf of Tonkin Resolution, which gave Lyndon Johnson the authority to wage war in Vietnam by executive fiat. We learned only years later that the president knowingly lied about what happened, how, and why. In the meantime, the American people were told repeatedly that the U.S. would stay the course in Vietnam, that victory was slowly but surely being achieved, that we would prevail. Only many years later — long after the war ended in American defeat and 58,000 American dead — did we learn that as early as March 1965, when there were only a few thousand American soldiers in Vietnam, and only a few hundred American dead, Johnson was telling Senate Majority Leader Mike Mansfield that we could not win the war in Vietnam. In 1995, former Secretary of Defense Robert McNamara finally admitted that "we were wrong, terribly wrong" in Vietnam, though we now know that he had reservations as early as 1966, the year I enlisted.

A war begun under false pretenses by a government that insists it is fighting for freedom, slowly but surely winning that fight, and determined to stay the course no matter what: does that sound familiar?

I'm not a believer in historical analogies. In the end, they never hold up. Iraq is not Vietnam, no matter how many similarities we might identify. But I should think my fellow citizens would have learned enough from history to make them more skeptical of the course of events since 1975 than many of them seem to be.

But as Hamlet says, "Aye, there's the rub." Because you can't learn from history if you don't know history. Or if what you know is false history: mythology masquerading as fact. And that's where we come in, my fellow historians. It is — or at least should be — the job of the historian to make people feel uncomfortable, to urge them to look beyond the easy platitudes and behind the vacuous assertions. Good decisions can only come from good information. Rather than assuming that "good fences make good neighbors," rather than acquiescing silently to the shallow cheapness of empty rhetoric and feel-good bluster, it seems to me our obligation to ask,

> *Why* do they make good neighbors?
> Before I built a wall I'd ask to know
> What I was walling in or walling out,
> And to whom I was like to give offense.

❖   ❖   ❖

What the Fuss Is All About

Senior Dinner Remarks
The Haverford School
June 8th, 2006

Thank you for inviting me to speak to you tonight. It is a singular honor that touches me deeply. I want to begin by sharing with you my newest poem; it's called:

What the Fuss Is All About

One wonders what the fuss is all about.
They say the flag is blowing in the wind.
They say the wind is blowing up a storm.
They say the moon is blue, the lies are true,
the bogeyman is here, we must believe
whatever we are told. So all for one
and one for all the money he can get
his sticky fingers on, him and all his
sticky-fingered friends. So what's new?
Just the other day, K Street three-piece-suit
walks into a bar and orders a beer.
Sorry, sir, the barkeep says, we don't serve

sleaze in here; FBI man overhears,
calls the IRS: barkeep's doing time
in Lewisburg. Let that be a lesson
to us all: Miller Lite can change your life.
Super Size me, praise the Lord, and give me
purple mountains' majesty, Hollywood
commandos, and a gas-guzzling SUV
with GPS and Power Everything.
Burn, baby, burn, some angry Black man said,
but I say what's the hurry? Soon enough
we'll burn the whole damned planet down, choke it,
strip it, starve it, melt it, pave it over,
blow it up, and bury it in empty
bottled water bottles, Pampers diapers,
plastic grocery bags, and last year's cellphones.
Then we'll see which way the wind is blowing,
whose flags are blowing in the wind, whose lies
are worth a big rat's ass, who's rich enough
to buy a one-way ticket out of Hell,
whose God is on whose side, and who's left
to wonder what the fuss was all about.

Okay, I realize that's pretty much of a bummer, even for me, and you're probably wondering what the heck it has to do with the happy occasion of your graduation from the Haverford School.

And this is certainly a happy occasion, one full of promise and hope and excitement and possibility. There is a reason why graduation is called "commencement." You are about to commence your lives as adults. You are the future and the future is yours. Your parents and families and teachers and mentors have high expectations for you, and with good reason. Go out and make your mark on the world. As your 2006 *Haligoluk* says, "Be not ordinary men; your talents are more."

So why do I find myself so sad tonight? So close to despair, even. Maybe it's because all of this talk about beginnings and futures and high expectations strikes me as less a reflection of reality than it is the stuff of Hallmark greeting cards. Do you realize that every graduating class in every high school in every community, not just all over America but all over the world, is hearing exactly the same stuff right about now? Tens of thousands of you, hundreds of thousands of you, all being told by proud families and teachers that you are not ordinary men and women. Can they all be telling the truth?

Especially when you consider that more thousands of graduates were told the same thing last year, and the year before that, and the year before that. It strains credulity. And I've got news for you: forty years ago to this very day, I and my 275 classmates at Pennridge High School were being told pretty much what you are going to be told tomorrow. I suspect the students of Plato and Aristotle heard pretty much the same spiel 2500 years ago.

All of which would be okay except that, though you haven't yet been around long enough to know it, we don't seem to be making any progress in spite of all those millions of not-ordinary graduates who've come before you. Indeed, the world into which you are about to commence is — how to put this delicately: royally screwed up, in ruins, dysfunctional, a chaos of greed and misery and suffering and ignorance and arrogance and intolerance and injustice. In case you haven't been paying attention, what with proms and sports and final exams and end-of-year parties: it doesn't look too good out there, boys.

And whose fault is that, you might well ask. A good question, and I think the answer is, "Mine." My fault. Me and my generation. None of us were ordinary men and women, our elders told us; we would go forth with our youth and our energy and our extraordinary talent, and we would fix the world our elders had left to us: perpetual war, nuclear Armageddon, corruption, hunger and poverty, disease, hatred and bigotry, intolerance — all that stuff that's still out there forty years later and going nowhere fast.

One might even make the case that the world is in worse shape now than it was when my generation took over: at least the polar ice caps weren't melting, and the Chinese and the Indians weren't all driving cars yet, and we knew who our enemy the Soviet Union was and where to find him.

True, if you spend any time at all around me, you soon learn that my glass is never half full but always half empty, so you may not be inclined to believe me when I say that things are worse now than they were 40 years ago or 400 years ago or 4,000 years ago, and I'm willing to concede that.

On the other hand, you can't really make the case that things are getting any better either. Generation after generation, century after century, millennium after millennium, we keep making the same choices, the same decisions, the same mistakes. Only a fool could believe that we can keep this up forever, of course, but even a cursory glance at any history book or newspaper readily reveals that the story of humanity is the story of folly. And one of these days, we really are going to burn the whole damned planet down, choke it, strip it, starve it, melt it, pave it over, blow it up, or bury it.

But here's the fun part. Me — I don't really care anymore. Whatever happens now is of little consequence to me. Given my ancestral gene pool, it's fairly safe to say that most of my life is already behind me. If the whole world goes to hell in a hand-basket tomorrow, I won't have missed much.

But you guys: you're just commencing. Your whole lives really are still in front of you. The future really is yours. Are you really just going to keep behaving the same way we've been behaving ever since we started running around naked on the Serengeti Plain? Or are you, for the first time in human history, going to demonstrate that you — you young men sitting right here in front of me — really are "not ordinary men"?

This is not about Republicans or Democrats, liberals or conservatives, Christians or Muslims, Jews or Palestinians, Americans, Armenians, Azerbaijanis, Angolans, Albanians, Arabs, Asians, atheists, agnostics, Anglicans, athletes, atomic physicists, or alligator wrestlers. Or rather, it's about all of those things, about all of us, about a fragile world that appears to be one of a kind in a vast cosmos, precious and irreplaceable.

Are you going to continue to make the same mistakes humanity has been making since time out of mind? Are you going to continue to think in terms of me and mine, us and them, my good fortune and your tough luck, my country versus your country, my way or no way, this is mine and I deserve it? Are you going to continue to live as the generations before you have lived, as if the future will always be there?

Or are you going to do what has never been done before: learn to think truly and genuinely creatively, imaginatively, globally, selflessly, beyond borders and boundaries and horizons, beyond old fears and comfortable truisms that are leading us inevitably toward irreversible disaster?

I love you all dearly. I have learned as much from you as you have learned from me. I have enjoyed these last four years with you more than I could ever make you understand. I will miss you. But I have to be honest with you: nothing in a lifetime of experience and knowledge, nor anything in these past four years among you, leads me to believe that you are going to be any more special, any different, any less ordinary than the long parade of generations that has come before you.

There it is. That's what I think. What are you going to do about it? Prove me wrong? Go ahead, I dare you: prove me wrong.

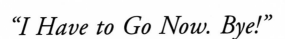

"I Have to Go Now. Bye!"

A Remembrance of Gloria Emerson

Gloria Emerson once described herself to a reporter as "bossy. Ill-tempered. Ferocious. Put all of that down. Do you have it?" And it was all true. Her telephone calls were famous. The phone would ring, you'd answer it, Gloria would launch into a monologue, after awhile you'd give up trying to get a word in edgewise, just hanging on for dear life. And then, with the abruptness of a meat cleaver slamming through a side of beef all the way to the cutting board, she'd say, "I have to go now. Bye!" And you'd be left, breathless and dazed, with the telephone receiver buzzing in your ear, feeling as if you'd just gone fifteen rounds with Joe Frazier.

She could be just as abrupt in writing and in person. Of the second edition of *Carrying the Darkness: The Poetry of the Vietnam War*, she wrote: "I didn't expect you in a new foreword to denounce the war because the poems do that. But I thought what you did write leaden and tedious, and I thought the dedication to your daughter was unnecessary. The world knows how much love you have for her." When I showed up for lunch one day wearing a small Purple Heart lapel pin on my jacket, she barked, "Why are you wearing that? What's the point?"

But she was also soft-hearted, generous, loyal, and courageous. She had nothing but contempt for generals and presidents, but spent her life giving voice to the voiceless: the privates and corporals and hapless civilians crushed by the powerful. And she was brilliant. Watching her speak with out notes to a spellbound audience on the folly of American policy in Vietnam was well worth the quirky late-night calls telling me to put my infant daughter on top of the washing machine and turn it on, I don't have to do any laundry, just turn on the machine and the vibrations will put Leela right to sleep. Bye!

She was one of a kind, and I was often thankful I only had one of her to cope with. But it was impossible not to love someone who could write, "I don't know even now, twenty years after I left [Vietnam], how to harden my heart so it won't be punctured yet again by the war." Someone who could say to a discouraged writer, "Don't keep track of where the other writers are, either behind or ahead. We are all doing what we can, no more no less. It isn't a race, is it?"

I don't remember when or how I first met Gloria. She had already become a part of my life long before that. I have a vague recollection of Jan Barry and Larry Rottmann talking about her support of their efforts to publish what became the landmark 1972 anthology *Winning Hearts and Minds: War Poems by Vietnam Veterans*. She contributed money to the publication of Jan's and my 1976 anthology *Demilitarized Zones: Veterans After Vietnam*. We corresponded when I was working on *Carrying the Darkness* in 1984 and '85. She sent a little blue dress with little white chickens all over it when my daughter Leela was born in 1986. And when the Five College Program in Peace and

Gloria Emerson, journalist, war correspondent, and author of *Winners and Losers*, *Some American Men*, *Gaza*, and *Loving Graham Greene* (courtesy the late Gloria Emerson).

World Security Studies invited her to participate in a scholarly conference called "Tet Plus Twenty: The Legacy of the Vietnam War," she said she'd do it only if the organizers also invited some Vietnam veteran-poets.

Which is how I ended up with Gloria in Amherst, Massachusetts, in February 1988. And she was spectacular that weekend. Riveting. Unforgettable. That was the time she spoke extemporaneously for over an hour on the folly of American policy in Vietnam. Not a single note, yet her presentation was seamless and compelling, the audience rapt.

The next day, when the redoubtable Colonel Harry Summers, Jr. (Retired) told another audience that the U.S. government had played no part at all in the 1963 overthrow of Ngo Dinh Diem, Gloria bluntly asked Summers to explain, then, why Lucien Conein, the veteran CIA operative, had told her that he had said to the Saigon generals who subsequently deposed and executed Diem, "If you don't get rid of Diem, we'll do it ourselves." Taken aback, Summers ponderously launched into a long-winded and convoluted obfuscation, but Gloria cut him off sharply. "How can you lie to all these people?" she asked, gesturing around the auditorium. The moderator intervened at that point, and Summers must have thought he had dodged a bullet, but later Gloria collared him in a corridor and repeated her question, shaking her finger in his face, Summers looking very much like a deer caught in the headlights before scurrying away with Gloria in hot pursuit.

How could you not love her? How could you not forgive her the quirks and foibles and idiosyncrasies, the irascibility and the bluntness? It was all, I think, perhaps just her way of hiding the tenderness of her heart, the weight of the pain she carried for the suffering of others, the innocent and the helpless. Way back in 1972, she had written, "One American was picked up with a head wound and lay on the floor, not dead and not alive. The medic could not stop the bleeding. It all becomes normal, the other correspondents, men, would say. In time, you'll see. They lied."

Nearly two decades later, in her stunning book *Gaza: A Year in the Intifada*, she wrote, "The Israeli Defense Forces maintained the position that consideration was always given" to Palestinian women, "but the witness knows better. A group of middle-aged women, their bodies shaped like old pillows, another choir of grief," are charged by soldiers whose faces reflect "high glee, as if now they were playing a favorite game and certain to win."

In contrast to her first book, *Winners and Losers: Battles, Retreats, Gains, Losses, and Ruins from the Vietnam War*, which earned her a National Book Award, *Gaza* earned her mostly a lot of grief. Writing sympathetically about Palestine and the Palestinians has never been a popular choice in the United States, and Gloria became the target of harassment at readings, the recipient of voluminous hate mail. Yet all she ever said to me about the firestorm her honesty and clear-sightedness had created was, "The whole year has been taken up either defending *Gaza* or trying to sell it. You know the struggle."

I never could figure out what was the point of her second book, *Some American Men*, which just never resonated with me. But her other three books are masterpieces made all the more remarkable by the fact that each is completely different from the others: *Winners and Losers* a sweeping account of the consequences and aftermath of the Vietnam War, *Gaza* a short hard punch in the solar plexus, *Loving Graham Greene* a work of fiction.

Loving Graham Greene, published late in her life, may be the most disturbing of all of her books, for me at least. I fear the novel's protagonist, Molly Benson, is Gloria herself as she saw herself in the last years of her life, a foolish idealist who accomplished nothing for all her good intentions. That Gloria chose to end her own life a few years later, though I will never know what led her to that decision, does nothing to dispel my fear.

And that makes me very sad because I hate to think of Gloria feeling so alone and useless and empty. She meant so much to so many people for so many years. Within days of her death, I got e-mails or phone calls from a host of friends — Wayne Karlin, John Balaban, Jan Barry, John McAuliff, Jack Laurence, John Ketwig, John Prados and Ellen Pinzur, Marc Leepson, John Baky, Martin Novelli, Bill Crandell, Dave Connolly: poets, writers, veterans, old VVAW guys, journalists, activists, teachers — most of whom had known and loved Gloria, and all of whom noted her passing with profound sorrow.

How often these days do I wish that my phone might ring and there would be Gloria on the other end, launching into another one of her lopsided conversations, telling me not to be so petit bourgeois or promising not to nag me anymore "because it doesn't do any good" or urging me to "overcome the bitterness, a form of poison." And then the famous, "I have to go now. Bye!"

❖   ❖   ❖

Concerning Memorial Day

When I was a boy, Memorial Day was my favorite holiday. Its arrival meant that school would soon be over for another year. It was also the day the local swimming pool opened for the summer. Best of all, it afforded me that only-once-a-year opportunity to decorate my bicycle with red, white and blue crepe paper, and join the high school marching band and the trucks of the volunteer fire company in the big parade up Fifth Street to the town's war memorial.

And the crowning moment, the apex of it all, was when the American Legion color guard fired its 21-gun salute for America's fallen heroes. That sharp crack was the real thing. Not the adolescent "Bang! Bang!" of our imaginary guns, but the genuine ear-splitting thunder of rifles. My playmates and I always waited impatiently for the bugler to finish playing Taps so we could scramble after the empty brass casings we treasured as souvenirs.

It simply wasn't possible for a 10-year-old to comprehend what Memorial Day really meant. Only when I got to Vietnam as an 18-year-old Marine volunteer did I come to understand that real guns shatter people's skulls and scatter their brains like spilled pudding, or rip their insides to shreds and leave them screaming for their mothers. Only then did I realize that all the pageantry every year is designed to make people believe that it is somehow noble and heroic to send our children off to be maimed, mutilated and butchered while attempting to inflict that sort of punishment upon others.

My grandfather's generation fought in the war to end all wars. My father's generation fought in the war to rid the world of fascism. My generation fought in Vietnam to — to what? What was it for that time? Nothing that mattered, we came to realize, but only after the damage had been done. And the killing just goes on and on. Since my generation stopped dying in Vietnam, American soldiers have died in Cambodia, Iran, Lebanon, Grenada, El Salvador, Panama, Kuwait, Iraq, Somalia, Yemen, Afghanistan, and now Iraq again.

And I begin to suspect that the politicians and generals who tell us that we must sacrifice our children for the cause of peace are perhaps being just a bit disingenuous. I didn't see any politicians in the ricefields of Vietnam, and precious few generals died there. Kenny Worman died there. Randy Moore died there. Kids who used to ride their bikes in Perkasie's Memorial Day parade with me. Kids who had no quarrel with the people who killed them. Kids who died merely because powerful people who would never have to face death in battle told them it was their duty to die.

More recently, we were told repeatedly that we had to send our children into harm's way because Iraq possessed weapons of mass destruction that posed a direct and immediate threat to the peace and security of our country. Four years later, 3,200 more young Americans are dead, 30,000 more have been wounded, we all know that we went to war for a lie, Mr. Bush asks us to be patient, Congress dithers over non-binding resolutions, and there is no end in sight.

Have the dead and wounded of our latest war sacrificed for their country? I don't think so. Nor do I think my friends Kenny and Randy died for their country in Vietnam. They died for the fantasies and machinations of arrogant powerbrokers the American people repeatedly and mistakenly put our confidence in, generation after generation, too ignorant ourselves, or too spineless, to separate the rhetoric of patriotism from the substance of patriotism.

I don't go to Memorial Day parades anymore. It seems to me that if we really want to honor our fallen heroes, we might try a little harder to keep any more of them from falling. We might try to be a little less gullible when politicians and generals tell us the next war is necessary. We might take a moment to consider that the ones who start these wars for peace are seldom the ones who do the killing or the dying.

"Knock Their Jocks Off, Boys!"

Just about every pre-meet locker-room pep talk Swarthmore College's men's swimming coach Jimmy McAdoo ever gave ended with some variation of those words. Considering that Jimmy coached the team from the fall of 1937 to the spring of 1972, that's a lot of knocked-off jocks. And if you say those words to anyone who ever swam for Jimmy, you're guaranteed to get a smile and a story for your trouble.

Jimmy was the kind of coach who changed lives for the better, who taught young men how to be men in the finest and most inclusive sense of the word. Here's a brief sampling of thoughts from those who swam for him:

Alden Bennett '40: "God bless him, he never gave up on me." David Alburger '42: "A cheerful, enthusiastic, and supportive man." Stephen Sickle '50: "Swimming for Jimmy was a pleasure." Joe Becker '66: "He treated his swimmers as though they were his sons." Mark Sherkow '67: "The kind of man you wish could live forever." Brad Lemke '70: "He had that special knack of making those around him feel important." Don Cassidy '75: "Jimmy McAdoo was one of the most important mentors in my life."

And the stories: oh, goodness. The time the team had to push their bus through Lancaster in a snowstorm. The season Jimmy persuaded Ken Landis '48 to become a diver. The night Jimmy treated his seniors to dinner at Bookbinder's. The meet at which the entire diving stand pulled out of the deck and ended up in the pool. The time Jimmy suckered the Johns Hopkins coach into thinking the meet would be a walk-over.

All of these reflections and stories are included in *Jimmy: Swimmer, Coach, and Dad* (iUniverse, 2007), a

James J. McAdoo, Jr., in his Red Cross field service uniform, circa 1945. McAdoo took a leave of absence from his job as men's varsity swimming coach at Swarthmore College to work with American occupation troops in Europe at the end of World War II (courtesy James H. McAdoo).

new book written by Jimmy's oldest son, James H. McAdoo (Jimmy the coach was James J.). Also included are Jimmy's family background and Irish roots, his stellar career as a competitive swimmer in his own right, his marriage and family life, his service with the Red Cross during World War II, and other aspects of Jimmy's life that few of his swimmers ever saw or were aware of.

But while the book is a biography of Jimmy, it is also the story of a man's search to understand his father. What most of Jimmy's Swarthmore swimmers saw was an upbeat, jovial, happy-go-lucky man who was always smiling, joking, encouraging. A man who was never angry. But that is not the man that young Jim and his two brothers grew up with.

There was a darker side to Jimmy that we swimmers never saw: the man who had grown up hardscrabble in working-class Germantown, who turned down a college swimming scholarship to read meters for Philadelphia Gas Works, who spent some forty years in an unhappy marriage, who could never make a living at the one thing he loved, who worked a succession of dead-end jobs just so he could coach, who struggled all his life with alcohol and sadness.

What's most remarkable about this book, however, is not what the son reveals about his father, but that the son is able to do so with profound love and affection and respect. What one learns about Jimmy does not diminish him, but rather makes one appreciate all the more the man that Jimmy was able to be for so many of us. And while I do not want to give the story away, I feel constrained to say that for all young

Bronze plaque that hangs in Swarthmore College's Ware Pool, built in 1981 to replace the ancient pool in Hall Gym where Jimmy spent his coaching years. With the support and assistance of Swarthmore's then–Vice President Kendall Landis, the plaque was initiated and funded largely by the swimmers Jimmy had coached during his 34 years at Swarthmore.

Jim's travails growing up with Jimmy, father and son did indeed come to an accommodation in the son's adulthood, an understanding of each other, and finally a deep and abiding friendship.

Jimmy's last season was my junior year, 1971–72. In the middle of the season, Jimmy suffered a heart attack and was hospitalized briefly. (Therein lies another good story: our surprise victory over Franklin & Marshall with Jimmy "coaching" us by telephone.) But he came back to finish the season, and I was looking forward to my senior year as Jimmy's team captain only to be told by the athletic director in September 1972 that Jimmy had decided to "retire."

Neither his son nor I nor anyone who knew Jimmy in those years believes that his retirement was voluntary. But that is water over the dam. Jimmy went on to coach at La Salle College for the last three years of his life, assisting a man Jimmy had himself coached four decades earlier at North Catholic High. It was typical of Jimmy that he did not bridle at becoming an assistant. One thing this book makes clear, the one thing that his swimmers always sensed, is that when Jimmy was coaching, Jimmy was happy.

What follows is an article from the Swarthmore College *Phoenix*, February 29th, 1972, giving an account of what would be Jimmy McAdoo's last regular season meet as Swarthmore's swimming coach, though none of us knew this at the time:

"S'more Sinks Soldiers as Swimmers Surface for Rare Successful Season" By Bill Ehrhart

Jimmy McAdoo's Marvelous Mermen blew Penn Morton/Pennsylvania Military Colleges right out of the pool Saturday afternoon. The victory brought the season's final record to 6–3 (5–1 in league competition), the best swimming season since 1958.

The meet began in a flourish of drums and bugles as the PMC cadet corps rolled out their traditional Civil War cannon, complete with caisson, six white horses, pumpkin, and gleaming gun crew.

It was discovered, when starting the first race, that the indoor pool complex did not provide sufficient running room for the 12-pound cannonball, which blew an 8x10 foot hole in the wall, so the usual starter's pistol was returned.

In the 200 yard freestyle, Don Cassidy picked his way through the rubble to finish in record breaking time, as Barney Voegtlen grabbed third. The 50 yard freestyle went to Bob Smith with Jeff Troy a close second and Bill Arden, swimming exhibition, also beating the PMC entries. Arden then came back to take third in the 200 yard medley.

Next, Colin "the Sleeper" Barnett, swimming the 200 yard butterfly for his first and last time in his four year dual meet career, took a resounding first. The meet had to be delayed until Coach McAdoo managed to bring his surprise under control. During the delay, the six white horses were removed for sanitary reasons.

Another surprise entry was Bill Ehrhart in the 200 yard backstroke. The crowd was on its feet as the first 25 yards went neck and neck. Ehrhart, however, unaccustomed to the 85 degree warm tropical water, soon went to sleep and finished only second with Pete Jacquette a close third.

Cassidy and Bobby McKinstry finished 1–2 in the 500 yard freestyle, with Cassidy setting another college record. At this point, the gleaming gun crew had to be removed after they tried to bayonet Super Don.

Arden took to the water again, this time with a bar of soap in each hand, finishing third in the 200 yard breaststroke. After the race, Arden remarked, "Would you look at the size of this bathtub?"

In the final event, the 400 yard freestyle relay, the PMC team was quickly left behind as the official Swarthmore entry of Smith, Voegtlen, Troy, and Craig Edwards battled an exhibition team of Cassidy, Stover Jenkins, Barnett, and McKinstry.

In the victors' locker room after the meet, above the din of popping champagne corks, an exuberant Cassidy was heard to say, "We knocked their jocks off, Jimmy!"

I last saw Jimmy in the spring of 1975. A few months later, he was dead. Here is the poem I wrote for him soon after I got the news:

Jimmy

> (for James J. McAdoo, Jr.
> Swarthmore College Men's
> swimming coach for 34 years)
> Age finally caught him from behind
> like a swimmer coming on strong
> in the last ten yards of the race
> nobody ever really believed
> would end.

> We all knew it was coming, of course,
> but it was hard to think of him
> as an old man; somehow, he was still
> just a kid, just one of us —
> "French 75s" and his lost jeep on VE Day
> just another campus prank. Jimmy
> with his "Knock their jocks off, boys!"
> and his soft eyes misting
> when you'd done your best
> and lost.

The last time I saw him
he was stooped and puffy, moving
with slow deliberate care —
but he went for a ride in my MG Midget,
muttered a curse in my ear,
and kissed me with an exuberant joy
ageless
as the love which binds him to us
even now.

❖   ❖   ❖

The Value of Your Name

Honor Assembly
The Haverford School
November 26th, 2007

All but the newest members of the Haverford School community know that I'm particular about my name. Faculty and staff have grown accustomed — perhaps I should say inured — to the e-mails correcting misspellings of my name on the bus duty list or the health screening list or the advisory roster. Those students who've had me for a teacher know it's not unusual to find, as a for-credit question on quizzes and tests, "How do you spell your teacher's last name?" Billy Annesley spelled my name wrong on a recent paper assignment, and got a dose of red ink for his trouble. I suppose it's a bit of a joke around here, the way I respond to misspellings of my name, but I don't think it's funny at all. Names matter. My name matters. Your name matters.

Though we mostly behave as if it isn't true, not a one of us human beings has much in this world that is ours. Really and truly ours. Go home today and take a look around you at what you have — your iPods and your iMacs, your hockey pucks and your DVDs, your Calvin Kleins and your SUVs, your athletic skills, your academic achievements, your wealth, your hopes, your dreams, your friends, and your families: everything and everyone you love — any or all of it you could lose tomorrow. Ask those folks whose homes burned down in the recent fires in California. Ask our recent graduate, Fred Robinson, or the family of Jack Berrittini. And even if you are lucky enough to get through life without those sorts of tragedies ever befalling you, sooner or later we all have to dance with the Reaper, and you will most assuredly take with you none of what you think you possess when you finally bid this earthly life farewell.

In truth, each of you possesses only two things that are truly your own. One of these things is your name. That's T. C. Gallagher. There's Travis Loving. That guy out there is Bobby Greco. And I'm William Daniel Ehrhart. I was Bill Ehrhart on the day I was born. I will be Bill Ehrhart on the day I die. My name is me. It is who I am. When you misspell my name, you are calling me something — or rather someone — that I am not. Which is why I take umbrage.

But while you can mangle my name, you cannot take it from me. Nor can you take from me that one *other* thing that is truly mine: my honor. My honor, like my name, is also mine alone. It belongs to no one but me. Call it dignity, call it self-respect, call it integrity, it is all the same, and it too is me. It is who I am. Whether I am rich or poor, young or old, alone or surrounded by family and friends, I have my honor. You can no more take my honor from me than you can take my name.

There is one great difference, however. Unlike my name, which I cannot give away, I can give my honor away. You can't take it from me, but I can give it away. And I can tell you — I will tell you — and from hard experience — that once you give your honor away, you will not easily regain it. Furthermore, once you give your honor away, your name alone is of little value. "My good name" is not just an expression.

I am going to tell you a story. An unpleasant story. A harsh story. One that may make many of you uncomfortable. I would like to apologize for that, but I won't because the truth is often uncomfortable, and what I am about to tell you is the truth. Before I do that, however, I need to give you a little background:

I've spent most of my life being pretty much an ordinary guy. I was an ordinary kid. Like most kids, I was mostly honest enough. Okay, when I was little, I lied to my Mom about where I got the 12 cents to buy that Tastykake apple pie — (12 cents for a Tastykake: that should give you some indication of just how old I am) — I didn't really go to the store for groceries for our next-door neighbor, old Mr. Moyer; I took the money from my mother's purse.

My mom called Mr. Moyer to check, and I got spanked on my bare backside. Oh, and yes, my pal Larry Rush and I told Mr. Druckenmiller, our junior high gym teacher, that I'd done three pull-ups when in fact I couldn't do even one.

We got away with that one, Larry and I. In fact, I got away with a lot of stuff, now that I think about it. Little stuff. Nothing that ever really mattered. A white lie here. A glance at someone else's quiz there. One year I collected money for the United Nations Children's Fund at Halloween and split the take 50–50 with the UN — hey, I wasn't rich growing up, and it's not like I kept *all* the money for myself. Another time, I faked the results of a project and won a yellow ribbon at the school science fair — but if I'd actually done the experiment, the laws of physics told me it would have worked the way I said it did, so where was the harm? And the only reason I told my folks I was going to watch TV at Jeff Apple's house is because they would never have let me hitchhike to a party in a town 15 miles away.

Don't get the wrong idea here. It wasn't as though I was a juvenile delinquent. I was a varsity athlete, a consistent Honor Roll student, vice president of my student council, a member of the National Honor Society, a student speaker at my high school commencement. Indeed, I don't think I was really any more dishonest than most of my peers. We all took the less-than-high road now and then. It was no big deal. Many of you do, too, I'll bet, and more often than you'd care to admit. After all, it's just the little stuff, right? When it matters, you do the right thing, don't you?

But unlike you — at least I hope it's unlike you — I eventually found myself in a situation that really did matter, that really was a big deal. Indeed, a much bigger deal than I had any way of realizing at the time.

Most of you know that I enlisted in the U.S. Marine Corps when I was younger than many of you VI Formers are now, and I ended up in the Vietnam War, still at an age younger than at least some of you are now. I'm not proud of anything I did during my thirteen months in Vietnam, but most of what I did was neither honorable nor dishonorable. It was just what happens in war, the object of which, in the end, is to kill, maim, cripple, and destroy until the people whose lives you are deliberately making miserable either give up or all die. This sort of thing is not honorable, one cannot avoid observing, but the dishonor lies with those who send soldiers to do these things, not with the soldiers themselves.

There is one thing I did, however, for which I and I alone am responsible, and which was very much a question of honor. A question of honor, and courage, and respect. One evening after I'd been in Vietnam for over a year — in fact during a lull in the biggest battle of the war — one of the scouts came into the building where some of us were resting after a hard day of fighting, and told us he'd found a woman over at the refugee collection center who would do the lot of us for one case of C-rations, twelve meals. That is: to have sex with us. Moreover, he had a friend in the weapons platoon who would let us use his 60mm mortar pit if we let him in on the deal.

I was tired, scared, dirty, and hungry, it was cold and raining, and getting laid, at that particular moment of my life, was not among the things on my to-do list. But we were young, we were Marines, we imagined we were men, and who was going to decline, in front of his comrades and peers, an offer to get laid? Not me. So off I went with five or six other guys to the mortar position up by the River of Perfumes. Together we lifted the gun tube out of the pit. Then, while the rest of us stood around smoking in the cold, dark rain, one after the other we took our turns. When my turn came, I lowered myself down into that pit and did what I'd come there to do.

All the while, I kept thinking to myself, "This isn't right. I shouldn't be doing this." I felt more than a little sick to my stomach, and the uneasiness only increased when, face to face with the woman, I discovered how young she was, how sullen and unresponsive. Maybe she was a prostitute. More likely she was a young mother with children to feed, or a daughter whose parents could find no food because the war had come to their city with a vengeance and turned their world upside down. Whoever she was, what I did that night — an act of conscious choice I had had at least half an hour to reverse before the choice became irreversible — what I did that night was disgusting. It was vile, repulsive, degrading. It was without honor.

So why did I do it? The explanation is simple: I did not have the courage to say to my buddies, "This is wrong. We should not do this." I did not even have the courage to say, "You guys go ahead if you want to. Count me out." Because I did not want my buddies to think of me as less than a man, or as some kind of Goody Two-Shoes, because I did not want to face their potential taunts and teasing, I went ahead and did something that, even as I was doing it, I knew was wrong.

But you see, I'd already spent years doing things that were wrong and getting away with it. Cutting corners here, going along with the crowd there. Not big things. Who got hurt if I lied to my parents about where I was going? Who got hurt if I lifted a book of Stephen Crane's poetry from our school library? Who got hurt if we partied at the house of whoever's parents happened to be away that weekend? Who got hurt if we called Barbara Hoffman "Barn"? Well, maybe Barbara did, but everybody does it. It's called being a teenager, isn't it?

And of course, I'd seen and done plenty of ugly things in the year I'd been fighting in Vietnam, so what was one more bit of ugliness? The war was insane. How was this any different? It made me uncomfortable at the time, I knew it was wrong at the time, but that would pass. It always had. What harm was done, really? It wasn't like we raped the woman.

The interesting thing is, just as Larry Rush and I had fooled Mr. Druckenmiller back in junior high and gotten away with it, my buddies and I got away with what we'd done, too. Nearly as I can tell, what we did wasn't even illegal. I didn't have to answer to anyone for it. It isn't like I got court-martialed, or had to go before the Honor Council, or explain myself to Mr. Rein.

But as time passed, as weeks became months became years, the memory of that night did not fade. Even a permanent tattoo will fade over time, but that night was tattooed into my soul, and it did not fade, and has not faded. It will be forty years come this February, yet I still remember that night, if anything, more vividly than ever: her silence, her passivity, my cowardice, my lack of self-respect, my weakness, and every time I remember, a great wave of shame washes over me, and I want to cry out, "No, that wasn't me! That was someone else. I couldn't have stooped so low. There must be some mistake. Give me another chance."

But that's not the way life works. Life doesn't come with a reset button. Or a bottle of White-Out. You don't get to re-write your first draft. At any given moment, you do what you do, and then you live with it. For the rest of your life. When I look in the mirror, there's only me. I had a clear choice to make that night. I knew right, and I chose wrong. The years have not eased the burden of that decision.

Some of you, maybe all of you, are wondering how I can stand up here and share with you the dirty linen of my life, the kinds of secrets that ought not to be talked about in polite company. Well, here's another little truth: what you think of me is of no great consequence. I'm the one who has to live with me. And if I have any chance at all of helping at least some of you boys to make better decisions than I did, you really need to know why I think it's important. You really need to understand the cost of choosing wrongly. I would just as soon none of you boys ends up dragging through his life the kind of baggage I've been dragging through mine.

And a great part of why I ended up forfeiting my honor that night in 1968 in Vietnam is because I had, even by the young age of 19, gotten accustomed to choosing wrong over right when expediency seemed to make that the better choice. The advance warning about the quiz questions from a buddy who took the quiz first period. The four-mile training run that turns into two miles and a medium fries. The book taken from someone else's locker. The Tastykakes eaten but never paid for. The silence when someone remarks, "That's so gay."

Mr. Patrylak has a sign in his room that says something to the effect of, "Be careful what you do, it becomes a habit. Be careful of your habits. They become what you are." Learn to value your honor now, while the stakes are still relatively small, so that you will know how to value your honor when the stakes are high. Learn to make good decisions here in this community that gives you shelter and support and love and concern, so that when you are alone and afraid, and no one around you cares, you will have the courage and integrity and self-respect to make the hard right choice rather than the easy wrong choice.

Right now, I suspect, the abstract concept of honor may not mean all that much to most of you. Strive to be honorable anyway. Someday, if not today, honor will mean a great deal to you, may be the most important thing in your life, and when that day comes, it will be on you and you alone to defend your honor — or to give it away. And upon that choice will rest the value of your name. The value of who and what you are. The measure of your life. In the beginning, in the end, and in between, you have only your name and your honor. You have only your good name. In no figurative way, what you do with your good name is entirely up to you.

❖   ❖   ❖

Words for John Balaban

Not every American can say he got lost one chilly Saturday afternoon in Hanoi. Especially not in 1985, when Americans in Hanoi were about as common as feathers on a fish. But I can. So can John Balaban.

We'd been walking all afternoon, mesmerized by this ancient city, by the fact of our being in it. Old Hanoi, the Rising Dragon of antiquity become sleepy French colonial outpost become the very heart of the indomitable people who had defeated the most powerful empire the world has ever known.

The Temple of Literature. The One-Pillared Pagoda. The Lake of the Returned Sword. Ho Chi Minh's Tomb. And the people: the noodle shops and bicycle repairmen and vegetable venders. The lotus cutters. The Red River with its dikes and paddy fields. We had been like kids in a candy shop. Like sponges in a bucket. Wide-eyed. Amazed. Enchanted.

But now we were hopelessly lost in spite of my repeated insistence that I knew how to get us back to our hotel. Cold and exhausted from five hours of walking, we finally concluded that there was nothing for it but to hire a cyclo — a rickshaw-like bicycle — to rescue us. Ubiquitous as they had seemed earlier in the day, it took another 45 minutes to locate one. Finally, with Balaban negotiating because only he could speak Vietnamese, we settled with the driver on a price of 50 dong (then about $3.50) and climbed aboard.

John Balaban (right) and me (left) flanking doctors and staff of Bach Mai Hospital in Hanoi during a tour of the facility in December 1985. Thirteen years earlier, the hospital had been bombed by an American B-52 during President Richard Nixon's furious final air campaign against North Vietnam, destroying one wing of the hospital and killing 28 members of the hospital staff (courtesy Commission of Investigation into War Crimes, Socialist Republic of Vietnam).

Which was no easy task: our third companion, Bruce Weigl, took up the entire wicker seat while Balaban and I perched on either arm of the chair. It was now pitch dark. As the driver pedaled along, working very hard to propel his 450-pound load, John tried to talk with him, but about all we could discover was that the driver liked "Hotel California," a song by the Eagles, an American rock band.

After awhile, I began to suspect that we were not going in the right direction. We seemed to be heading out of the city, rather than into it. But my directional credibility had long since evaporated, and I was rudely and gaily told to shut up. Perched precariously on the narrow arm of the cyclo chair, my rear end and left leg were by now asleep, which sounds more benign than it felt.

Soon, however, I was sure we were going in the wrong direction. Only a few hundred yards up ahead stood the Thang Long Hotel, where we had eaten dinner a few nights earlier with a group of disabled Vietnamese veterans. The Thang Long Hotel was on the edge of the city, a very long way from the Thong Nhat Hotel, where we were staying.

There followed a brief but energetic burst of shouting and general pandemonium. Then Balaban began to talk to the driver. I couldn't, of course, understand anything he was saying. Except the words "Thang Long."

"What hotel are you asking for, John," I interrupted.

"The Thang Long."

"That's the Thang Long," I said, pointing. "We're staying at the Thong Nhat."

"Oops," Balaban replied.

"You want to try explaining this one to the driver?" I asked.

"No," he replied. But he did. And it clearly wasn't what the driver wanted to hear. He was panting hard and drenched in sweat. At first he refused to budge, as if he couldn't believe what Balaban was saying. Then he shook his head, as if to say, "No wonder we beat them." But he turned around, and off we went again.

At one point we were stopped by a policeman. There was a brief conversation between the cyclo driver and the cop, and then we were off again. "I think it's illegal to ride three to a cyclo," John said, "But the guy explained that we're Americans and we're lost, and the cop told him to beat it."

Our driver was pedaling furiously now, anxious to be rid of us. On one narrow street, we overtook one of the old French-built trolley cars, the three of us cheering and urging our driver on, the trolley passengers hanging out the windows and laughing and pointing, and when we finally drew up even with the trolley driver, he waved and smiled and rang the trolley's bell.

And then we were cruising around the far side of the Lake of the Returned Sword, and past Indira Gandhi Park and the Central Bank building, and finally there was our hotel. Our driver was whipped. He leaned over the handlebars, breathing like he'd just gone fifteen rounds with Smokin' Joe Frazier. Then looked up and grinned. Even as I write this, he's probably telling his grandchildren about the three crazy Americans he met one cold December night long ago.

I no longer remember when I first met Balaban — the late 1970s, or maybe 1980. But I'd first encountered his poetry in 1974, years before we finally met, when Jan Barry and I were putting together *Demilitarized Zones: Veterans After Vietnam*. Barry had come across a collection of Balaban's poems published earlier that year called *After Our War*, and we were both deeply taken with Balaban's work. We ended up including seven of Balaban's poems in our anthology, and Balaban's writing has been a staple of my life ever since. In

1987, in the course of an essay called "Soldier-Poets of the Vietnam War," I had this to say about him and *After Our War*:

"Balaban is an anomaly: a soldier-poet who was not a soldier; indeed, he opposed the war and became a conscientious objector. But he chose to do his alternative service in Vietnam, first as a teacher of linguistics at the University of Can Tho, then as field representative for the Committee of Responsibility to Save War-Injured Children. Later returning to Vietnam independently in order to study Vietnamese oral folk poetry, he spent a total of nearly three years in the war zone — learning to speak Vietnamese fluently and even getting wounded on one occasion — and he is as much a veteran of the Vietnam War as any soldier I have ever met.

"Because of his unique situation, however, Balaban brings to his poetry a perspective unlike any other. 'A poet had better keep his mouth shut,' he writes in 'Saying Good-bye to Mr. and Mrs. My, Saigon, 1972':

> Unless he's found words to comfort and teach.
> Today, comfort and teaching themselves deceive
> and it takes cruelty to make any friends
> when it is a lie to speak, a lie to keep silent.

"While Balaban's poems offer little comfort, they have much to teach. Years before Agent Orange was widely acknowledged for the silent killer it is — the deadly seed sown in Asia only to take root at home among those who thought they'd survived — Balaban wrote in 'Along the Mekong':

> With a scientific turn of mind I can understand
> that malformation in lab mice may not occur in children
> but when, last week, I ushered hare-lipped, tusk-toothed kids
> to surgery in Saigon, I wondered, what had they drunk
> that I had drunk.

And his 'The Guard at the Binh Thuy Bridge' is a frightening exercise in quiet tension — the way it was; the war always a hair trigger away, just waiting to happen:

> How still he stands as mists begin to move,
> as morning, curling, billows creep across
> his cooplike concrete sentry perched mid-bridge
> over mid-muddy river.
>
>   * * *
>
> Anchored in red morning mist a narrow junk
> rocks its weight. A woman kneels on deck
> staring at lapping water. Wets her face.

> Idly the thick Rach Binh Thuy slides by.
> He aims. At her. Then drops his aim. Idly.

"Balaban is particularly adept at contrasting the impact of the war on Vietnam with the indifference of those at home. In 'The Gardenia in the Moon,' he writes: 'Men had landed on the moon. / As men shot dirty films in dirty motel rooms, / Guerrillas sucked cold rice and fish.' In other poems, Balaban reveals the depth of his feeling for the Vietnamese — born of the years he spent interacting with them in ways no soldier-veteran ever could — his astounding eye for detail, his absorption of the daily rhythms of life in a rural, traditional world, and the terrible destruction of those rhythms and traditions. In 'Orpheus in the Upper World,' he offers perhaps an explanation for the hundreds and even thousands of poems written by those who fought the war:

> For when his order had burst his head
> like sillowy seeds of milkweed pod,
> he learned to pay much closer watch
> to all things, even small things,
> as if to discover his errors.

"Not all the poems in *After Our War* deal with Vietnam. But if some of the non–Vietnam poems occasionally reveal the graduate student laboring to flex his intellectual muscle, they also reveal the poet's ability to transcend Vietnam and reach out to the wider world around him."

As I look back now, I realize I've written a lot about Balaban's poetry over the years, and that last sentence above is just about the harshest thing I've ever had to say about it — not because I can't see the flaws and weaknesses, but because there are so few. Later in that same essay, "Soldier-Poets of the Vietnam War," I had this to say about Balaban's second collection, *Blue Mountain*: "Here are poems ranging from the American West to the southern Appalachians, from Pennsylvania to Romania, along with eloquent elegies to friends and family members.

"Still, lingering memories of the Vietnam War persist. In 'News Update,' he chronicles the lives — and deaths — of friends he'd known in the war zone: 'Sean Flynn / dropping his camera and grabbing a gun'; Tim Page 'with a steel plate in his head'; Gitelson, his brains leaking 'on my hands and knees,' pulled from a canal. 'And here I am, ten years later,' he muses:

> written up in the local small town press
> for popping a loud-mouth punk in the choppers.
> Oh, big sighs. Windy sighs. And ghostly laughter.

In 'For Mrs. Cam, Whose Name Means *Printed Silk*,' he reflects on the dislocation of the refugee boat people:

The wide Pacific flares in sunset.
Somewhere over there was once your home.
You study the things which start from scratch.

And in 'After Our War' (the poem, not the book), he writes:

After our war, the dismembered bits
— all those pierced eyes, ear slivers, jaw splinters,
gouged lips, odd tibias, skin flaps, and toes —
came squinting, wobbling, jabbering back.

After observing wryly that 'all things naturally return to their source,' he wonders, 'After our war, how will love speak?'

"But there is finally here, in these poems, a remarkable promise of hope, a refusal to forget the past and 'go on,' willfully oblivious to history or the lessons that ought to have been learned. In 'In Celebration of Spring,' he insists:

Swear by the locust, by dragonflies on ferns,
by the minnow's flash, the tremble of a breast,
by the new earth spongy under our feet:
that as we grow old, we will not grow evil,
that although our garden seeps with sewage,
and our elders think it's up for auction — swear
by this dazzle that does not wish to leave us —
that we will be keepers of a garden, nonetheless.

More than transcending the Vietnam War, in *Blue Mountain* Balaban absorbs Vietnam and incorporates it into a powerful vision of what the world *ought* to be."

In another essay, "Praise the Poet," I wrote of *Blue Mountain* that "one expects poems about the Vietnam War from the author of *After Our War*, of course. Indeed, those who insist that it is time to put Vietnam behind us may well deserve to be convicted of a felony. But beneath the expected bitterness and cynicism and irony of poems like 'News Update,' there is also a remarkable willingness not only to acknowledge that terrible past, but to build something lasting and good out of it [as he demonstrates in 'In Celebration of Spring']. It is this affirmation of what is worthwhile, and the refusal to knuckle under to all that is not, which carries Balaban far beyond Vietnam into the more general and ultimately more durable realm of shared experience.

"Balaban manages to deliver sentiment without sentimentality, emotion without embarrassment. Although his elusive Blue Mountain is 'only as large as a thought,' the range to which it belongs stretches from Ovid's Black Sea city of exile to the Pueblo ruins of New Mexico, from antebellum Charleston to Kate and Gary's Bar in Red River. And Balaban covers that territory with authority and conviction.

"I have seldom, in fact, encountered a collection of poems so consistently solid. Each poem in *Blue Mountain* is a mother lode so rich that it is likely to take one weeks to finish the book. Particularly impressive is Balaban's knowledge of the flora and fauna that surround him wherever he is; his poems read like botanical and biological catalogues. Moreover, he observes keenly and in great detail all that he sees. The best part of *Blue Mountain*, however, is its constant insistence upon the dignity of the human will. Insane we may be. Certainly foolish and shortsighted and capable of brutishness. But if he finds despair and sadness in the worst that we are capable of— and he does — he finds also courage and hope in that human will which has thus far permitted us to survive.

"'Into that peculiar silence which only parents have, / she retreated, and, now, she has entered forever,' Balaban writes of his mother in 'Words for the Dead':

> But if all things crave themselves more clearly,
> we who issued from the cells of her body, whose
> first impulses flexed with the rhythms of her heart,
> are each partial flesh and seed of her craving
> for wistful things. That are her. And will not die.

It is this continuity, however tenuous and vulnerable, that Balaban celebrates. One worries about heaping praise so lavishly as not to be believed. But this book is good, and there is no way around it. 'Praise the poet,' says one of the 'Inscriptions from the Black Sea Tombs.' And indeed, *Blue Mountain* proves John Balaban worthy of praise."

In the twenty-five years since *Blue Mountain* appeared, Balaban has published three additional collections: *Words for My Daughter*, *Locusts at the Edge of Summer*, and *Path, Crooked Path*. Each subsequent collection only confirms and renews what was so evident in his first two books: that here is a poet of great power and tremendous range, an exceptional poet, a poet of lasting worth, a poet for the ages. The poems he wrote thirty and, now, even forty years ago still resonate while the newer poems are exactly that: new, fresh, exciting, each one a discovery.

The war in Vietnam, for better or worse the touchstone experience of our lives, is never far from mind, whether it be an old Viet Minh fighter reminiscing with three American veterans young enough to be his sons, or the tiny Green Beret at Balaban's front door on Halloween night, or the dog meat served to the vegetarian American by the Vietnamese district chief who'd been sent home from the war to die years ago but hadn't.

But vying for attention, indeed, bumping the old war off the front pages, are Balaban's cancerous and beloved dog Apples, an Arab emissary encountering Vikings on the Volga in the 10th century, the teachers who rescued Balaban from mental poverty when he was a high school boy, Van Gogh, Hurricane Andrew, snails, parrots, alligators, Eddie the homeless paraplegic shot by a cop while trying to steal a car. These along with poems translated from Vietnamese, from Bulgarian, from Romanian, from Latin.

Translations, in fact, are another whole facet of Balaban's life as a poet. In addition to his extensive work with Vietnamese *Ca Dao*, traditional folk poetry, he spent years translating the 18th century Vietnamese poet Ho Xuan Huong, in the process helping to retrieve the nearly-lost-forever ancient Vietnamese script called *Nom* in which she wrote. And he's the only guy I know personally who's ever been awarded a medal declaring him a Hero of Bulgaria — for his work translating Bulgarian poetry.

As if all that weren't enough, Balaban has also written fiction for both adults and adolescents, *Coming Down Again* and *The Hawk's Tale* respectively, a nonfiction memoir, *Remembering Heaven's Face*, and the text for a book of photographs, *Vietnam: The Land We Never Knew*, in addition to editing *Vietnam: a Traveler's Literary Companion*. Not to mention teaching full-time all these years at Pennsylvania State University, the University of Miami, and now North Carolina State University.

Best of all, for me at least, Balaban is as decent and great-hearted a human being as his poetry suggests. Let me speak again, if I may, from personal experience: I know for a fact that I was, for much of that 1985 trip to Vietnam, a most unpleasant traveling companion. For reasons I could not begin to understand at the time — though I came to believe after the fact that I was experiencing a kind of post-traumatic stress, a sort of "short-timer's syndrome" flashback with all the uncertainty and anxiety those last days in combat seventeen years earlier had entailed — I became pathologically homesick during the trip.

I mean, for much of the trip, I was no fun at all. A pain in the ass would be a polite way of putting it. In retrospect, I wouldn't be surprised

John Balaban with his daughter Tally, circa 2011 (courtesy John Balaban).

if I had never heard another word from Balaban as long as we both lived. But aside from one brief remark a year later when my book about the trip, *Going Back*, was published — a book that didn't begin to convey either my emotional tumult during the trip or Balaban's patient forbearance — he's never even mentioned it, though we have had occasion to be together often in the years since.

Most recently, in the spring of 2006, Balaban came to the Haverford School, where I teach, to give the annual Edward R. Hallowell Lecture, a series that has attracted the likes of Norman Mailer, Derek Walcott, Donald Hall, Edward Hirsch, and Tim O'Brien. A year later, my students and colleagues are still talking about his visit, about his rambling shuffling of papers between poems, about his affable and unpretentious demeanor, about his lilting rendering of the sing-song rhythms of the Vietnamese language, about his breath-taking, heart-stopping poems.

Indeed, I've heard him read "Words for My Daughter" on more than one occasion, as he did that night, and I cannot for the life of me figure out how he manages to get through it without choking up or bursting into tears. It gets me every time I read it. Or hear it. Every single time.

❖   ❖   ❖

Good Wars, Bad Wars, Forgotten Wars and Poetry

Keynote Address
Netherlands American Studies Association
International Conference "War and War's Aftermath: Ethical
Dilemmas of the American Witness" Vrije Universiteit
Amsterdam, June 11th, 2009

In 1985, Studs Terkel published an oral history of the Second World War that he titled *The Good War*. By then, a decade after the final end of our once-seemingly endless "bad war" in Vietnam, Americans were ready and eager to wax nostalgic over a war whose most iconic images are of Marines victoriously raising the Stars-n-Stripes over Mt. Suribachi and a sailor exuberantly kissing a nurse in Times Square on VE Day. And as the 20th century has come to a close and the 21st century unfolds, for Americans at least, World War II has become firmly entrenched as America's last good war.

One is hard-pressed to find, however, anything good about that war in the poetry of World War II combat veteran John Ciardi. One poem of his called "A Box Comes Home" begins like this:

> I remember the United States of America
> As a flag-draped box with Arthur in it
> And six marines to bear it on their shoulders.

After ruminating on how other countries and other cultures in other times might have remembered their war dead, Ciardi returns to the present:

> Once I saw Arthur dressed as the United States
> Of America. Now I see the United States
> Of America as Arthur in a flag-sealed domino.
>   * * *
>   ... I would pray
> An agreement with the United States of America
> To equal Arthur's living as it equals his dying,

but Ciardi finally gives the reader little expectation that the United States of America will either make or keep such an agreement.

It is not exactly the kind of poem one might expect from what has become fixed in the American cultural and historical landscape as "the Good War." But if World War Two was a good war, it certainly did Arthur no good, nor did it do much good for Randall Jarrell's more famous ball turret gunner who "woke to black flak and the nightmare fighters" and who was washed "out of the turret with a hose" when he died. It did no good for Van Wettering or Averill, "gone to early death" in Richard Eberhart's "The Fury of Aerial Bombardment." In what way was World War Two — which devastated Europe and Asia and cost the lives of some 40 million human beings, the majority of them not even armed combatants — in what conceivable way was World War Two a good war, and for whom was it good?

Joe Rosenthal's famous photograph — still seen everywhere in almost every imaginable form and medium, and as fresh and uplifting today as it was when it first appeared on the front pages of newspapers all over the world almost 65 years ago — doesn't tell us that 27 more days of hard fighting remained after that flag went up, or that three of the six men who raised it never left Iwo Jima alive, or that another drank himself to an early death, or that only one lived out what could be called a "normal life." And while Alfred Eisenstadt's photograph of the sailor and the nurse amidst the tickertape and happy crowds captures one image of the end of World War II, Howard Nemerov captures a very different image in "Redeployment":

> They say the war is over. But water still
> Comes bloody from the taps, and my pet cat
> In his disorder vomits worms which crawl
> Swiftly away. Maybe they leave the house.
> These worms are white, and flecked with the cat's blood.

Later in the poem, Nemerov mentions a man he knows "who keeps a soldier's dead blue eyeballs that he found / Somewhere," a grisly reminder of the dehumanizing affects of war on those who do the killing and the dying. Unlike Eisenstadt's photo, Nemerov's poem is hardly celebratory. Indeed, it is not much different in what it has to say than John Balaban's "April 30, 1975," a poem about that bad war of ours in Vietnam:

> The evening Nixon called his last troops off,
> the church bells tolled across our states.
> We leaned on farmhouse porch pilings, our eyes
> wandering the lightning bug meadow thick with mist,
> and counted tinny peals clanking out
> through oaks around the church belltower.
> You asked, "Is it peace, or only a bell ringing?"
>
> This night the war has finally ended.
> My wife and I sit on a littered park bench
> sorting out our shared and separate lives[.]

Balaban goes on to describe an urban American landscape that seems "a city at war," where a ski-masked man who tried to attack a girl is, in his own turn, attacked by yet another predator, and where "kids have burnt a bum on Brooklyn Bridge."

Despite each being about the end of a war — different wars at that, with seemingly different outcomes — in neither poem does one come away with any sense of peace. Both poets suggest a world still out of kilter. Both poems are possessed of a profound sadness. Even their closing lines, in both imagery and intent, are strikingly similar, though the poems were written thirty years apart:

> I heard the dust falling between the walls.
>
> — — — — — — — — — —
>
> By the Lo waterfalls, free and high,
> you wash away the dust of life.

Nor does the passage of time seem to bring with it any greater peace. Consider Reg Saner's "Re-Runs":

> All that flying iron was bound to hit something.
> His odd nights re-visit a stare, let a torn head

trade looks with him, ...

* * *

... alone inside a nameless grief holding
nothing: their faces, grass shrapnel — which some field
on the world's other side bothers with. Like seed,
the shapes that won't go away without tears.
They just lie where they fell, and keep going.

Or Keith Wilson's "The Ex-Officer, Navy":

> the man, in whose eyes gunfire
> is a memory, a restless dream
> of stuttering mouths, bright flame
> a man, who no matter how long the days
> faces still the combat, the long night's terror —

Saner and Wilson are both veterans of the Korean War — our so-called Forgotten War — though neither Saner nor Wilson have forgotten it. Moreover,
both men would surely know instinctively exactly what Gerald McCarthy is
talking about in "The Sound of Guns":

> At the university in town
> tight-lipped men tell me the war in Vietnam is over,
> that my poems should deal with other things:
> earth, fire, water, air.
>
> * * *
>
> I don't know what it is that's kept me going.
> At nineteen I stood at night and watched
> an airfield mortared. A plane that was to take
> me home, burning; men running out of the flames.
>
> Seven winters have slipped away,
> the war still follows me.
> Never in anything have I found
> a way to throw off the dead.

No doubt, McCarthy could change his fourth last line to read "forty-three
winters have slipped away," and the poem would still be just as true. He could
change the word "Vietnam" to "Korea" or "Guadalcanal" or "Salerno," and
the poem would still be just as true.

For Hayden Carruth in "On a Certain Engagement South of Seoul," a
newspaper story about a battle in the Korean War triggers a reverie of his own
experiences in the Second World War:

> we were a few,
> Sprawled on the stiff grass of a small plateau,

Afraid. No one was dead. But we were new —
We did not know that probably none would die.

He describes in moving detail the terrible fear of these young soldiers before
shifting his attention to "another campaign ... in another land," admitting
that this brief account of an engagement in Korea "can make my hand tremble
again." Of the men who were with him on that small plateau, "one limps.
One cannot walk at all." One has nightmares. Carruth concludes:

Is this a bond? Does this make us brothers?
Or does it bring our hatred back? I might
have known, but now I do not know. Others
May know. I know when I walk out-of-doors
I have a sorrow not wholly mine, but another's.

Carruth is not the only poet to make connections between and among
the three major American wars of the mid-20th century. While his poem
touches on both the Second World War and Korea, in "The Long March"
William Childress connects Korea to Vietnam:

North to Pusan,
trailing nooses of dust,
we dumbly followed
leaders whose careers
hung on victory.

Childress seems haunted by the misery of war, especially the suffering of children who line the roads, begging, many of whom, nothing more than "bones
in thin sacks," will be picked up by "the dead-truck" in the frozen dawn. "A
soldier fished a bent brown stick/from a puddle," Childress writes, "the arm
of someone's child," before concluding:

Not far away, the General
camps with his press corps.
Any victory will be his.
For us, there is only
the long march to Viet Nam.

As if to bring the three wars full circle, Joseph A. Soldati associates the
Vietnam War with World War Two in "Surroundings." Ostensibly a poem
about the destruction of Soldati's old neighborhood, including the house he
and his brother grew up in, it takes us back to 1944, when the poet and his
brother were five and three, before returning to the present:

Long trains were going to Asia then,
And still are. Two small boys,

Who rushed to see them pass, are men —
Have been there and come home again.

Over the years since I came home from my own war, I have read thousands of poems from the Second World War, the Korean War, and the Vietnam War, and what is most striking about these poems is that, almost to a poem, they have nothing good to say about the experience of war. Furthermore, whether a poet is writing about the war we won, the war we tied, or the war we lost, the tone, the feel, the sensibilities of the poetry from war to war bear stunning similarities.

Indeed, I find it truly astonishing that among all the poets who have faced the ordeal of war and lived to write about it with any seriousness of purpose, the prevailing themes to be found in their poems are sorrow, loss, anger, fear, pain, dislocation, isolation, emptiness. There is nothing uplifting about Louis Simpson's "Carentan, O Carentan":

> I must lie down at once, there is
> A hammer at my knee
> And call it death or cowardice
> Don't count again on me.
> * * *
> Carentan, O Carentan,
> Before we met with you
> We never yet had lost a man
> Or known what death could do.

There is nothing inspirational about Rolando Hinojosa's "A Matter of Supplies," which begins:

> It comes down to this: we're pieces of equipment
> To be counted and signed for.
> On occasion some of us break down,
> And those parts which can't be salvaged
> Are replaced with other GI parts, that's all.

And I certainly hope there is nothing heroic about the "ruined faces" and "putrifying bodies/bloated like Macy's Parade balloons" in my own poem "The Bodies Beneath the Table."

This is not, however, because the poets of our 20th century wars cannot see the uplifting, the inspirational, or the heroic in the wars they have fought, but rather because there is, quite simply, nothing uplifting, inspirational, or heroic about war in the 20th century. And from what little I've seen of American veterans' poetry from Iraq and Afghanistan — Brian Turner's *Here, Bullet*, and the poems collected by Lovella Calica and the Warrior Writers' Project —

war in the 21st century is shaping up to be equally ugly, the poetry equally honest.

In the 18th century, Benjamin Franklin said, "There never was a good war or a bad peace." A century later, William T. Sherman added, "War is hell, and you cannot refine it." Both men were right. So was Walt Whitman when he wrote that "the real war will never get in the books." The books Whitman was talking about, however, are the history books. Whitman himself wrote what I think is the first modern war poem, "The Wound-Dresser," a poem that deals unflinchingly and ungloriously with the ugly truth of war. And it is in the poetry of war that you will find not "the good war" or "the bad war" or "the forgotten war," but rather the truth of war.

❖   ❖   ❖

"They Want Enough Rice": Reflections on the Late American War in Vietnam

Teachers College
Columbia University
July 1st, 2009

At the outset, I need to make clear several key points. Firstly, though this conference is focused on using digital media to teach the Vietnam War, I am myself seriously technologically challenged. It would be, in fact, more accurate to call me technologically befuddled. The Haverford School in sub-urban Philadelphia, where I teach, only last year opened a brand-new state-of-the-art upper school. I have a classroom that is equipped with a Smartboard, projector, and computer. Theoretically, my students and I can do power point presentations, video conferencing, and distance learning. The operative word there is "theoretically." I do my best to make use of these resources, but I am like an old sailing ship: I don't tack easily, and make a lot of noise when I do. My students are constantly having to show me how to do even the most basic stuff. They give power point presentations. I do not. I spend a lot of my time feeling like a 19th century man who somehow wandered into the 21st century and can't get out of it.

Secondly, the Vietnam War remains a volatile and controversial subject. As I've often said before, I suspect we will reach a consensus on that war only after the last members of my generation are dead and buried and can no longer argue with each other. No one — and I am absolutely certain of this — no one can be objective about the Vietnam War, certainly no one who lived through those years. As with most things touching on the human experience, objectivity is an illusion.

Take one of the fundamental principles of American journalism, for instance, that there are two sides to every story. That is nonsense. Most stories have six or eight or twenty-seven sides. And not all sides deserve equal weight. Should we accord the same credibility to Richard Nixon's assertion that he was not a crook as we do to John Dean's assertion that there was a cancer growing on the presidency? Should we accept at face value the statements of Robert McNamara while he was Secretary of Defense when thirty years later he balefully admitted that "we were wrong, terribly wrong"?

History may be, as Napoleon claimed, nothing but a fable agreed upon, but some things are true and some things are not true. The attack on the USS *Maddox* in the Gulf of Tonkin in early August 1964 was *not* unprovoked, and the Johnson Administration knew it at the time. The second attack a few days later never actually happened, and the Johnson Administration knew it at the time. The Johnson Administration knowingly and flagrantly lied to the American people and the Congress of the United States. This is not speculation. This is fact, provable by examining the documents compiled at the order of Robert McNamara himself and commonly known as the *Pentagon Papers*.

And this is only one small example in a history that is filled with arrogance, ignorance, half-truths, obfuscations, falsehoods, deceptions, and lies. If you are going to teach the Vietnam War accurately and honestly, you are risking serious trouble because a lot of people will not like what you have to say. A lot of people will accuse you of bias, of grinding your axe, of failing to be impartial, perhaps even of being unpatriotic and anti–American. Indeed, some of you may already not be liking what I've said about the war in these first few paragraphs.

Which brings me to a third point I'd like to make at the outset. The syllabus describes me as a Vietnam War veteran, which is true. But that is not why you should listen to what I have to say. There was not one Vietnam War. There were many different Vietnam Wars. It had to do with when you were there, where you were stationed, what your job was, how lucky or unlucky you were. The war in the Mekong Delta in 1965 was very different from the war in the Central Highlands in 1971. An aircraft mechanic at Tan Son Nhut had a very different experience from a rifleman at Con Thien. It is the old fable of the blind men feeling an elephant: each person knows only what little part of the experience was his.

At his trial for treason, Socrates declared that the unexamined life is not worth living, but a great many of the Vietnam War veterans I've known over the years either never heard Socrates' admonition or decided that, since Socrates was found guilty and executed, they'd do well not to take him too seriously. Let me give you one example among many:

In the early 1990s I was teaching a course on the war at La Salle University and one of my students was another Marine Corps veteran of the war. It was clear during the first few classes from his body language and facial expressions that he didn't like what he was hearing, but he wouldn't say anything. Finally, after class one evening, I said I could tell he didn't agree with me, so why didn't he speak up? The younger college-age students who made up most of the class could learn something from such a dialogue. He told me that indeed he didn't agree with what I was saying, but he had not responded — indeed, could not respond — because, as he said, "I don't know what to say. I don't know anything about the war." He had gone to Vietnam at the age of 19, been badly wounded after only four months, spent a year in a hospital recovering, and then became a local cop. Twenty years later, he was hearing for the first time about the arrogance, ignorance, half-truths, obfuscations, falsehoods, deceptions, and lies that had nearly gotten him killed, and it all conflicted hideously with the beliefs he had carried for two decades, beliefs that were entirely divorced from knowledge, fact, or historical reality.

He and I developed a healthy respect for each other over that semester: I because he was willing to stick with the course in spite of his discomfort; he because he recognized that I was not just some bleeding heart pinko who hates America, but a serious scholar who has spent decades examining and reflecting upon the history of the American War in Vietnam, using my own experience only as a touchstone and a springboard. And that is why you, too, should not dismiss me out of hand, though I may make you uncomfortable, perhaps even angry. I have not made up the facts. I have only discovered them, and drawn inferences and conclusions based on them. You may disagree with my inferences and conclusions, but you will be hard pressed to dispute my facts.

The first fact you should consider is the long history of Vietnam and China. From the 2nd century BCE to the 10th century AD, China occupied and ruled Vietnam. Maps of China all through this long millennium show what was then Vietnam, extending down as far as Hue, as a province of China. The Vietnamese saw things differently, however. All through this period, there was rebellion after rebellion after rebellion, each one crushed, until finally in

938 the Vietnamese rebelled yet another time, and this time succeeded in defeating their Chinese occupiers and throwing them out. Three successive Chinese invasions, along with two Mongol invasions and a Siamese invasion, were all defeated over the next nine centuries before the arrival of the French on Vietnamese shores. A thousand years of resistance to Chinese occupation, nine hundred years of successfully defending Vietnamese independence, and — what I have not yet mentioned but will now — immediate and unceasing resistance to French colonization even before French rule had been fully consolidated. Keep all of this in mind.

I cannot give you an entire history of the Vietnam War today, but I would like to suggest some of the crucial turning points and milestones that you might want to examine with your students. The first missed opportunity, it seems to me, came at Versailles in 1919. Woodrow Wilson had brought the United States into World War I with his inspiring Fourteen Points, one of which was self-determination for all peoples and all nations. Ho Chi Minh, who had been living and working in the West for much of the previous decade and had come to admire the American Revolution, Thomas Jefferson in particular, actually thought Wilson meant what he said. Ho, then using the name Nguyen Ai Quoc — Nguyen the Patriot — traveled to Versailles to try to meet with Wilson and obtain his support for Vietnamese independence from French colonial rule. Need I say that no one in the American delegation would give Ho so much as the time of day? Who was this little scraggly fellow, anyway? As Tom Buchanan says of Jay Gatsby, "Mr. Nobody from Nowhere." Only then did Ho turn to the French Socialist Party, which opposed its own country's colonial empire, subsequently becoming a founding member of the French Communist Party after reading Lenin's writings denouncing European colonialism. Yes, Ho Chi Minh was a communist, but was communism his first choice, or did he turn to communism only after he and his country had been subjugated by one western capitalist democracy and utterly rejected by another?

A second crucial turning point came at the end of World War II. With the fall of France to Germany in 1940, Vietnam effectively came under the military control of Imperial Japan, and Ho Chi Minh and his compatriots, organized as the Viet Minh — the League for the Independence of Vietnam — proceeded to resist Japanese occupation as they had resisted the French and the Chinese before them. By early 1945, an American team from the Office of Strategic Services — the forerunner of the Central Intelligence Agency — was working with Ho's forces, providing training and equipment to the Vietnamese while the Vietnamese provided them with intelligence on the Japanese and assistance in rescuing downed American pilots. On September 2nd, 1945, when Ho Chi Minh declared independence for Vietnam in the main square in Hanoi, he paraphrased our own Declaration of Independence, helped in the wording by Major Archimedes Patti, a member of the OSS team, who stood on the reviewing stand beside him while a U.S. Army Air Force fly-over saluted the new nation. That should have been the end of it.

How then did it come to pass that a British general released and rearmed thousands of Japanese soldiers, almost simultaneously to that ceremony in Hanoi, and sent them into the streets to keep the Viet Minh from taking control of Saigon? How did it come to pass that French Foreign Legionnaires returned to Vietnam aboard American ships a month later? Why did the U.S. government ignore the findings of its own emissary, Abbot Low Moffat, who, after spending months in the company of Ho Chi Minh in 1945 and 1946, concluded that while Ho Chi Minh was indeed a communist, his primary concern was independence for Vietnam, and he was taking orders neither from Joseph Stalin nor from anyone else? Why did Harry Truman leave unanswered each and every one of the seven letters Ho sent him in 1945 and 1946, begging for U.S. support of Vietnamese independence, Ho even going so far as to offer Vietnam up as a United Nations Trust Territory for as long as the UN thought it necessary for Vietnam to demonstrate the ability to govern itself? Did the U.S. decision not to block French reoccupation of Vietnam even have anything to do with what was going on in Vietnam itself, or was that decision based entirely on the situation in Western Europe at the end of World War II?

In any event, France went ahead and tried to re-conquer and re-colonize Vietnam (along with Laos and Cambodia — what the French called Indochina), but after eight bloody years of war that led only to continually escalating stalemate, the French finally took to heart what Ho Chi Minh had told the French prime minister in March 1946 — "You will kill ten of our men for every one of yours we kill, but in the end it is you who will tire of it." After their humiliating and decisive defeat at Dien Bien Phu, the French ran up the white flag.

That was on May 7th, 1954, and that should have been the end of it. Again. But by then, though few Americans had ever heard of Vietnam and fewer still could have found it on a map, the U.S. was already committed to waging war in Vietnam. Unbeknownst to the American people, by the end of the First Indochina War, U.S. taxpayers were footing three-quarters of the French war bill. How and why did this come about? What were American policymakers thinking? Yes, the Soviet Union had rapidly gobbled up all of Eastern Europe in the years immediately after World War II. And yes, Mao Zedong and his communists had finally won the Chinese Civil War. And yes, the Cold War was in full swing by 1954, as was the domestic communist witch hunt in the U.S. But did Vietnam's war for independence from France have anything at all to do with any of that? Did the prospect that Vietnam might become a communist state really have any impact on the balance of power between East and West, U.S. and USSR? Remember Abbot Moffat's assessment back in 1946. He was not the only one to voice such an opinion over the next eight years. Why were these voices ignored? Not just ignored, but vilified and excoriated.

In the wake of France's withdrawal from Vietnam, the so-called great powers — the U.S., USSR, Britain, France, and China — divided Vietnam in half. This was to be a temporary military demarcation only with national elections to be held two years hence to reunify Vietnam under one government. Ho Chi Minh and the communists, of course, took control of the north immediately, but only after much wrangling, maneuvering, and outright fighting, and only with American support, did Ngo Dinh Diem emerge as the leader of South Vietnam.

This presents yet another interesting question: what could possibly have induced American policymakers to imagine that a mandarin Catholic French-educated elitist who had spent the First Indochina War in a Maryknoll seminary in New Jersey might stand as a viable alternative to a man who had devoted his entire life to the freedom and independence of his country? Indeed, American policymakers and CIA intelligence analysts knew perfectly well that Diem stood no chance at all of winning a free and fair election in Vietnam. So did Diem. That's why Diem, with the full support of the Eisenhower Administration, refused to participate in those elections. That's why those elections never took place. Did the Republic of Vietnam, more commonly called South Vietnam, ever really exist, or was it, from beginning to end, a figment of the imaginations of a succession of powerful men who could not accept their powerlessness?

I would call those missed elections a third crucial turning point except that it seems certain that, even at the Geneva Convention of 1954 that called for the elections, the U.S. had no intention of ever allowing them to take place. By then, U.S. policymakers were already caught in a trap of their own making: Ho Chi Minh was the only person the overwhelming majority of Vietnamese would accept as their leader, but Ho Chi Minh was a communist and therefore unacceptable to the Americans. How to resolve this impasse? The death and destruction and misery and waste, the damage and heartache and hatred and pain that transpired over the next twenty-one years is the result of the insistence of a succession of U.S. administrations on finding a resolution to an irresolvable dilemma.

And all of what I've discussed so far — all of it — comes practically a decade before most people think of the beginning of the Vietnam War. History doesn't function in a vacuum. The Vietnam War didn't begin when JFK sent Special Forces to Vietnam in 1961 or Thich Quang Duc burned himself to death in 1963 or the Marines landed at Danang in 1965. Long before any of those events took place, American policymakers, in secret and behind closed doors, had staked their reputations and what they imagined to be the nation's reputation on a particular outcome in Vietnam. Long before the 1960s, any realistic possibility of the U.S. choosing a different course in Vietnam had been lost. No, not lost. Actively and completely rejected.

The United States would wage war, at first indirectly but eventually directly, rather than allow Vietnamese independence from foreign control. Thanks to French incompetence (in the opinion of U.S. policymakers), North Vietnam was beyond U.S. reach, but there still remained the south. The *Pentagon Papers* reveal that simply allowing South Vietnam to come under control of the North, to stop fighting, stand aside, and allow Ho to have all of Vietnam, was never — never — seriously considered.

When the fiction of Ngo Dinh Diem with his "personalist regime" and "one-man democratic rule" (these are the actual terms used by supposedly responsible politicians and journalists) — when the fiction of Ngo Dinh Diem collapsed, the U.S. sanctioned a coup d'etat that led to a succession of unstable and incompetent military regimes, culminating in the iron-fisted rule of Air Vice Marshal Nguyen Cao Ky. When Ky, with his tailored purple flight suits (with matching attire for his ravishing wife) and his openly expressed admiration for Adolph Hitler, proved too much of an embarrassment, the U.S. switched its support to the quieter, more publicly palatable general, Nguyen Van Thieu.

Meanwhile, on the battlefield, when South Vietnamese military forces proved incapable of effectively fighting the Viet Cong, the U.S. sent ever-increasing amounts of aid, along with the vaunted Green Berets and other so-called advisors. When these proved ineffective, the U.S. sent major air squadrons. Then came the Gulf of Tonkin Incident, which I've already discussed and which led to the sustained bombing of North Vietnam, the little-discussed but even more massive bombing of South Vietnam, and the deployment, ultimately, of nearly three million U.S. military personnel, maximum U.S. troop strength in-country reaching 548,000 by January 1969. It is important to realize that a generic version of the Gulf of Tonkin Resolution, giving Lyndon Johnson a free hand to wage executive war in Vietnam, was drafted by National Security Advisor Walt Rostow four months prior to the incident itself. The Johnson Administration was only waiting for the opportunity to fill in the blanks and foist it on Congress and the American people. When an opportunity did not readily present itself, the Johnson administration created one. Once again, this is not a matter of opinion. You can find the documentation in the *Pentagon Papers*.

I knew none of this, of course, when I arrived in Vietnam in February 1967, having volunteered for the U.S. Marine Corps on graduation from high school at the age of 17. My first memories of television were of Soviet tanks crushing the Hungarian Revolution in 1956. I'd seen and heard Nikita Khrushchev pounding his shoe on the podium at the UN while shouting, "We will bury you." I'd awakened one morning to the Berlin Wall, and I'd lived through the Cuban Missile Crisis. When Lyndon Johnson said that if we didn't fight the Reds in Vietnam, we'd be fighting them in Waikiki, it sounded very much as if my country needed me.

I didn't know that Roosevelt had all-but-handed Eastern Europe over to the Soviets at Yalta in 1945. Or that the Soviet Union had lost as many people

Corporal Bill Ehrhart, 1st Battalion, 1st Marine Regiment, Operation Pike, Republic of Vietnam, August 1967.

in World War II as all other nations combined, and was not about to see this slaughter repeated in another war with the West. Or that the Soviet Union was, by 1962, completely encircled by U.S. nuclear ballistic missiles. Most of all, I did not know that what was happening in Vietnam had nothing to do with whatever worldwide struggle between communism and capitalism was actually taking place. I did not know that Ho Chi Minh had spent a lifetime trying to free his country from foreign domination. That the Americans had simply replaced the French in that struggle. That in fact Ho Chi Minh was deftly playing Russians and Chinese off against each other in order to navigate between them and pursue his own agenda, which remained what it had always been: independence for his country. I did not know that the nation I thought I was defending from the scourge of communism never really existed. I did not know that Vietnam posed no danger either to my mother or to my country, nor that I was in danger only because I'd gone half way around the world to make trouble for the Vietnamese. Interestingly enough, as soon as I went home, the Vietnamese communists stopped trying to kill me. But I digress.

These two photographs were taken from the body of a Viet Cong guerrilla in the summer of 1967. The woman in the upper photo, who also appears in the group shot, may have been the dead man's wife, girlfriend, or sister. The Americans could kill people with this kind of determination, but we were not going to defeat them.

Because of what I did not know when I got to Vietnam, imagine my confusion when I discovered that the people I was sent to help didn't welcome me with open arms, didn't seem to like me, didn't seem to want me there or appreciate my help. Imagine my confusion when my allies, the South Vietnamese army, seemed to be indifferent cowards with no will to fight while my enemies, the Viet Cong, seemed willing to fight to the bitter end, though they possessed only the most rudimentary of resources

Once, for instance, we killed a man in an ambush who was dressed in thin cotton shirt and pants with sandals made from discarded tires (we called them Ho Chi Minh sandals). He had in one pocket a few balls of rice wrapped in a banana leaf. His weapon was a 1936 French bolt action MAS-36 with a bent hide-away bayonet, a stock held together with wire, and a bamboo strip to replace the leather sling that had rotted away a decade or more earlier. He had five bullets, and the barrel of his rifle was so pitted that I dared not fire it for fear it would explode in my face. And that is how that man had gone out to do battle with the most powerful army on earth. You can kill people like that, but you cannot defeat them.

One has to wonder why one side that seems to have everything going for it won't fight while the other side that has nothing going for it won't surrender, and I sure as hell did wonder. But I had no way to find my way through the myriad welter of information and experience that was pouring in on me as my time in Vietnam unfolded. It simply did not make sense. Nothing made sense. It was all just crazy. Or seemed so.

Only some years later, after the Ohio National Guard killed four students at Kent State University, two of whom were not even part of the demonstration that was fired upon, when I realized that the war was not ever going to go away, but instead had come home to America with me, did I finally decide — not so much consciously as by default — that I needed to understand what had happened to me in Vietnam, and what was happening to my country. I read just about everything I could get my hands on. I no longer recall the order, but over the next few years I read *Street Without Joy* and *Hell in a Very Small Place* by the French journalist Bernard Fall, Jean Larteguy's *The Centurions*, David Halberstam's *The Best and the Brightest*, Frances FitzGerald's *Fire in the Lake*, along with other books that put the Vietnam War into a larger historical context, among them Marine Corps Major General Smedley Butler's *War Is a Racket* and Dee Brown's *Bury My Heart at Wounded Knee*.

In the spring of 1971, several thousand Vietnam War veterans came to Washington to return their medals to Congress. They called their demonstration "a Limited Incursion into the Country of Congress," mocking the invasions of both Cambodia and Laos, protesting the war they themselves had fought, and making an indelible impact on the nation — including me. Then, only two months later, the *Pentagon Papers* became public, much to the consternation of just about every American official who had ever had anything to do with creating and perpetuating our quarter-century war in Vietnam.

I can only urge you again and again to read as much of those documents as you can. Never before, and probably never again, will the inner workings of government be made so fully available to the governed. Never before, and probably never again, will we mortal folks be given such an opportunity to see the emperor without his clothes.

Since then, I have poured through, quite literally, hundreds of books and articles and monographs on the Vietnam War, but nothing I have ever read has given me reason to change the opinions I had formed by about the time of my graduation from college in 1973. What that additional knowledge has given me is only more reason to believe that the Vietnam War was unnecessary, wrongheaded, misguided, and counterproductive. Decades before former Secretary of Defense Robert McNamara admitted that "we were wrong, terribly wrong," that fact had become obvious. I've heard few people express the corollary of McNamara's belated conclusion: that if "we were wrong, terribly wrong," then those who opposed the war were right, terribly right. But again, I digress.

Let me return to the teaching of the Vietnam War. If you are unwilling to believe that your government will lie to you, if you are unwilling to believe that your government considers its less influential citizens expendable, if you are unwilling to believe that your leaders make decisions based not on rational logic and available information but on irrational wishes and insupportable beliefs, then you will never understand the disaster of the Vietnam War and should not be teaching it. What you will teach may be comfortable and well within the parameters of our national mythology, but it will not be true. It will not be history, but only fantasy. And you will, deliberately or inadvertently, be preparing your students for the kind of fall from grace that I experienced when I found my life on the line in Vietnam for no good reason and with no way out but forward.

I present all of this with more than a little trepidation because I know that for many people the Vietnam War remains an open wound, and over the years I have encountered more than a few people who do not like what I have to say about it. If I have gotten this far today without anyone throwing anything solid at me, I thank you for your patience and forbearance, and urge you to be strong and keep up the good work.

This topic — the Vietnam War — is virtually inexhaustible, of course. There is so much to say, so much to explore, so much to debate. As I said at the outset, I can't begin to cover it all or even a small portion of it. But there are two more points I would like to make before I finish. The first is the issue of our Saigon allies, those who chose our side in this war: the men and women left standing outside the gates of the U.S. Embassy on the morning of April

30th, 1975; the boat people; the ones who ended up in re-education camps; the many Vietnamese émigrés who are now citizens of the U.S. or France or other countries. There may be some here in the audience today. You may know some. Most of you at least have heard their stories, which are true and heartbreaking. They paid a terrible price for casting their lot with us.

But the cold truth is that the Saigon regime that the U.S. created never had the support of more than a tiny minority of the people of South Vietnam, that most of these supporters were Catholics in a country that is overwhelmingly Buddhist, and that a significant proportion of them were French-educated urbanites. Many were northern Catholics who had come south in 1954 after the Catholic Church officially began preaching that the Virgin Mary had gone south and all good Catholics should follow her. Most of the senior leadership of the Saigon government and military had served the French colonial administration and had fought on the side of France against the Viet Minh and Vietnamese independence during the First Indochina War.

Meanwhile, the 95 percent of southern Vietnamese who were rural, Buddhist, and poor, who had suffered for decades at the hands of the French and their Vietnamese hirelings, never held any allegiance to the government in Saigon, nor had any reason to. This is not to say that the Viet Minh and their Viet Cong successors were "the good guys"—that is a different discussion—but merely to argue that they represented far more accurately the true aspirations of the overwhelming majority of the Vietnamese people, who wanted little else than for us to stop killing them and go home. As Graham Greene wrote so prophetically in *The Quiet American*, most Vietnamese "want enough rice. They don't want to be shot at. They want one day to be much the same as another. They don't want our white skins around telling them what they want."

It is also worth remembering our own history. During and immediately after our own rebellion against Britain, fully 20 percent of Americans—those who remained loyal to their country and their king—left or were driven out by the winners. The British Caribbean islands and the Canadian Maritime Provinces are populated by their descendants. This is a far higher percentage of émigrés than have left Vietnam since 1975. Shall we draw the same inferences from that fact as so many people draw from the fact of the Vietnamese boat people?

Finally, I want to come back to a point I made earlier and asked you to keep in mind: the long Chinese occupation of Vietnam. Over the past 35 years, I have heard time and again that the U.S. could have won the war in Vietnam if only.... As former Secretary of State Dean Rusk once put it, if only the American people had not lacked the will to see it through. Or as others have argued, if only the meddling politicians had let the military fight to win. If only the traitorous antiwar movement had not betrayed the troops. If only the liberal media hadn't turned the American people against the war.

All of these "if onlys" are, upon examination, sheer gossamer. Dr. Lawrence Lichty of Northwestern University has convincingly proven that the overwhelming percentage of news coverage about the war, from start to finish, remained uncritical of U.S. policies and sympathetic to the official U.S. government version of the war. Vietnam War veteran Jerry Lembcke has exhaustively demonstrated in his book *The Spitting Image* that the antiwar movement neither attacked nor blamed the soldiers who were doing the fighting. And to argue that the U.S. fought "with one hand tied behind its back," as has become the fashionable phrase, is to ignore the magnitude of the destruction rained down upon Vietnam, Laos, and Cambodia over multiple decades: the millions of tons of napalm and high explosive bombs and white phosphorous and dioxin, the millions of rounds of artillery, forced draft urbanization, Search & Destroy (later renamed the more benign Search & Clear), the Phoenix Program, Operation Menu.

Indeed, there were only two restraints placed on U.S. warmakers: 1) the U.S. did not invade North Vietnam because the last time we invaded a country bordering on China — in the fall of 1950 — we got our noses bloodied rather badly; and 2) we did not nuke North Vietnam because we feared that the Russians would feel obligated to retaliate in kind. Both of these decisions were not made by the meddling politicians, but rather by U.S. policymakers at the highest levels of government.

Moreover, what would "winning" the Vietnam War have meant? That North Vietnam would forever abandon its claim that Vietnam was and is one country? That the Vietnamese peasantry would accept the alien Saigon regime with its absentee landlords and corrupt representatives sent to govern the provinces like viceroys from Imperial Rome? That the Viet Cong would vanish into the mangrove swamps and be no more, or turn their weapons into plowshares and live happily ever after? Where were they going to go? What peace would they ever have accepted, these people who fought with antiquated weapons and lived in tunnels for years on end and spent months combing American garbage to collect enough discarded flashlight batteries to generate enough electricity to set off a single mine before beginning to collect again?

And keep in mind that we could not win that war with over half a million soldiers. Might we have won if we'd sent one million soldiers to fight in Vietnam? Even then, would we have been able to stop the occasional grenade thrown into the Saigon restaurant, the occasional rocket fired into the U.S. base, the occasional soldier with his throat slit on his way home from a night of liberty? How long would we be willing to bear the financial and emotional and physical burden of keeping an army of occupation one million strong halfway around the world, all the while sending a steady stream of them home in body bags, week after week, month after month, year after year?

Would the American people have been willing to sustain such an occupation for five additional years? How about for fifty more years? Five hundred years? The Chinese left their army of occupation in Vietnam for one thousand and forty-nine years, but still the Vietnamese never gave up their notion of themselves as their own people, never relinquished their hatred of foreign domination, never stopped resisting, and in the end, the Chinese were expelled. There's a lesson in that, I think.

The history of the Vietnam War begins as far back as 111 BCE. To look at it from any less encompassing a vantage point is to misunderstand what you are seeing. Tactics, strategies, who did what to whom, who was right and who was wrong, whatever other questions you want to raise or points you want to argue — none of it matters. The Vietnamese had nowhere to go and all the time in the world. Viewed from this perspective — the perspective of Vietnamese history — the idea that the United States could ever have "won" the Vietnam War in any meaningful sense begins to appear chimerical.

Samuel Exler: The Poet as Historian

World War Two veteran Samuel Exler died in April 2008 at the age of 85. After a career in New York City as an advertising copywriter, he had moved from Woodstock to Philadelphia in 1998 to be close to a woman to whom he'd become very attached. In those last ten years, he'd lived only ten blocks from me.

I can't remember the exact circumstances under which I first became aware of Exler. I think he read something of mine that he liked, and either called or wrote to me. Subsequently, I recall that he introduced himself to me at a talk I gave with Paul Fussell at Friends Center here in Philly. Somewhere along the way, he mentioned that he, too, wrote poetry.

People often send me poetry. Unsolicited. Most of it is — well, the kindest thing I can usually say is — sincere. Why they send it to me, I don't know. It is generally an unwanted burden. So when Exler said he wrote poetry, I didn't bite. To my great relief, he was too gracious or too shy to press the issue.

Then in the early spring of 2008, I got a phone message from Exler's close friend Regina Holmes, who said that Exler had recently read my poem "Mostly Nothing Happens" and wanted me to know how much he liked it. When I returned the call, Holmes initially answered, but then Exler himself got on. His breathing was very labored and we only talked for a few moments before he was too exhausted to continue.

A few weeks later, Holmes called to say that Exler had died. She mentioned again his poetry. Wishing to respect her grief and to be polite, I asked if I could see some of it. Only after I'd read the poems did I realize what a mistake I'd made not to have taken more interest in Exler while he was alive. Not withstanding his slim list of publishing credits, Exler was not some rank amateur but a genuinely accomplished poet.

Private Samuel Exler, U.S. Army, World War Two (courtesy Regina Holmes).

Between 1970 and his death, Exler published several dozen poems in journals such as *Plainsong*, *New York Quarterly*, *Poetry East*, and *American Poetry Review*, and in a dozen or so anthologies. (Indeed, we share space in two of those anthologies, *We Speak for Peace* and *Who Are the Rich and Where Do They Live?*, though I didn't notice until after he'd died.) In 1957, he published a children's book called *Growing and Changing*, illustrated by his first wife and published by Lothrop, Lee & Shepard, and in 1982 he published a collection of poems called *Ambition, Fertility, Loneliness* from an outfit called Lintel. One of his children's poems appears in the 1995 Random House anthology *Ghosts and Goose Bumps*.

But it is the poems based on his experiences as an infantryman

Sam Exler in Philadelphia in the late 1990s (photograph by Regina Holmes).

in World War Two that most caught my attention. Exler served in the U.S. Army from December 1942 to December 1945, and fought in Belgium, Holland, and Germany with the 104th "Timberwolf" Infantry Division from October 1944 until the end of the war in Europe, earning the Combat Infantry Badge and a Bronze Star.

In a 1999 op-ed piece in the *Mt. Airy Times Express*, Exler said of the film *Saving Private Ryan*: "Instead of truth, we get the same old uplifting story about young men winning a battle against great odds to defeat an evil enemy. Instead of feeling horrified, we come out feeling somehow ennobled. Perhaps, for a little more reality, we should revive Stanley Kubrik's *Paths of Glory*."

On a scrap of paper Holmes gave me along with Exler's poems, he had written: "My belief that our history should not be forgotten lies behind these poems." I wish I had paid more attention to Exler when I'd had the chance to get to know him. Exler understood the relationship between poetry and history. I am grateful to have his poems, and grateful for the opportunity to share some of them with others.

Be All That You Can Be

I barely remember what it was
drilled into my bones. Barely remember
the boring words of abuse

harrowing my mind. Barely
remember how the boots
of close order drill
stomped across my thoughts —
pride skinned off, training's blunt knife
carving me into a dogface — an animal
taught
to suppress its whimper
at death's approach.

Taught cursing, taught fear, taught
not to speak, not to have thoughts;
taught to have no will, to make
no decisions, taught
ass kissing for small favors,
taught to pick spittle-soaked
cigarette butts from the ground
every morning.
　　　　Taught to kill.

First Casualties

The mortar shell bursts in the forest.
Pieces of shrapnel go flying, edges slicing
like scissors cutting fabric
for a boy's shirt.

The surgeon bends over the arm, ready to amputate,
but the arm resists. Smashed, bent, fingers curled,
it returns to the squad,
holds a baton, leads a hundred voices
in the "Ode to Joy."

The young soldiers lie on the ground
like scattered sacks of grain.

Someone is shouting, "Medic! Medic!"

Solomon Grundy

Solomon Grundy
Inducted on Monday,
Drilling on Tuesday,
Rifle range on Wednesday,
Shipped out on Thursday,

Shot up on Friday,
Last breath was Saturday,
Statistic on Sunday,
This is the end
Of Solomon Grundy.

One, Two, Three, Four

One, two, three, four,
Mother, we are off to war.
How many coming home, my son?
Four, three, two, one.

When I was Young

When I was young I put on another life
with my olive drab uniform, and I slept
under Government Issue blankets.
On the bare rifle range, barren
As a parking lot, I learned to *squeeze*
The trigger, a study precise
As a formal table setting.

Beyond the rifle range, the ocean.
Beyond the ocean, another continent
where cannon fire grumbled
like an advancing giant striding
the mountains. Sunrise tugged
at young men who slept with rifles
and dreamed of home; at night the moon
searched the rubble of cities.

I arrived on an ocean liner, free passage,
as though I had won a prize,
like the prize in the Cracker Jack box
when I was a boy. I'd lost
the girl I loved. And the sun paused
over the concentration camps
and the dead bodies behind
the barbed wire fence, like chess pieces
toppled, swept from the board.

Shipped back from the Elbe River, I slept again
under Government Issue blankets.
My sleep was blank, like a movie screen

before the show comes on,
and dreams did not return
till much later.

Backpacking Ammunition

Squeezed
against the building's red brick wall,
back
     bent,
bearing a box of caliber .30 cartridges,
box heavy
as
my
own
skinny body, pressing myself
flat as a notebook page
into red brick,
I see a medic stooped
over one of our wounded boys.
Then
a vast silence, like a spot of blood
spreading on a white bandage,
overtakes the world.
      ***

It's sixty years later. No
body's
there.

Our boys were wounded.
They were lying in the street.

Bad Dreams

I keep dreaming that I'm back
in combat; the dead are like black rocks
small boulders, they lie
strewn all around me, all over
the countryside, in the fields, in the Normandy
orchards; I've been called back
to war, to the cold that walks through the bones,
to my consciousness narrowed to a pinpoint
in a universe that is nothing but death;
I've returned to marches, to mess halls, to my

young life shrunken like a fallen crabapple,
and I see my friends receding,
crying out to me, their voices
thinning, growing transparent, crying
that they don't understand — their arms
outstretched, vanishing back in time,
calling out that our lives
exist like a war, like black rocks;
that our lives are stones, that there is no peace,
that we died with the dead whom we loved
a long time ago.

One, Two, Many Vietnams?

Lately there has been a lot of talk about whether or not our current undertaking in Afghanistan will turn into another Vietnam. And though Iraq is less in the headlines than Afghanistan recently, that war too is hardly over. But are either of these wars "another Vietnam"? Does either have the potential to become another?

The fact is that historical analogies never hold up under examination. Our present wars in Iraq and Afghanistan neither resemble each other nor the late war in Vietnam. The differences are almost too myriad to enumerate.

Nevertheless, there are some similarities worth pondering. Each war seems to have been entered into by powerful leaders acting on unexamined assumptions about their own righteousness and infallibility. Each war seems to have been justified on the basis of what at best could be called "misleading" information. Each involves a staggering ignorance of the history and culture of the countries against whom we were going to war.

Consider the Bush administration's insistence that the secularist Saddam Hussein was in league with the radical religionist Osama bin Laden, and then recall that American leaders insisted Ho Chi Minh was only doing the bidding of the Soviet Union and China. Consider the Bush administration's insistence that Saddam had weapons of mass destruction he could use within forty minutes, and then recall Lyndon Johnson's insistence that our ships had been attacked, unprovoked in international waters, in the Gulf of Tonkin. Consider the recent elections in Afghanistan, and then recall the repeated and transparently bogus elections held in South Vietnam. Consider President Obama's latest commitment of 30,000 more soldiers to Afghanistan, and then recall the incremental escalations of the Westmoreland years in Vietnam.

Have you ever heard of Scott Ritter, the former Marine officer and UN weapons inspector who tried to tell the American people that Saddam had no weapons of mass destruction? Have you read journalist Thomas Ricks's account of the Iraq War, which he titled *Fiasco*? Have you read former Marine Clint Van Winkle's Iraq War memoir *Soft Spots*?

Historical analogies, as I said, are suspect at best. Iraq — with its three major factions: Sunni, Shiite and Kurd — looks almost simple compared to Afghanistan with its dozens of competing tribal, religious, and political factions, and neither looks like Vietnam. The people of Vietnam, for the most part, share a common culture and identity. Iraq is the invention of post–World War I British and French diplomats, and Afghanistan is an all but ungovernable illusion of cartography. If you don't believe me, ask the British. Or the Russians.

But whatever vast differences separate the Vietnam War from our present wars in Iraq and Afghanistan, there are two fundamental — and insurmountable — similarities. Firstly, in all three cases, the U.S. military has been tasked with achieving goals that are simply and utterly unattainable — certainly not by force of arms and probably not at all. Secondly, when you send heavily armed frightened young soldiers into an alien world they cannot understand, nothing good will result.

I hope that I am wrong about the prospects for success in our current wars. But after eight years of fighting in Afghanistan and almost seven years of fighting in Iraq, I do not see much reason to feel encouraged. Calls for more troops, training the Iraqis and Afghanis to defend themselves, giving them the breathing space to create viable democratic government — we've heard all this before.

Meanwhile, to a degree unimaginable even during the Vietnam War, the blood burden of military service falls ever more unfairly on a smaller and smaller segment of our citizenry. How long can our armed forces sustain the unrelenting stress? How long will the young men and women on the pointy end of the stick be willing to go back and back and back?

During the Vietnam War, proud and powerful leaders relinquished their fantastical illusions only when the political cost of continuing that war finally came to outweigh the political cost of disengaging. That tipping point was reached only after 58,000 Americans had come home dead. What will be the tipping point in Iraq, where the American death toll is currently under 4400?

What will be the tipping point in Afghanistan, where the American death toll is currently under 800? In each of these wars, we have a long way to go before we reach 58,000 dead Americans. Will the death toll finally climb that high? Will our current leadership exercise humility and wisdom in place of arrogance and righteousness before that awful tipping point is reached? Or will these wars end in triumph and victory, our goals achieved, our policies vindicated? Anyone taking bets?

The Origins of Passion

Senior Dinner Remarks
The Haverford School
June 10th, 2010

Thank you very much for inviting me to speak tonight. I have the sneaking suspicion, of course, that the reason you chose me is because you figure there's a good chance I'll say something entertainingly outrageous. And I wouldn't want to disappoint you, so I thought I'd start with one of my own poems, a favorite of mine called:

The Origins of Passion

I am eight years old and naked
in my mother's bedroom: lipsticks,
brushes, combs and stockings fragrant
with her blessing hands, the vanity
an altar, I her secret acolyte.
A white lace slip drapes carelessly
across a chair; I take it in my hands,
press my face too deeply in its folds,
lift my trembling arms and drop it
over me, aching with desire
I can't articulate or understand,
immersed in her, burning with loss.

In all the years to come, I will
make love to women smelling softly
of lavender and talc, blessing me

with hands adept at rituals I want
to share but don't know how or why:
lipsticks, brushes, combs and stockings.
I will beg my wife to leave
her slip on; I will press my face
between her breasts and thighs and buttocks
too deeply, burning
to immerse myself in what I love,
still inarticulate, uncomprehending.

I'm not allowed to read that poem when my wife is in the audience because it embarrasses her, but I learned a long time ago that you cannot be a poet if you are not willing to be honest, and that poem's about as honest as poetry gets. I sent a draft copy to a friend of mine who's been critiquing my poems since our college days, and he sent it back about a week later with a short note that said only, "Billy, this is a wonderful poem, but if you ever publish it, you'll be sorry." I thought about that for a day or two, and then I called him up. "Why?" I asked.

"Why what?" he replied.

"Why will I be sorry?" It turns out he was afraid that readers might question my sexual orientation. This made me laugh because by that point in my life I had long since ceased to give a big rat's backside if people think I'm a gay transvestite fan dancer or a left-handed Belizian parrot lover. I've included the poem in two subsequent books of mine, and as nearly as I can tell, publishing the poem hasn't ruined my life.

Besides, this poem isn't about sexual orientation at all. It's a poem about loss. It's a poem about what our culture forces boys to deny in and about themselves as they mature into what our culture tries to pass off as manhood. (Girls have their own losses, but since you are all boys, I will stick with the masculine persuasion here.) When is the last time you heard an adolescent girl accused of being a "crybaby"? How many times have you hurt yourself only to have some adult male say to you, "Rub some dirt on it"? How many of you hate athletic competition because you simply are not gifted athletes and don't enjoy being the objects of scorn and ridicule? Yet our culture tells us we males are supposed to thrive on competition, strive to excel in athletics, shake off our wounds "like men," and never, ever get caught crying.

Haverford, I think, does a pretty good job of creating pathways for those among you who love art, literature, music, and drama. But even here, all too often I hear comments like, "You throw like a girl," or "That's so gay," or "He's a sissy." Cultural stereotypes, deeply ingrained patterns of belief and behavior, are not easily overcome. One of our worst fears is to be perceived by our peers as something other than masculine.

What's the most masculine image you can think of? How about a United States Marine Corps sergeant? Back in the days when I was your age and we didn't have computers or digital enhancement, the Corps's recruiting pitch was a life-sized poster of a huge Marine sergeant in that gorgeous dress blue uniform, hands on hips and stern eyes staring forward, with only the caption, "The Marine Corps Builds Men."

But what does it mean to build a man? At Parris Island, I was taught how to eat, how to dress, how to walk, how to speak. I had to tuck my shoelaces into the tops of my boots at night. I had to align my zipper, my belt buckle, and my shirt front just so. I had to shout the Lord's Prayer in unison with 79 other recruits every night — except when Drill Instructor Evans was on duty; then our nightly prayer was simply, "Pray for war!" How any of this made me a man remains a mystery to me still, 44 years later.

Me with artwork done by Haverford School graduating VI Former Billy Bourke, Class of 2010. The charcoal portrait is drawn over a background consisting of excerpts from my poetry. I did not know Bourke was doing this project until it was finished and put on display at one of the school's semi-annual Open Mic Nights (photograph by Scott Waldman).

And as for combat, I quickly discovered that it was a harrowing, horrifying, mayhem of fear and confusion, and that the only thing worse than being killed or maimed would be to have my buddies find out just how afraid I really was — scared witless and wanting Mommy to come and get me out of this terrible nightmare I'd somehow awakened into. There was nothing manly about it. I functioned because I was afraid to reveal the true depths of my cowardice.

Just about the only good thing to come out of that disaster was a real-ization that most of what I'd been taught to believe was largely untrue. That had all sorts of ramifications, but the one I want to concentrate on here is this notion of what it means to be a man. I did that manly thing, and it turned out to be, quite frankly, bullshit. So I started looking for my own definition of manhood.

You guys all know about my Marine Corps service, but how many of you know that I am the only male ever to receive a four-year award from the Women's Physical Education Department of Swarthmore College? Water bal-let, called synchronized swimming these days, is now an Olympic sport, but only for women. Our culture tells us, by the mere absence of men in the sport, that it's not the sort of thing a real man does, but I did water ballet for four years in the early 1970s, and I could care less what the International Olympic Committee thinks of me; I had fun.

But here's an even better example. Our culture tells us that men are the breadwinners, the providers, the bring-home-the-bacon partners in a mar-riage. To a lot of people, a man who makes less than his wife isn't quite a man, and there is something seriously wrong with a man who has to be sup-ported by his wife. Yet that is exactly what happened between my wife and me for nearly 20 years. My wife worked as a computer programmer while I sat home and wrote poetry. I also did the laundry, washed the dishes, cleaned toilets, watered the plants, and went grocery shopping — all those things the mommies do.

I don't know what others thought of that arrangement; my wife and I were the only people whose opinions mattered to me. And as I said, I'd done that manly thing, and no longer cared to play by those rules. Instead, my wife got to feel a sense of accomplishment that her mother never had the chance to experience, and I wrote a dozen books that wouldn't have been written if I had had to work five days a week for someone else.

Even more importantly, when my daughter was born I got to be a "house daddy." For years, more often than not I was the one who got Leela up in the morning, fed her breakfast, changed her diaper, took her to feed the ducks on Wissahickon Creek. When she started school and her class would go on field trips, there I'd be, zooming down the slide at Smith Playground with fifteen Munchkins glommed onto me. Not many men get the opportunity I had to play so active a role in raising our daughter. Think MasterCard: you want to talk priceless?

There's a lot more I could tell you — the day in 1970, for instance, after I heard about the killings at Kent State, and I sat on a street corner in Swarth-more, Pennsylvania, and cried and cried until I couldn't cry anymore, and when I finally stopped crying, I found my mind more clear and focused than it had ever been in all my 21 years.

But I've already spoken too long. The point I'm trying to make from all of this is that I hope all of you in the years ahead will challenge yourselves to recognize and question the cultural and societal baggage that comes along with being an adult male. Step outside your comfort zone. Don't be afraid to follow your heart and your instincts. Open your mind to the full range of what is possible. Go out and learn the difference between being a man and being your own man. Your lives—and the lives of those around you—will be so much richer if you do, and the opportunities you allow yourselves may lead in directions you cannot now even begin to imagine.

Thank you again for asking me to speak. Thank you for all you have given me these past four years. I will miss you. Have a nice life, and when you get to the end of it, I hope you will be able to look back and know this world is a better place because of you.

❖   ❖   ❖

The Pity of War Poetry

(In response to a request to contribute to the 18 March 2011 opening of The Wilfred Owen Story and Gallery, Birkenhead, Wirral, Merseyside, U.K., Britain's only permanent exhibition commemorating Wilfred Owen's formative years in Birkenhead and his life in the trenches, *http://www.wilfredowenstory.com.*)

I was very familiar with Wilfred Owen's poetry while I was still in high school. I even had—and still do—a book of his, *The Collected Poems of Wilfred Owen* (New Directions, 1963) edited by C. Day Lewis and with an essay by Edmund Blunden. I was much enamored of Owen, finding him heroic, tragic, magnetic. Even his death, a week short of the armistice, was romantic to a starry-eyed schoolboy.

But knowledge without experience is at best an empty thing, at worst a disaster. I read Owen's poems, but I didn't begin to understand what he was trying to tell me. Instead, imagining that I might become the Wilfred Owen of my own war (while avoiding death, of course), I enlisted in the United States Marine Corps when I was just seventeen. And by the time I was able to connect experience with knowledge, it was too late.

By the grace of chance, I survived my war, and in an odd way I have indeed become a Wilfred Owen of sorts, a chronicler in verse of the war I fought. But I often wonder, when people — especially young people — read my poetry, do they understand what I am trying to say any better than I understood Owen when I was young? Sadly, I don't imagine they do.

Indeed, years ago, when I was still in college after I'd come back from my war, I wrote a poem called "Imagine." In a 1988 edition of Owen's selected poetry and prose, an Owen scholar took umbrage with my poem, thinking that I was somehow reducing Owen's poetry to "a stereotype in the public's response to war," but my poem is only trying to express this terrible gulf between those who have known war and those who have not, the gulf between knowledge and experience. Owen, I think, would have understood my poem:

Imagine

The conversation turned to Vietnam.
He'd been there, and they asked him
what it had been like:
had he been in battle?
Had he been afraid?

Patiently he tried to answer
questions he had tried to answer
many times before.

They listened, and they strained
to visualize the words:
newsreels and photographs, books
and Wilfred Owen tumbled
through their minds.
Pulses quickened.

They didn't notice, as he talked,
his eyes, as he talked,
his eyes begin to focus
through the wall, at nothing,
or at something inside.

When he finished speaking,
someone asked him:
had he ever killed?

"That Damned Bad": Fragments from the Life of Robert James Elliott

When we think of the British poets of World War I, we think of Wilfred Owen, Siegfried Sassoon, Isaac Rosenberg, Edmund Blunden, Robert Graves, perhaps Charles Hamilton Sorley, Rupert Brooke, and a handful of others. All of them were officers, excepting only Rosenberg, who was of the "other ranks," articulate and educated men with a sense of literary tradition whose poetry has been anthologized and analyzed and remembered for nearly a century.

But have you ever heard of Robert James Elliott? Of course you haven't. Nor had I. Why would we? The record of his life, the impact he made on history, did not extend beyond has family and friends. He was just an ordinary man among millions of ordinary men who got caught up in what was then known as the Great War. Recently, however, a friend and colleague of mine at the Haverford School, Gerard Rooney, shared with me a small collection of documents his cousin in Scotland had come upon while sorting through their maternal grandfather's papers, and I was once again reminded that, when one takes the time to listen, there is no such thing as an ordinary life. Here is what Rooney shared with me:

Robert James Elliott was born into a working-class family in 1880. At the age of 18, he enlisted in the 14th Light Highland Infantry, serving seven years on active duty and another five years of reserve duty. Employed as a laborer when the Great War began, he voluntarily re-enlisted in the 14th Light, leaving behind his wife Catherine and a growing family in Paisley, Scotland. On a postcard dated May 17th, 1917, he wrote to his wife:

> Dear wife, Just a few lines to let you know that I have been in hospital these last few days with trench fever but is going on all right and will be out in a day or two. I took bad on Sunday and rose to 103° — so they sent me away at once. We were washed out of our dugout with one of the greatest rainstorms ever I seen. All our stuff was washed away. It was that damned bad that it clean took Eddy's address off the paper so you will have to send me another one. I hope you and the children are doing all right for I am about all right myself. This life is something hellish — we never see anything but shells and hard biscuits. I have told my pal to keep any letters that come for me and I am sorry to say that I have not got your tobacco yet but you need not trouble about more as you have not

money to burn. This is only a few notes when I get you[1] I will write a bigger one. Best wishes to Mary and family — love and kisses to yourself and children. I remain your loving husband till death. Bob

A second postcard is dated June 7th, 1917:

> Dear wife. The old story — I am going on all right and hopes these few lines find you and the children the same. I am still in the next station and as soon as I get out I will write you a letter and let you know if all yours has come all right. It will soon be a month since I had your last. Again hoping this finds you well, I remain your loving husband Bob.

Another postcard, undated, reads: "Dear Kate. I had nothing else to do so I thought I would compose these lines. I hope you get some amusement out of them." The poem follows:

> I am fighting for my home in 9 Back Sneddon[2]
> With my wife and children always on my mind
> And I very often wonder what would happen
> If by any chance with rent you lag behind
> For the factor[3] is a dirty sort of fellow
> He is always on the spot to get the rent
> And the clubman[4] gets a move on every Monday
> He is at the door before the money it is spent
> The bravest men of Paisley went to war
> And from the Sneddon quite a few has fell
> But we left behind a couple of dirty scoundrels
> Who try to make our home a perfect hell
> It's the factor and the clubman that I mean
> The type of men I call The British Huns
> And if I had my way, well, I would do it
> And send them out as fodder for the guns
> There's a pair of what the women call shirkers
> Who never knew a decent hour's work
> And if I was the women in the Sneddon
> I'd send them out as targets for the Turks.
> The next to pop his dirty dial[5] in the house
> Is an animal — they call him Davie Rodgers
> He gives his nose a blow but his eye is on the door
> And he whispers 'how is hubby in the sodgers?'[6]

Three other poems are included among this small batch of papers, one titled, two untitled. The first two are clearly addressed to his wife:

Faces In The Fire

Mid the glamour of the twilight when the dusk of evening falls,
And the shadows grow and lengthen in the old oak paneled walls,
In the corner by the chimney in her old accustomed place,
Sits a gentle little lady with the firelight on her face,
And her eyes adream and wishfull watch the flames and never tire,
She is seeking always seeking for the faces in the fire,
Oh my lady, there's a face that's more to you than all the rest,
Mid the many dear and precious there is one you love the best,
Oh it's not so very handsome but it's honest and it's true,
And of all the world of faces it's the handsomest to you,
For your eyes grow soft and tender as a tongue of flame leaps higher,
And his steady eyes smile back among the faces in the fire,
Little lady are you dreaming of his coming back some day?
On his kneeling down to kiss you on the day he marched away,
Are you weaving dreams of glory tinged with flames effulgent glow?
Or do memories rise to haunt you of your baby, no not so?
Do you see him chilled and weary, stumbling on the Flemish mire?
That has dimmed your eyes dear Kate in your picture in the fire.

* * * * * * * * *

When I come home to you dear
What will your welcome be?
Tired by long months of waiting,
Will you have changed to me?
Or will your love have grown dear
A stronger purer tie,
Caused by these months of waiting,
That have passed so slowly by.

When I come home to you dear
What will your welcome be?
The hours you've found so weary,
How dread they've been for me
Yet midst the mire of battle,
One hope has urged me on
And that fond hope I'll cherish, till
My work is wholly done.

When you come home to me dear,
My heart will gladden'd be,
These long months of waiting,
Have made me yearn for thee.

Though weary on the lonesome hours,
To you I still belong,
God bring you home to me dear,
And crown my life with song.

Rooney surmises that perhaps Elliott sent the third poem to his two daughters on the occasion of the birth of a third daughter:

Only a baby small dropped from the skies
Only a laughing face two sunny eyes
Only two cherry lips one chubby nose
Only two little hands ten little toes
Only a golden head curly and soft
Only a little tongue that wags loudly and oft
Only a little brain empty of thought
Only a little heart troubled with naught
Only a tender flower sent us to rear
Only a life to love while we are here
Only a baby small never at rest
Small but how dear to us we knowest best.

At the bottom of this poem, Elliott added, "I suppose this will be about it — Kate and Harriet."

One can only speculate about what he meant when he wrote, "I suppose this will be about it." Was it a premonition? A postcard from Catherine to Robert, dated December 14th, 1917, reads:

Dear husband,

Just a postcard hoping it will find you well. It is five weeks since I got a letter from you and I have been waiting every day. For God's sake write and let me know if there is anything wrong with you — for I have sent three letters and never got an answer. If you get this write at once and ease my mind.

From you loving wife.

But Catherine Elliott would not hear from her husband again. Instead, more than five months later,[7] she would receive this letter from the British Red Cross. Headed: "Pte. Robert Elliott 8869, H.Q. Coy, 14 H.L.I.," it read:

"Dear Madam,

Ever since your request for news of your husband, we have been doing our best to find out something about him for you, but we regret to say that the following sad report which came today is the only one we have had about him.

Pte. Wm. Mooney 20772 14th H.L.I. H.Q. at present in St Luke's War Hospital, Halifax and whose home address is 24 Paisley Road West, Glasgow states:—

'I had known and been with Elliot for 12 months. He belonged to Paisley. He was one of the Battn. Police. Twenty of us, including Elliot, left Bourlon Wood[8] at 4 o' clock on the morning of Nov (I cannot remember the exact date but it was between 24 and 28). We were being shelled all the way down when we were relieved by another Batt. And Elliot was killed by one of the shells.'

We never like to form a definite opinion on the evidence of one man, but Pte. Mooney appears to have been an eye-witness and it is now so long since your husband was heard of that we very much fear it may prove to be true.

We are continuing our enquiries and we will send you on anything further we may get.

Assuring you of our very sincere sympathy.

Yours faithfully,

On behalf of the Earl of Lucan"

At the time of his death, Elliott was 37 years old. He left behind his 37-year-old wife, and five children: Harriet, 9; Kate 7; James, 5; Mary, 3 (eventually to become Gerry Rooney's mother); and Robert, 3 months. Catherine Elliott lived another thirty years, raising the family on her own. She never remarried.[9]

Notes

1. Grammatical errors, spelling errors, and omissions all appear in the original documents.
2. 9 Back Sneddon: the address of the rental property where the Elliotts lived.
3. factor: the rent collector.
4. clubman: cross between a company store person and a loan shark.
5. dial: face
6. sodgers: soldiers, aka the army.
7. The letter is dated April 18, 1918, but apparently was not sent until May 29.
8. The fighting in and around Bourlon Wood was part of the Battle of Cambrai.
9. Robert Elliott had four brothers, three of them also killed in the Great War.

Con Thien and Dancin' Jack

I don't know where or why the Vietnam War got the nickname "the rock-n-roll war." That certainly wasn't my experience during my thirteen months with 1st Battalion, 1st Marine Regiment from early February 1967 to late February 1968. I never heard a broadcast of Armed Forces Radio, let alone watched

Armed Forces TV, and the only USO show I ever saw starred Mrs. Miller, an overweight middle-aged housewife whose one claim to fame was an AM radio spoof of a hit by Petula Clark.

My memories of music in Vietnam are so memorable precisely because they are so rare. I first heard the Doors' "Light My Fire" and the Iron Butterfly's "In-A-Gadda-Da-Vida," played on battery-powered portable turntables during down time in the battalion's command post southeast of Danang in the summer of 1967. I remember hearing Buffy Saint Marie singing "Codeine" and "Now that the Buffalo's Gone," And when we were up near Quang Tri in January 1968 — it might have been New Year's Day — someone had a copy of the Beatles' Sgt. Pepper album, and played it over and over again until the batteries on his turntable wore out.

The one exception to this paucity of music came during the weeks our battalion spent at Con Thien up on the demilitarized zone. Con Thien was a miserable lump of mud and barbed wire where there was little to do except sit inside the two sandbagged bunkers occupied by the battalion scouts and play cards and talk and just pass the time while waiting for the next barrage of incoming North Vietnamese artillery to arrive from the other side of the DMZ, which it did with nerve-wracking regularity. And when it did, we'd all double up inside our flak jackets and helmets, and put our fingers in our ears, and hold our breath, and shiver, and hope like hell none of the stuff landed in our neighborhood.

You didn't walk around outside any more than you absolutely had to. Getting caught in the open by incoming was both mentally harrowing and physically uncomfortable. The telltale whistle of the rounds didn't give you much warning, and the heavy mud made it impossible to run for cover, so you'd just have to flop yourself down right where you were and try to bury your body in the mud like a pig wallowing down on the farm. Then you'd have to spend the next few hours trying to scrape the mud off your one pair of jungle utilities, and out of your nose and rifle.

There weren't too many places to go anyway, except maybe to the helicopter landing zone to get the mail, when the weather was good enough to allow a chopper to land, or over to the supply dump to get a few more cases of C-rations. And it was almost always raining. Who wants to walk around in the rain when you don't have to?

Nighttime was different. More relaxed. You could unclench your jaws and unwind your fists. The NVA didn't fire at night because the flashes would reveal the locations of their guns. Of course, there was always the possibility of getting hit with a ground assault some night, but our bunkers were far enough inside the perimeter wire that we would have plenty of time to say our prayers before some NVA soldier flipped a grenade through the door. Nighttime actually got to be sort of fun, and I soon came to look forward to it through the long daylight hours of ducking and cringing. Here's why:

About the fourth or fifth night we were at Con Thien, several of the scouts in the other bunker came pouring into our bunker in a tangle of arms and legs and laughter. "Get on the Bullshit Band!" Mogerdy shouted, all excited, "They got tunes!"

"Get outta here, you assholes," said Wally, wrapping his arms protectively around his PRC-10 radio. "You're trackin' mud all over our goddamned house."

"Come on," said Mogerdy, "turn on the radio. They're playin' music on the Bullshit Band. I kid you not. We were just listening to it in the S-3s' bunker. Somebody's playing music."

On military radios, there's a frequency way near the top of the band that's left unassigned at all times, and is supposed to be used only in emergencies. It was regularly used, however, as an open conference line among enlisted men, and anybody with a spare radio and a little time to kill would get on the air and try to find somebody else from Podunk, Iowa, or Bumfart, Maine, or wherever. "Hey, hey, hey, this is Cool Albert from Detroit," you could hear on any given night. "Any Motor City Soul Brothers out there? Who knows a good joke?" Thus, the frequency had acquired the nickname of the Bullshit Band.

After much cajoling, bribery, and threats, Wally finally consented to turn on his radio. Nothing but static. "Fuck you guys," he said.

"Put on the whip and run it out the door," said Hoffy. "You can't get nothing in here with a tape antenna." Wally got out the ten-foot long whip antenna, plugged it in, and stuck it out of the bunker. He fiddled with the radio. "Baby, baby, where did our love go?" Diana Ross and the Supremes were singing to us right through the radio's handset speaker, clearly audible in spite of the static.

"Hot damn!" shouted Morgan.

"Wha'd I tell you!" said Mogerdy.

"Run next door and get Kenny and them, Rolly," said Wally. "Let's have a party." The song ended, and a voice came over the box:

"Diana Ross and the Su-premes," said the voice. "Ain't they wonderful? Eat the apple and fuck the Corps; that's what I always say. And who am I? Why, I'm Dancin' Jack, your Armed Forces Bullshit Network DJ, comin' to you from somewhere deep in the heart of the heart of the country. Do I have any more requests out there, you jive motherfuckers?"

"You got 'Dancin' in the Streets'?" another voice broke in.

"All right! Martha and the Vandellas," said Dancin' Jack, "an excellent choice. Anybody out there in Radioland got 'Dancin' in the Streets'?"

"Yo!" came in a third voice. "I do."

"Well, spin it, comrade!" Another song began: "Callin' out around the world, there'll be dancing in the streets..."

"How are they doin' that?" asked Wally.

"Must be guys down around Dong Ha and Camp Carroll with turntables and tapedecks and stuff," said Mogerdy. "All you gotta do is put your headset up to the speakers and the airways fill with music."

The bunker got very crowded when several more scouts piled in from next door, but we all squeezed in together and pulled up our knees and made room because we only had the one PRC-10 assigned to the scouts. We smoked cigarettes, and laughed and listened, and sometimes we got real quiet — like when the Beatles were singing, "Yesterday, love was such an easy game to play; now it seems as though it's gone away" — and sometimes we all shouted along at the tops of our lungs: "Gimme a ticket for an airplane!"

Con Thien was also the first and only place I smoked marijuana in Vietnam. Most of the time, it just didn't pay to be high because out where we were most of the time, if you were high you were likely to end up in a body bag. But at Con Thien, as I said, the scout bunkers were well inside the wire. If we got hit by a ground assault, and the NVA got as far as the scout bunkers, we might as well be stoned out of our minds because we were all going to be dead meat anyway.

For awhile, then, we had it pretty fine. Daytime was no fun, but we spent our nights getting stoned and listening to Dancin' Jack, hour after hour after hour. When Otis Redding sat on the dock of the bay, I could really see the tide rolling away, and the kicks just kept getting harder to find for Paul Revere and the Raiders, and the Lovin' Spoonful insisted, "What a day for a daydream." Whatever anybody wanted to hear out there in Radioland — which consisted, I assume, of far northern I Corps from Gio Linh to the Rock Pile — somebody else seemed to have it: rock-n-roll, blues, jazz, soul, country.

Eventually, the no-sense-of-humor screw-the-enlisted-men military brass caught up with the whole operation and chased everyone off the air. I've no idea how they managed to do it. Maybe they used radio direction finding equipment to track down the guys with the music and threatened to throw them in the brig. Maybe Adrian Cronauer got jealous of Dancin' Jack. Who the hell knows? Whatever happened, the Bullshit Band fell silent, and we spent our last nights at Con Thien sitting in our silent bunker, listening to the occasional air strike, or outgoing artillery, or the pop and hiss of illumination rounds.

But the music had been fun while it lasted — just about the only fun I ever remember having in Vietnam — and I can still hear the driving beat of the Rolling Stones thumping through the static, the whole bunker screaming in unison: "I can't get no! Satisfaction! Oh, no, no, no!"

❖   ❖   ❖

Dead on a High Hill: Poetry from the Korean War

Every war leaves in its wake, along with destruction and misery and sorrow and death, a body of literature. From Homer's *The Iliad* to Virgil's *Aeneid*, from Philip Freneau's "The American Soldier" to Walt Whitman's "The Wound-Dresser," from Mark Twain's "The War Prayer" to James Jones's *From Here to Eternity*, war and literature are each a subset of the other. Moreover, no longer does war have to wait for a Homer or a Tennyson or a Kipling to be translated into literature. As soldiers increasingly have become more literate, there has been a marked increase, beginning in the early 20th century, in the body of literature written by the soldiers and veterans themselves.

Consider, for instance, the British poets of the Great War: Charles Hamilton Sorley, Wilfred Owen, Siegfried Sassoon, Edmund Blunden, Isaac Rosenberg. Among Americans, e. e. cummings, Alan Seeger, John Peale Bishop, and Malcolm Cowley all wrote important poems about the Great War.[1] American veterans of World War II produced such classic novels as Norman Mailer's *The Naked and the Dead* and Joseph Heller's *Catch 22*, along with poems like Randall Jarrell's "The Death of the Ball Turret Gunner," Howard Nemerov's "Redeployment," John Ciardi's "A Box Comes Home," and Richard Eberhart's "The Fury of Aerial Bombardment."[2]

The Vietnam War has produced a huge body of literature written by those who fought in it, including such canonical works as Philip Caputo's *A Rumor of War*, Ron Kovic's *Born on the 4th of July* and Tim O'Brien's *The Things They Carried*, the plays of David Rabe, and powerful poems by an assortment of poets from John Balaban, Bruce Weigl, and Walter McDonald to Yusef Komunyakaa, David V. Connolly, and Dale Ritterbusch.[3]

Even our Iraq and Afghanistan Wars are beginning to produce literature, as evidenced by Brain Turner's 2005 poetry collection *Here, Bullet* and Clint Van Winkle's 2009 memoir *Soft Spots*.[4]

Then there's the Korean War. It lasted three long years, cost 37,000 American lives (more than the Revolutionary War, the War of 1812, the Mexican War, the Spanish American War, and the Filipino-American War combined), and has never officially ended.[5] A major American war by any definition of "major." But ask yourself to name three writers from the Korean War. Two? How about one? There is more than one reason why the Korean War is called the Forgotten War, and this is one of them.

Because if the body of literature from the Korean War is much smaller than that of the American wars that straddle it, which it is, it is far from inconsequential. It includes novels such as Pat Frank's *Hold Back the Night*, William Styron's *The Long March*, and Richard Kim's *The Martyred*, memoirs like James Brady's *The Coldest War* and Martin Russ's *The Last Parallel*, Rod Serling's play *The Rack*, and short stories such as Donald Depew's "Indigenous Girls" and John Deck's "Sailors at Their Mourning: A Memory," along with an assortment of poets whose work I will shortly discuss. Yet for much of the last fifty years, continuing to this day, this literature has been all but ignored.[6]

It is not my purpose here to explore in depth the differences between Korean War literature and the literatures of the two American wars on either side of it, the Second World War and the Vietnam War. But without going into great detail, a few observations are appropriate. The Second World War was the kind of experience that literally transformed an entire generation of Americans. One need only read Studs Terkel's *The Good War* or Tom Brokaw's *The Greatest Generation* to get a sense of that. And in its own way, though for very different reasons, the Vietnam War did that to another generation, as is readily apparent in Gloria Emerson's *Winners and Losers: Battles, Retreats, Gains, Loses, and Ruins from the Vietnam War* or Myra MacPherson's *Long Time Passing*.

The Korean War simply did not have that kind of impact. It was not the central event of the '50s, and most Americans remained untouched by it from start to finish. "People had other things to do and unless your son was there, nobody seemed to care much about Korea," writes Korean War veteran Charles F. Cole in *Korea Remembered*, and when it ended, he adds, "the Korean War vanished from view like a lost football game."[7]

The reasons are multiple and complex, but like the war itself, I would suggest that the literature of the Korean War has never been recognized or widely read precisely because that experience was not the kind of transformative experience that the other two wars were. Put briefly, as Phil Jason and I write in *Retrieving Bones*, "The Korean War did not capture the American popular imagination."[8]

But why? The soldier-poets themselves offer some possible answers.

"Korea was a 'non-war,'" says William Childress, "being alternately a 'police action' and 'Harry Ass Truman's war.' Korea was no war to inspire poetry or fiction. It lacked all nobility and didn't settle a damn thing."[9] Keith Wilson calls the war "a very dirty and murderous joke."[10] Reg Saner's answers take the form of questions: "Is it because Korea wasn't officially a war, just bloody murder on both sides, while being officially termed 'a police action'? Is it because for a long time people referred to it as 'the Phoney War'?... Or, finally, and perhaps most likely, had World War II made us small potatoes by inevitable comparison — among even ourselves?" In spite of "all the ink spilt about poor public support for Vietnam veterans," Saner believes that "we Korean veterans got neither respect nor disrespect. Except amid our immediate families, there was no reaction."[11]

Beyond the level of popular culture, however, even within the highly specialized world of those who actually study war and the literature of war, Korean War writing, and especially the poetry, remained invisible for nearly fifty years. Paul Fussell's *Norton Book of Modern War*, for instance, includes no poetry from the Korean War, nor does Jon Stallworthy's *Oxford Book of War Poetry*, though both books include poems dealing with the Second World War and the Vietnam War. Carolyn Forche's *Against Forgetting* misidentifies Etheridge Knight as a Korean War veteran while including no one who actually is a Korean War veteran.[12] Not until after the 1999 publication of *Retrieving Bones: Stories and Poems of the Korean War* has a major American war poetry anthology included work from the Korean War.[13]

Ignored and unrecognized even by these specialists on war literature are magnificent poems by Thomas McGrath and Hayden Carruth, two of the most important American poets of the 20th century, along with the work of half a dozen veterans who fought in Korea and later went on to become prolific and serious poets.

Both Carruth and McGrath are, coincidentally, World War Two veterans, not Korean War veterans. Carruth has been called "one of the lasting literary signatures of our time" by *Library Journal* and "a national treasure" by *The Nation*,[14] while the *New Republic* considers McGrath to be "one of the best American poets extant," and *Poetry East* says, "McGrath is, quite simply, one of the very best American poets."[15]

Though Carruth's "On a Certain Engagement South of Seoul" did not appear in book form until 1959,[16] the poem was probably written in 1950 and first published in *The Nation*.[17] Consisting of sixteen stanzas of loose iambic pentameter, the poem is written in *terza rima*, and begins: "A long time, many years, we've had these wars." Carruth then goes back to his high school days "when Italy broke her peace," a reference to the 1936 Italian invasion of

Ethiopia, before describing how, when he was nineteen (which would have been 1940), he "saw/A soldier in a newsreel clutch his ears//To hold his face together." Such images, "so raw and unbelievable," were "enough to numb us."

But that was before Carruth had experienced for himself the "bark and whine" of battle. Ten years later,

> ... the news of this slight encounter somewhere below
> Seoul stirs my remembrance: we were a few,
> Sprawled on the stiff grass of a small plateau,
>
> Afraid.

Carruth makes that fear vivid, elucidating how war — combat — transforms literally everything, altering perceptions of self and others, warping emotions, leaving men isolated from themselves and each other:

> My clothing was outlandish; earth and sky
> Were metallic and horrible. We were unreal,
> Strange bodies and alien minds; we could not cry
>   * * *
> Nor could we look at one another, for each...
>   * * *
> ... sat alone, all of us, trying to wake
> Some memory of the selves beyond our reach.

There is a weariness to the poem, a sense of sad inevitability. It is evident in the opening line, and recurs throughout the poem in lines such as "the nations undertake/*Another* campaign now ... and we forsake//The miseries there that we can't understand/*Just as we always have*" (italics added). But this is not entirely true because Carruth, at least, does understand the miseries of those soldiers caught in that "slight encounter somewhere below/Seoul," just as he is aware of the toll combat takes on those who survive it, and even this brief glimpse

> Of a scene on the distant field can make my hand
> Tremble again. How quiet we are. One limps.
> One cannot walk at all. Or one is all right.
> But one owns this experience that crimps
>
> Forgetfulness, especially at night.

This is what war does to body and mind. This is the curse of memory. And for what? One war merely gives way to the next in an endless succession. And Carruth can find no saving grace, no redeeming qualities in his own experiences or the misery of others, but only a loss of certitude. Unlike many

veterans, who insist on a sense of comradeship and brotherhood forged under
arms, however terrible the circumstances, Carruth asks:

> Is this a bond? Does this make us brothers?
> Or does it bring our hatred back? I might

> Have known, but now I do not know. Others
> May know. I know when I walk out-of-doors
> I have a sorrow not wholly mine, but another's.

And here the poem ends, the questions unanswered, the sorrow unmitigated.
Carruth is doubly cursed, once for the burden of his own sorrow, and again
for "a sorrow not wholly mine, but another's."

McGrath's "Ode to the American Dead in Korea," first published in
1955,[18] but almost certainly written while the war was still going on, consists
of three stanzas of 14, 15, and 14 lines respectively, and is an unusual combination of rhymed and blank verse. In the first stanza, 8 of 14 lines rhyme, or
four pairs of lines; in the second, 8 of 15, or four pairs; and in the third, 10
of 14, or five pairs. Five of the rhyming pairs are couplets, one couplet each
in the first two stanzas and three in the last; at other times, rhymes are separated by one or two other lines. The stanzas are numbered.

How does one even begin to take apart a poem so dense, so intricate, so
perfectly balanced as this one is? McGrath manages to weave into his poem
the loneliness of war ("God love you now, if no one else will ever"), the bleak-
ness of death in Korea ("Corpse in the paddy, or dead on a high hill"), the
naiveté of ordinary citizens ("All your false flags were/Of bravery and ignorance"), the venality of those who take advantage of that naiveté ("the safe
commanders"), the common humanity of soldiers ("ready to kill ... your
brother"), and the insignificance and anonymity of the dead ("tumbled to a
tomb of footnotes") to those who send them to die ("distinguished masters
whom you never knew").

And this is only in the first stanza. In the second and third stanzas, he
likens those ordinary Americans who answer the call of duty to bees and moles
("happy creatures") running on "blind instinct," neatly condemns church and
state ("the state to mold you, church to bless") and school, too ("No scholar
put your thinking cap on"), offers perhaps the bleakest and most succinct
explanation of evolution ever put forth:

> ... in dead seas fishes died in schools
> Before inventing legs to walk on land[,]

dismisses the Christian belief in a benevolent and caring God ("whose sparrows
fall aslant his gaze/Like grace or confetti"), implicates Big Business ("the stock

exchange /Flowers"), and disparages politicians ("the politic tear/Is cast in the Forum").

Conversely, McGrath's poem pays loving tribute to the American dead in Korea "who did not know the rules." It is a lament for those who die for the interests of those who risk nothing, certainly not their own lives. Above a bleak dawn landscape, "the lone crow skirls his draggled passage home" while God blinks "and you are gone" as quickly as that. Back home, "your scarecrow valor grows/And rusts like early lilac while the rose/Blooms in Dakota." But McGrath vows that after "the public mourners" have done with their empty rituals, "we will mourn you, . . : brave: ignorant: amazed:/Dead in the rice paddies, dead on the nameless hills."

Among those who actually fought in the Korean War and later came to write about it in verse are Childress, Saner, Wilson, Rolando Hinojosa, and James Magner, Jr.[19] Magner and Saner, with eighteen books between them,

have also between them no more than a dozen poems that deal with the Korean War, though some of those, such as Magner's "Zero Minus One Minute" and "To a Chinaman, in a Hole, Long Ago," and Saner's "Re-Runs," "They Said," and "Flag Memoir," are stunning. Hinojosa, primarily a novelist, is the author of *Korean Love Songs*, a 38-poem sequence that is essentially a novel-in-verse.[20] The experiences of these men in Korea, and the writing that came out of those experiences, deserve far more attention than they've ever gotten. Childress and Wilson in particular have produced work that warrants close examination.

Sergeant Rolando Hinojosa, Fort Buchanan, U.S. Army, Puerto Rico, 1948 (courtesy Roland Hinojosa).

William Childress grew up in a family of sharecroppers and migrant cotton-pickers. He joined the army in 1951 at

age 18 and was sent to Korea the following year, where he served as a
demolitions expert and secret
courier. He subsequently earned
Bachelor of Arts and Master of Fine
Arts degrees, and has worked a variety of jobs from college teacher and
juvenile counselor to newspaper
columnist and freelance writer.

Childress's two books of poetry
appeared within a year of each
other—*Burning the Years* (The
Smith, 1971) and *Lobo* (Barlenmir
House, 1972)—and his most active
years as a poet came between 1960
and 1970. A 1986 reprint combining
both books, *Burning the Years and
Lobo: Poems 1962–1975* (Essai Seay),
includes few poems not in either of
the earlier two.

Childress takes his subject matter from a wide variety of sources:
the natural world and its inhabitants,
the agricultural west and southwest
of his childhood, the unnatural

Poet, novelist, professor, and Korean
War veteran Rolando Hinojosa (courtesy the Office of Public Affairs, University of Texas at Austin).

world of urban poverty and button-down America, and the whimsy of his
own imagination. But war occupies a significant percentage of the total body
of his published work, and his Korean War poems are wedged in between
World War Two (in the form of his eight-part poem "Hiroshima") and the
Vietnam War (in poems such as "The War Lesson" and "Washington Peace
March, 1969").

Indeed, while those who fought the Korean War were closer in age and
temperament to the veterans of World War Two, the Vietnam War seems to
have been a catalyst for both Childress and Wilson, releasing pent-up feelings
that had perhaps been held in check by the personal and cultural stoicism
bequeathed to them by their generational older brothers and by the stultifying
atmosphere of the Fifties created by Senator Joseph McCarthy and the House
Un-American Activities Committee.

While Childress, for example, did write several of his best Korean War
poems prior to the vast American air and ground commitment in Vietnam

Private First Class William Childress, 11th Airborne, U.S. Army, Germany, 1957 (courtesy William Childress).

("The Soldiers" in 1961 and "Shellshock" in 1962), his poems become more pointed, more cynical, and more bitter as the Sixties — and the Vietnam War — advance. And while Childress can say, with what sounds very much like pride, resentment, and envy all at once, "Korean veterans did not come home and start throwing tantrums like many Viet vets did. We simply faded back into civilian life — no monuments, and not even a doughnut wagon to meet the [troop ship] I came home on,"[21] his poems suggest that the price of simply fading back into civilian life was very dear indeed.

In one of his finest poems, "Korea Bound, 1952," Childress emphasizes the unwillingness of those who are being sent to fight. The soldiers on the troop ship are "braced" against the railing as they listen to the "shrill complaining of the waves." Ostensibly free men in a democracy, they are likened to Pharaoh's slaves, and the ship itself to Pharaoh's burial tomb. And in the poem's final irony, they sail past Alcatraz Island, then a federal prison, where the prisoners' "lack of freedom guarantees their lives."

As often as not, Childress uses both rhyme and meter, sometimes altering the pattern of the rhyme scheme within a given poem, or rhyming in some

places but not in others, an admixture
of free verse and fixed form that is oddly
pleasing and reminds me of Gwendolyn
Brooks. Occasionally he gets into trouble or forces a rhyme, but for the most
part he handles form skillfully.

"Letter Home," however, is free
verse, and in it he assumes the persona
of a young American soldier, newly
arrived and still able to see beyond himself and his own misery to the misery
of "children with bellies swollen,/and
O, the flowers/of their faces, petals all
torn." Such empathy will not survive
what is to come. In "The Soldiers,"
Childress reminds us that "lives nar-
row/around living's uncertain center"
and "soldiers can't be soldiers and
be/human." A well constructed poem
of six rhymed sestets, each line with
nine syllables, it offers a cold, hard
world where only the dead are resolute.

Poet, writer, troubadour, and Korean
War veteran William "Chilly" Childress (courtesy William Childress).

In "Shellshock," Childress moves
from generic soldiers to a soldier with
a name: MacFatridge. A poem about the cost of war on those who survive,
it immediately suggests those men in John Huston's 1946 documentary *Let
There Be Light*, which was filmed in the psychiatric ward of a military hospital — though that film was withheld from public release by the U.S. government until 1979, seventeen years after Childress's poem first appeared in *Poetry*.

Childress's empathy for his fellow soldiers is matched and more than
matched by his contempt for the generals who commanded them. Both "Combat Iambic" and "Death of a General" are scathingly unrelenting, reminiscent
of Siegfried Sassoon at his angry best. And in "The Long March," a soldier
pulls from a puddle

> the arm of someone's child.
> Not far away, the General
> camps with the press corps.
> Any victory will be his.
> For us there is only
> the long march to Viet Nam.

Here, suddenly, in the last line of a poem that begins "North from Pusan," Childress makes explicit what must have been a steadily rising horror among many Korean War veterans as the Fifties became the Sixties and the Sixties became the Vietnam War. The "we" in the third line of the poem, and the "us" above, are not just the soldiers themselves, but the American people "dumbly follow[ing]/leaders whose careers/[hang] on victory."

"For My First Son," a bitter poem over which hangs an air of resigned helplessness, appears in several variants. I prefer the version in his 1971 collection in which, after enumerating the "future of steel" toward which his son's "tiny fingers grope" — a flamethrower's blast, trenchfoot, worms, gangrene, shrapnel, empty eyes — Childress concludes:

> ... these are
> the gifts of male birthdays,
> the power and glory, and
> the lies of leaders send them.

"Trying to Remember People I Never Really Knew" also deals with the wreckage of war and the future that awaits male children, but this time, after detailing the fates of three men he had once known, he refuses to say if they have left sons behind or not. It is as if, if he does not acknowledge that they had sons, he might somehow protect their sons from those who would train them "as hunters of men" and the "dark forests/where lead rains fall." It is only a gesture, his trying to shield the sons from the fate of their fathers, and Childress leaves little doubt that it is a useless gesture, that those who would train them will find them in any case, but in its uselessness it is also powerfully loving and affirming of life. For whatever he might have thought when he was "still a boy [with] fists full of detonators and TNT" smiling "murderously/for the folks back home," as he writes in "Burning the Years," war and the years have taught him that "duty changes with each job,/and honor turns ashes soon enough."

"I was a regular Navy officer," writes U.S. Naval Academy graduate Keith Wilson. "I came from warrior stock, right out of the Highlands of Scotland, and the Welsh Marches."[22] He went to Korea the first time as a 22-year-old ensign in 1950, and returned from his third tour in Korean waters in 1953. "I expected nothing from war. I was a professional. I didn't, however, expect to be lied to and betrayed. I was very proud of the UN flag at our mast head when we went in to launch attacks. I thought, and still do think, that the only way I can see for the planet to survive is to have an effective world-wide government. When I found out that Korea was all a very dirty and murderous joke, I was silenced for many years."

Wilson got out of the navy and returned to his native New Mexico, earning a Masters degree before commencing careers in both academia and as a prolific poet and writer. Working entirely in free verse, much of his work is rooted in the American Southwest, and he has a particular affinity for Native American and Spanish-American cultures. But Wilson's experiences in the Korean War provide the foundation for perhaps his most important book: *Graves Registry*. "I started writing *Graves Registry* in the winter of 1966 in anger that our government was again fighting an undeclared war in a situation that I, from my experiences in Korea, knew we could never win," he says. "I was one of the first combat veteran officers to protest Vietnam because I knew it to be unlawful, and could only lead to another disgraceful stalemate, ... [but] I had no poems about war at all — I had buried it inside.... It took the pressure of rage and fear for the young men [of the Vietnam Generation] that made me write it and it poured out, page after page."

U.S. Naval Academy Midshipman Keith Wilson with his dog Poochie, 1946 (courtesy the late Keith Wilson).

First published by Grove Press in 1969 as *Graves Registry & Other Poems*, it contained the Korean War poems along with poems about the Southwest. In 1992, Clark City Press published an updated edition called simply *Graves Registry* and containing the original Korean War poems, additional poems from his 1972 *Midwatch* (Sumac Press), and some fifty newer poems. Taken altogether, they weave the literary and the political into a single tableau that moves across time and geography, but my attention here must necessarily be limited to the poems dealing with Korea, which are grouped together at the beginning of the book.

The sequence begins with a love poem to his wife, "Echoes, Seafalls for Heloise," followed by three poems dealing more with the remnants and reminders of World War Two than with the Korean War. The first Korean

War poem is "The Captain," in which Wilson encounters a U.S. Army officer with "the kind eyes/of somebody's uncle." But as the captain describes the raids he and his Korean Commando team conduct, Wilson records "what happened to his eyes":

> the changes when he spoke of their raids
> of villages flaming, women & children
> machinegunned as they ran
> screaming from their huts.

It isn't all blood and guts. One of the virtues of Wilson's poems is the way they traverse a wide range of experiences, all of them belonging to war. In "...*ganz in Waffen*,"[23] a deck officer, firmly but without humiliating, bolsters the courage of a young sailor on the verge of breaking as their ship comes under fire from enemy shore batteries. "The Singer" recounts an incidence of accidental gunshot (in any war, though for obvious reasons it is seldom given much attention, large numbers of soldiers are killed not by the enemy but by their own and their comrades' mistakes). "Waterfront Bars" in Japan offer temporary relief to sailors between 90-day battle cruises "north of the bombline." And in "Combat Mission," three officers "in a ruined house" ten miles behind the lines drink Scotch while squatting around an oilcan stove, lifting "their cups against/the darkness, the rumbles rolling forward."

But if it isn't all blood and guts, there is plenty and more than enough of both. In "Guerilla Camp," Wilson is confronted first by the dead and wounded "from the/raid the night before," then by "a retired fighter" no older than himself whose hand has been ruined by a bullet and who demands to know "how a man/could farm/with a hand like that." In "The Circle," Wilson's ship steams for hours through hundreds of Korean bodies floating "in faded blue lifejackets," victims of a sunken troop ship, no survivors: "We sailed on. I suppose that's all/there is to say." But one body in particular remains fixed in his mind:

> God knows why
> but his ass was up instead
> of his head; no pants left,
> his buttocks glistened
> greyish white in the clear sun.
> the only one.

Whatever illusions of service and nobility Wilson entered the war with are evaporating. By "December, 1952," once again "back in the combat zone," he recalls the heroism of great naval commanders of the past and the grand enterprise to which he'd thought himself attached:

A blue United
Nations patch on the
arm, a new
dream. One World.
One
Nation.

Peace.

But now he realizes that nothing has
changed since the days of Nelson and
Farragut, that "the old bangles" still
work, allegiances are still bought,
and "tracers hit a village,/the screams
of women, children/men die." And
while the "New York Stock Market
[rises] and cash registers/click," Wilson is finally forced to confront

> the cost of
> lies, tricks
> that blind the eyes
> of the young.
> *Freedom.*
> Death. *A life safe
> for.* The Dead.

Keith Wilson, poet, professor, and
Korean War veteran (photograph by
Everett Campbell).

"Commentary" is equally scathing, a recitation of what has become, for
Wilson, only the squandering of lives, especially Korean lives, in the name of
Americans back home

> whose enemies
> are always faceless, numbers
> in a paper blowing in the
> Stateside wind.
> How many bodies would
> fill a room
> living room with TV, soft
> chairs & the hiss
> of opened beer?

> We have killed more.
> The children's bodies alone
> would suffice.

Wilson's poems are not about the big battalions and the pitched battles, but about coastal operations and guerilla raids, shattered villages and shattered ideals. They are peopled by Americans, yes, but also by Koreans and Japanese, refugees and cripples, and by warriors, yes, but also and more so by the defenseless and the innocent who always become the wreckage of war. They are Wilson's explanation of how he began life expecting to kill people and ended up dedicating it to teaching people instead.

So there is indeed a poetry of the Korean War, and there are at least three good reasons why it should not be ignored, dismissed, or forgotten. Firstly, it offers valuable insights into the Korean War itself and the experiences of those who fought it. As I wrote a quarter of a century ago about the poetry of the Vietnam War:

> Scholars and politicians, journalists and generals may argue, write and re-write 'the facts.' But when a poem is written, it becomes a singular entity with an inextinguishable and unalterable life of its own. It is a true reflection of the feelings and perceptions it records, and as such it is as valuable a document as any history ever written.[24]

This is no less true of the poetry of the Korean War.

Secondly, much of this poetry is first-rate writing, be it war poetry or not, as I hope I've demonstrated with the poems I've discussed here. Good writing is always worthy of attention, and the best of these poems can stand up to the best poetry written about any war in any generation.

Finally, the poetry of the Korean War helps to make sense of what otherwise appears to be a baffling and mystifying juxtaposition. The poets of World War II hardly celebrate or glorify their experiences. Jarrell's ball turret gunner is "washed out of the turret with a hose." Nemerov's cat "vomits worms" in "Redeployment." Ciardi's "A Box Comes Home" with Arthur inside. Eberhart's students in "The Fury of Aerial Blombardment" are "gone to early death." Yet none of these poets suggests that the war they fought was unnecessary or unjustified, let alone that it was wrongheaded, arrogant, evil, unforgivable.[25]

But only a generation later, Vietnam War poets do exactly that. Jan Barry compares American soldiers to the Mongol hordes in "In the Footsteps of Genghis Khan." Steve Hassett compares them to Hessian mercenaries in "Christmas." In "The Hooded Legion," Gerald McCarthy wonders, "What hand did not turn us aside?" Bryan Alec Floyd's "Private Jack Smith, U.S.M.C." came to feel "that his politicians were garbage/who should have been wasted."[26]

But an examination of the poetry from the Korean War suggests that this transition from "Good War" (or at least necessary and justifiable war) to "Bad

War" is not so abrupt as it seems. In "Combat Iambic," Childress writes of his commanding general, "I pray Beelzebub, Lord of the Flies,/to rear his maggot children in your eyes." In "A Matter of Supplies," Hinojosa coldly observes, "we're pieces of equipment/to be counted and signed for." Saner's American flag in "Flag Memoir" flutters over a hometown stadium, "Explaining. Trying to Explain." And Wilson, in "December, 1952," laments, "It is when the bodies are counted/man sees the cost of lies, tricks/that blind the eyes of the young."[27] If the Korean War poets are closer in age to their World War II counterparts, they respond to their experiences in the Korean War with a sense of disillusionment and betrayal that much more closely resembles the poets of the Vietnam War.

At the larger historical level, to skip from World War II directly to the Vietnam War is to fail to understand both the Vietnam War and the Cold War within which the Vietnam War unfolded, the parameters for each having been determined by the Korean War. Just so, on a literary level, there is much to be learned from the poetry of the Korean War, and much to be appreciated. Yet for most readers, students, teachers, and scholars, this literature remains, in Tom McGrath's words,

> dead on a hill,
> Dead in a paddy, leeched and tumbled to
> A tomb of footnotes.[28]

Notes

1. For these American poets, see, respectively: "I sing of Olaf glad and big," "Rendezvous" and "On the Aisne," "In the Dordogne," and "Chateau de Soupir, 1917." See Hedin, Robert, ed. *Old Glory* (New York: Persea Books, 2004). The work of the British poets can be found in multiple sources.

2. An excellent selection of American poetry from World War II, including these poems and poets, can be found in Stokesbury, Leon, ed. *Articles of War* (Fayetteville, AR: University of Arkansas Press, 1990).

3. Many of the Vietnam War poets are represented in Ehrhart, W.D., ed. *Carrying the Darkness* (Lubbock, TX: Texas Tech University Press, 1989). For Connolly's poems, see Connolly, David V. *Lost in America* (Woodbridge, CT: Vietnam Generation & Burning Cities Press, 1994).

4. Alice James Books and St. Martin's Press, respectively.

5. A truce was signed in July 1953, but there has never been a peace treaty ending hostilities.

6. Depew's and Deck's stories, along with other stories and a solid selection of the poetry, are included in Ehrhart, W. D., and Philip K. Jason, eds. *Retrieving Bones: Stories and Poems of the Korean War* (New Brunswick, NJ: Rutgers University Press, 1999).

7. Cole, Charles F. *Korea Remembered: Enough of a War!* (Las Cruces, NM: Yucca Tree Press, 1995), 212 & 273.

8. Ehrhart & Jason, *Retrieving Bones*, xix.

9. Ehrhart, W. D., "Soldier Poets of the Korean War," *War, Literature and the Arts*, vol. 9, #1, Spring/Summer 1997, 33. This special edition of *WLA*, which I guest-edited, is the first substantial exploration of any kind into the poetry of the Korean War.

10. Ehrhart, *WLA*, 9/1, 33.

11. Ehrhart, *WLA*, 9/1, 39–41.

12. See Ehrhart & Jason, *Retrieving Bones*, xlii, for a detailed discussion of Etheridge Knight.

13. Both Hedin's *Old Glory* and Lorrie Goldensohn's *American War Poetry* (New York: Columbia University Press, 2006) include substantial sections on Korean War poetry, and both acknowledge in print their debt to my research on the poetry. (Phil Jason's interest was in the fiction of the Korean War, and it was his expertise in that genre that enabled us to do an anthology combining fiction and poetry.)

14. Both quoted in Martha T. Mooney's *Book Review Digest 1993*, 322.

15. *New Republic* quoted in *Contemporary authors New Revision Series*, v.6, 341. *Poetry East* quoted in the 1999 Copper Canyon Press Catalog (www.ccpress.org).

16. Carruth, Hayden. *The Crow and the Heart* (New York: Macmillan, 1959).

17. In a letter to WDE dated December 9, 1999, Carruth writes: "I can vaguely recall writing the poem you ask about, 'On a Certain Engagement South of Seoul,' and I'm quite sure it was after I read a newspaper account of a group of soldiers who got lost somewhere and were ambushed, and it made me think of feelings I had had as a GI in World War II. I think this was in about 1949 or 1950, but I can't be sure of that. [Note: It could not have been in 1949 since the Korean War did not begin until June 1950.] It might have been originally published in *The Nation*, because I was writing for that magazine then and the topic would have been congenial to the editors there, but again I can't be sure."

18. McGrath, Thomas. *Figures from a Double World* (Denver, CO: Swallow Press, 1955).

19. All of the poems by these Korean War veterans can be found in Ehrhart, *WLA*, 9/1. A smaller selection of their poems is included in Ehrhart & Jason, *Retrieving Bones*. See the essay on "Reluctant Poets of the Korean War" for a discussion of Magner and Saner.

These poets are all, of course, Americans. Though 60,000 British troops served in Korea between 1950 and 1953, I know of no significant poetry written by British veterans of the fighting. If it exists, I would be grateful to have it brought to my attention.

20. Hinojosa's original *Korean Love Songs* (Berkeley, CA: Justa Publications, 1978) is long out of print, as is a 1991 German-English bilingual edition published jointly by the University of Osnabruck and VC-Verlagscooperative. The entire sequence appears in Ehrhart's *WLA*, 9/1, but that, too, is now not easy to obtain. A small selection from the sequence appears in Ehrhart & Jason's *Retrieving Bones*.

21. Letter to Ehrhart dated June 13th, 1997.

22. This and subsequent statements by Wilson are taken from his letter to Ehrhart dated February 21st, 1997.

23. The title means "complete in armor." This and the German epigraphs that Wilson uses with a number of his poems come from Rainer Maria Rilke's *The Lay of the Love & Death of Coronet Christopher Rilke*.

24. Ehrhart, W. D. *Carrying the Darkness: The Poetry of the Vietnam War*. (Lubbock, TX: Texas Tech University Press, 1985), xxvi.

25. See Stokesbury, *Articles of War*.

26. See Ehrhart, *Carrying the Darkness*.

27. See Ehrhart & Jason, *Retrieving Bones*.

28. Ehrhart & Jason, *Retrieving Bones*, vii.

Ken and Bill's Excellent Adventure

Part 1: The War

I. THE HOUSE IN HUE, 1968

The weapon that got Kenny and me was an RPG, a rocket-propelled grenade. You've probably seen RPGs in news footage of Afghan mujahedeen or Taliban fighters. The launcher is a long thin tube that the gunner rests on his shoulder like a bazooka, and the projectile sticks out the front end of the tube like a bulbous cone-shaped piece of nastiness. RPGs are light, cheap, and powerful. A guerrilla army's artillery.

We didn't call them RPGs back when Kenny and I were fighting in Vietnam. We called them B-40s. I don't recall ever hearing the term "rocket-propelled grenade" until many years after the fact. But a rose by any other name still has thorns, and whatever you call it, one B-40 can screw up your whole day. Just ask Kenny.

Talk about irony. The North Vietnamese gunner who fired the rocket wasn't even aiming at Kenny. He didn't even know Kenny was there. He was aiming at me. Sitting in a heavy overstuffed armchair by the window, a cup of C-ration coffee brewing at my feet, cranking rounds off now and then at the shadows in the buildings across the street, at figments of my imagination, at whatever might be over there, I was the only one that NVA gunner could see.

Kenny was sitting on the other side of the room under the canopy of a four-poster double bed cleaning his rifle. He wasn't even wearing his body armor. After several days of hard fighting with little progress, we were waiting for the flame tanks to come and burn down the block across the street. Hue City or not, Tet Offensive or not, it was a slow morning in our neighborhood.

Or seemed like a slow morning until the world exploded. Later, we figured out that the rocket came through the window on a rising trajectory, missed both the side of the window frame and my face by no more than a couple of inches either way, and detonated against the wall four and a half feet above and behind me. It blew the chair apart, shattered a heavy wooden table, turned my rifle into junk, imbedded 50 or 60 pieces of jagged metal, concrete chunks, and wood splinters into the back of my flak jacket, and punched in the back of my helmet so badly that I couldn't put it back on my head, like somebody had taken a 20-pound sledgehammer to it.

I must have been knocked out momentarily, but by the time Graves and Mogerdy got to me, I was conscious enough to tell them that Kenny was in the room, too. But Kenny was already gone. And by the time Graves and Mogerdy got me downstairs, Kenny was already on his way to the battalion aid station. By the time I got to the battalion aid station, Kenny was on his way to the LZ to be medevaced out.

I never saw him again. Kenny was sitting on the bed cleaning his rifle, and then the world exploded, and when the smoke cleared and the dust settled, Kenny was gone.

That's just the way it happens sometimes. Bobby Ross flew to Tam Ky one day and never came back. Gerry Gaffney headed off to the LZ at Con Thien and never got there. Mike Bylinoski got put on a chopper to Da Nang and was dead before it landed.

I knew Kenny hadn't died. The corpsman at the aid station said he would live. But he also said they'd never save Kenny's arm. It was hanging by a few shreds of tissue just below the shoulder, the bone shattered and exposed. No way he'd keep it.

Though I'd been much closer to the blast, Kenny had gotten hit much worse than me. A doctor cleaned up my wounds, which weren't much to speak of, and gave me a couple of shots, and then I slept for a few hours. Later that same day, I went back to the war, stone-deaf but otherwise reasonably functional. A few weeks later, I made my rotation date and got out of Vietnam in one piece, and a year after that I completed my enlistment, got out of the Corps, and embarked on the rest of my life.

I always felt badly about Kenny losing his arm because that NVA gunner was aiming at me, not Ken. Not that I lost any sleep over it. I'd seen enough of war to know that's just how it happens sometimes. But I often thought about Kenny, and wondered where he was and how he was doing. He'd paid a hell of a price for joining the Marines, and he wasn't even an American.

II. LOST & FOUND

That's the thing about Kenny. He was Japanese. Not Japanese-American. Just Japanese. A card-carrying natural-born Japanese citizen. As the years passed, I wished ever more frequently that I could find him again. But I didn't know where or how to begin looking for him. Was he still in the U.S., or had he had enough of America and gone back to Japan? I didn't even know his full name. His last name was Takenaga, but none of us could ever remember his first name, so we just called him "Ken." If there's a way to find somebody when all you've got is a last name, I never discovered it in all those years.

Then in the summer of 2000, a man named William L. Myers asked if he could publish an essay of mine called "Places and Ways to Live" in a book he was editing called *Honor the Warrior: The United States Marine Corps in Vietnam*. My essay described the combination sleeping quarters/fighting hole/reinforced bunker that Roland Maas, Kenny and I built the day after the night the VC mortared the bejesus out of us north of Quang Tri in October 1967.

At the end of every essay in his book, Myers included the full name and service number of every person mentioned in that essay. I don't know how Myers found that information about Kenny, but there it was: Cpl. Kazunori Takenaga 2320456. Now I could write to the Veterans Administration, and if Ken had ever applied for disability — which seemed highly likely, having lost his arm — the VA would forward a letter to the last address they had for Ken.

Ten days after I wrote to the VA, Kenny called me from Japan. It had been thirty-two years and seven months since we'd last spoken.

Almost immediately, I apologized to Ken for getting his arm blown off. "Oh, no," he replied. "I've still got my arm. Works pretty good, too, and I've been collecting twenty percent disability all these years. I owe you a share." He then went on to tell me how, when he finally got out of the hospital, he'd been assigned as a gate guard at the U.S. navy base at Pearl Harbor. "Can you imagine?" he said, the combination of wonder and mirth evident in his voice across the 8,000 miles between us, "A Japanese guy guarding Pearl Harbor!"

Over the next decade, Ken has come to Philadelphia many times to visit, and I gradually began to learn what I'd forgotten about him, or had never known.

III. KEN'S STORY

Ken's father had been trained as a *kamikaze* pilot during the Second World War, but the war had ended before he'd gotten his chance to die for the Emperor. Eking out a living as an itinerant actor, he had met and wooed Ken's mother, took her on the road with him, and gotten her pregnant. But he was a man struggling with demons, and was never going to be a husband or a father. There was no future in Japan for an unmarried young mother, so Katsuko left Ken with her parents and set out on her own, eventually ending up in New York and starting a new family.

Ken's grandfather was a fish merchant in the coastal city of Yatsushiro,

Kumamoto Prefecture, Kyushu, and by the time Ken was fifteen, he realized that was likely to be his own future if he stayed where he was, so he joined his mother and her new family in the U.S., finishing high school in three years and enrolling at City College of New York. As a permanent resident, however, he was subject to U.S. draft laws, and in 1966 Uncle Sam came knocking.

Ken's father and grandfather had both served in the Japanese navy, so Ken decided he'd join the navy, too, even if it was the American navy, but he discovered that he'd have to enlist for four years. When he pointed out that the army only required two years' service, the recruiter told him he could join a special branch of the navy for just two years. It was called the Marine Corps. Kenny joined. When he got to Parris Island, Ken says he told the drill instructors, "I think I'm in the wrong place. Where are the ships?"

Lance Corporal Kazunori "Ken" Takenaga (left) and Corporal William Ehrhart, near Hoi An, Vietnam, July 1967 (courtesy Ron Kincade).

With an introduction like that, I do not to this day understand how Ken ever got off Parris Island alive. But he did, and in April 1967 he was assigned as my fellow intelligence assistant with 1st Battalion, 1st Marines, replacing Bob Ross, who'd died on a hospital ship ten days after getting shot in the lung during an operation in Tam Ky. I'd hardly gotten to know Ross before he was killed, but Kenny and I spent ten months together before that morning when the world exploded. That's a long time when people are trying to kill you.

Kenny introduced me to *kimchi*, fiery hot fermented cabbage some relative of his used to send him in cans. I'd always be right there by his side whenever another "Care" package came for him at mail call, knowing there'd be *kimchi* in it. Some years later, I learned that *kimchi* is a Korean specialty, not Japanese. I spent many more years wondering why Kenny's relatives were sending him Korean food. Only after I found Ken again was this small mystery solved: I'm sure I must have known at the time, but I'd long since forgotten that Kenny was already married when he got to Vietnam — and his wife was Korean.

After Ken got out of the Marines, he stayed in the U.S. for the next twelve years, working for Pan Am and becoming a U.S. citizen (he has dual citizen-

Corporals Ehrhart and Takenaga filling sandbags near Quang Tri, Vietnam, October 1967.

ship these days). In the early 1980s, he returned to Japan. But he continued to work, as he does to this day, in the travel and tourism industry. Along the way, he's been married and divorced seven times — the first time he told me this, he looked at me deadpan and asked, "Do you think I have PTSD, Bill?" — and has nine children ranging in age from the early forties down to elementary school-age. He has a huge scar on his upper right arm, though you don't notice at first that his use of that arm is limited, and another big scar on his head.

IV. GOING BACK

What most amazes me, however, is how strong the bond between us has remained through all those decades when neither of us knew what had become of the other, how little effort it took to renew that bond, how obviously happy we both are when we have the chance to be together. But those chances have come only when Ken has reason to be in the U.S. and time enough to detour to Philadelphia for a day or two: visits on the fly, always too brief. So when Ken suggested that the two of us return to Vietnam, he didn't have to ask me twice.

Me sharing my poem "Making the Children Behave" with General Vo Nguyen Giap during an audience with the general in Hanoi, 1990. Though General Giap and I communicated through a Foreign Ministry interpreter (pictured center), I learned later that Giap understands, reads, and speaks English flawlessly.

This was not my first trip back to postwar Vietnam. I'd been back in 1985, when the devastating effects of the war were everywhere evident, and it was rare indeed for an American to be there. Children would point and say, "*Lien Xo*" (Soviet), and when I would reply, "*My*" (American), their eyes would become huge round saucers. I'd been back again in 1990, this time as part of a delegation of veteran-writers. The American War (as the Vietnamese call it) was still visible everywhere, but modern Vietnam was clearly beginning to emerge from the wreckage.

This trip would be special for two reasons, however: I'd be able to take my wife Anne with me this time, to share with her a place she had only — but endlessly — heard about during our thirty years of marriage. And I'd be traveling with my buddy, my comrade, who'd literally been where I'd been and knew what I knew and needed no explanations.

Part 2: Japan

YATSUSHIRO

Our journey began, however, not in Vietnam, but in Japan. Having been a guest in our home in Philadelphia on many occasions, and having seen where I grew up in Perkasie, Pennsylvania, Ken wanted to share with us his own roots. In Yatsushiro, Ken's hometown, we stood on the walls of the ruined feudal castle where Ken had climbed and played as a child, watching a single black swan float slowly by below us. Built in the 1600s by the Lords of Yatsushiro, it had been destroyed after the war of the Last Samurai against the Meiji Restoration. On its foundation, in 1874, a shrine was built to honor the then-crown prince of Japan. We also visited the nearby *Shohinken* or Pine Beach House, an elegant tea house built in 1688 by the third Lord of Yatsushiro for his mother, the pond behind it filled with lily pads and rimmed by irises.

As we walked the streets of Ken's old neighborhood, he pointed out the local jail where Ken's grandfather had once been locked up for "overspending" on election day (long before Ken was born). The jailers, Ken says, were sorry to see his grandfather released because every day his wife would bring a sumptuous feast for her husband and for them. We stood on the corner where Ken's house had once stood. Though it has since been replaced by a newer structure, just across the street is Kangyo-ji, the Buddhist temple where his grandparents' graves are, and where his will be some day. Later, Ken arranged for Anne and me to be decked out in traditional kimonos by a dressmaker and her two teenaged

Anne and me in Yatsushiro, Ken's home-town, dressed in traditional Japanese kimonos, a process that took a dressmaker and her two teenaged daughters nearly an hour to complete (photograph by Sachiko Akama).

daughters (the process takes nearly an hour). Having thus arrayed us, the three of them and an assistant then gave us a traditional tea ceremony.

VI. IWAKUNI

We spent eight days in Japan, flying into Osaka on China Airlines (for the long trans–Pacific flight, scrape up the $$$ for business-class if you possibly can; it is worth every penny), and traveling by bullet train first to Iwakuni, Yamaguchi Prefecture, in southern Honshu (far to the south of the recent earthquake and tsunami that devastated northern Honshu). In late 1968 and into 1969, after my time in Vietnam, I had been stationed at the Marine Corps Air Station in Iwakuni, and wanted to see the place again. We were given a personal tour by the Executive Officer of Marine Aircraft Group 12, Lieutenant Colonel Thomas E. Frederick, a close friend of my Haverford School colleague Jamie Griffin, who graciously gave us several hours in the midst of a busy day when the Commandant himself was on-station. Not surprisingly, almost nothing was recognizable after 42 years except the above-ground heating pipes and a few old quonset huts. The shabby one-story squad bays have been replaced by four-story barracks that could pass for college dormitories. The F-4 Phantoms of Marine Fighter Attack Squadron 122 have been replaced by the F/A-18 Hornets of Marine All-Weather Fighter Attack

Kintai Bridge, Iwakuni, Japan. In the distance, at the top of the hill in the center of the photo, is Iwakuni Castle (photograph by Sachiko Akama).

Squadron 242. The young MP who met us at the front gate, PFC Scheibelhut, was a poised and self-confident young woman. Talk about changes.

After we left the base, we drove to the other side of the city and walked across the graceful Kintai Bridge, whose five wooden arches span the Nishiki River in the shadow of Iwakuni Castle, home of the local lord in feudal times. This part of Iwakuni had hardly changed since last I'd been there to celebrate the Cherry Blossom Festival amidst the thousands of colorfully dressed Japanese who lined both banks of the river with blankets, picnic baskets, and magnum bottles of *sake*.

VII. Kumamoto

Then it was back on the bullet train and on to Kyushu Island and Kumamoto Prefecture, where Ken currently works for the prefectural tourism division promoting American awareness of Japanese culture. (Train travel in Japan, by the way, is wonderfully comfortable and efficient. Trains arrive on time. Trains leave on time. The conductors and the ladies who come through with snack carts bow when they enter a car, and bow again when they leave. The trains have names. The "slow" bullet train we rode on is called *Kodame* [Echo]; the newer and faster one, *Sakura* [Cherry Blossom].

Another thing you notice are the tunnels, which are ubiquitous. Japan is a mountainous land with very little flat ground, so trains and highways require bridges and tunnels in order to be viable. Between Osaka and Iwakuni, we passed through 75 tunnels; between Iwakuni and Kumamoto, another 63.)

The premier attraction in Kumamoto City is its castle, originally built by Lord Kato Kiyomasa in the early 1600s. One of the three most elaborate, well-preserved, and magnificent feudal castles in Japan, it dominates the city and the surrounding countryside, the walls massive and intimidating, the towers soaring, the living quarters of Honmaru Goten Palace — room after room — brilliant with gold leaf and multi-colored murals. The forces of Saigo Takamori, the Last Samurai, besieged the castle during the war against the Meiji throne, but could not take it. When you see it, you realize why they failed, a failure that led to Saigo's ultimate defeat.

Just beyond the castle walls is Kyu Hosokawa Gyobutei, usually referred to as Samurai House, a beautifully preserved 17th century residence built by Tadatoshi, the first Hosokawa lord of Kumamoto, for his younger brother Okitaka. And not far away is Suizenji Jojuen Park. Built by another of the Hosokawa lords, it sports a residence, multiple shrines (including one honoring foxes), a gorgeous lake with koi fish and turtles, a manicured landscape complete with miniature Mt. Fuji (indeed, small armies of landscapers and tree-trimmers seem to work non-stop at all of these sites), and a flock of pigeons so tame they perched on our hands and arms and shoulders, hoping for a handout.

VIII. Aso

We spent the next two days in the Aso Caldera, a vast bowl some 80 kilometers across left by the collapse of a prehistoric volcano, out of which protrude five newer peaks, one of them — Nakadake — still active. The area is extremely fertile, the caldera floor planted with rice, while red beef cattle particular to Aso graze on the slopes of the volcanoes. Freshwater springs are everywhere, gushing up from the ground and free for the drinking in front of every little streetside shop, at least on the street that leads away from (or to, depending on your direction) the Shinto Shrine in Aso City.

At Shirakawa Spring, where 60 tons of fresh water pour out of the ground every minute, Anne and I made rice paper and decorated it with dried flowers, leaves, colored dyes, and gold flecks. We spent a night luxuriating in the natural hot springs (called *onsen*) at Hizenya Hotel in the Tsuetate Onsen resort area that straddles the border of Kumamoto and Oita Prefectures, Anne and I in a roomy tub on a 9th floor balcony overlooking a steep, narrow, but incredibly lush valley with a river rushing noisily by below us. (*Tsuetate* means "no need for walking stick," the name given to this area 1300 years ago by a Buddhist monk who watched sick people taking hot spring baths and emerging without their walking sticks.)

The next day, while visiting Aso Shrine, we happened by chance upon a traditional Shinto wedding, bride and groom in kimonos, but with the bride's head hooded to hide her horns — an ancient Japanese custom — and the union sealed with *sake*, first drunk by bride and groom, then by their parents, and finally by the other members of their families.

We passed on the opportunity to check out Cuddly Dominion, though the billboard in the shrine's parking lot, complete with adorable-looking chimpanzee and dog, looked intriguing, opting instead for lunch at Aso Kougen, a restaurant featuring buckwheat soba noodles where female employees were helping half a dozen different groups of children to make their own noodles. Though I couldn't understand what the children were saying, it was clear that making the noodles was at least as much fun as eating them.

IX. Speaking of Food

Did I mention eating? Here is a typical dinner, this one served to us at the Grandvrio Hotel, built in the middle of a golf course and with a statue of an elk on the fairway right below our window:

1st course: lotus root, ham, aspic, seaweed, tuna, red snapper, and yellow
  fin (all of the fish raw);
2nd course: eggplant with green beans, okra, seaweed and radish wrap;
3rd course: mussels and cooked red snapper;
4th course: beef, potatoes, broccoli, carrots, okra, rice, miso soup, Japanese "pickles" (much more varied than the cucumber pickles we're
  used to);
5th course: chocolate cake, watermelon, honey dew melon.

All of this washed down, of course, with beer and *sake*. Not every meal was
this elaborate, but many were, and we often could not finish what we were
given. The meal above had the special grace of coming in small portions for
each course, which, after days of overeating, we came to see as a blessing. (On
the other hand, the lobsters we were served at the Amakusa Prince Hotel were
the largest I have ever seen. They were gigantic. Breath-taking. Brobdingna-
gian. Magnificent. I ate all of mine and half of Anne's.)

All of this luxury, by the way, is surprisingly affordable. Once you get
away from Tokyo and Kyoto — which are the only cities most Americans ever
visit, if they visit Japan at all — the pace of life slows, the congestion eases,
and the prices come down. One of the points Ken tries to emphasize in his
work is that Tokyo and Kyoto are about as representative of Japan as New
York City and San Francisco are of the U.S.

X. Amakusa-Shimabara

From Yatsushiro, an hour's ferry boat ride took us to Amakusa, a group
of 120 islands (only six of which are inhabited) off the Kyushu mainland and
part of Kumamoto Prefecture. There we visited the newly renovated Christian
Museum. Portuguese Jesuits had brought Christianity to Amakusa and neigh-
boring Shimabara in 1566, and the religion had spread rapidly among the peasantry. Indeed, by 1637, the Tokugawa Shogunate saw it as a threat, expelled the
Europeans, and outlawed Christianity. Led by a 16-year-old mystic, Amakusa
Shiro Tokisada, the peasants rose in rebellion, but were defeated after 123 days.
Some 37,000 Christians were killed in the final battle or slaughtered in its aftermath, and the survivors, who came to be known as the Hidden Christians, had
to disguise and practice their religion in secret and at great peril. Not until 1873
was the ban on Christianity lifted. The museum contains such items as Buddhas
that are actually Madonna and Child, Buddhas that have crosses etched into
their backs and are thus not visible from the front, and ceramic images of Jesus
and Mary that shogunate authorities would make people step on to prove they
weren't Christians (many refused and were summarily executed).

Christians are no longer persecuted in Japan, but Japan gets a lot of bad press for killing and eating dolphins. The fishermen of Amakusa and Shimabara (in Nagasaki Prefecture), however, have learned that there's more to be made by watching dolphins than by catching them, and many have converted their fishing boats into tour boats. The day we went out into Hayasaki Strait between Amakusa and Shimabara, we were joined by dozens of other dolphin-watching boats and anywhere from 50 to 200 zooming, leaping, surfing, cavorting dolphins (I gave up trying to count). The sea was rough that day, with large swells coming from multiple directions, but our skipper worked his small boat with a consummate skill that bespoke years of experience on the water.

Equally interesting — and as chilling as the dolphins had been uplift-ing — was Shimabara's Unzen Volcanic Area Global Geopark, built amid the ruins of the 1990 eruption of Fugendake, which killed 43 people, and its aftermath. In Memorial Park are the remains of eleven houses crushed, muti-lated, invaded, buried, or partially buried by a subsequent 1992 landslide, left exactly as they were when a debris field from the volcano destroyed them. In the nearby museum, you can experience a multi-media recreation of what the eruption would have been like using Imax-style visuals, motion, sound, heat, and smell.

Bill and Ken giving a presentation to the congregants of Toko-ji Zen Buddhist Temple in Amakusa. The Japanese writing at the top of the banner reads: "The Vietnam War from the point of view of a Soldier" (photograph by Sachiko Akama).

XI. Toko-ji Temple

Among the coolest things Ken and I did together was a talk about the Vietnam War to the congregants of Toko-ji Zen Buddhist Temple in Amakusa. Five years ago, at the request of Morinobu Okabe, 31st priest of the 350-year-old temple, Ken and I had translated and adapted a poem by the late Shinmin Sakamura, which Okabe-san makes available free for visiting English speakers (along with the original in Japanese for Japanese speakers). Here's what we came up with:

> The sun comes up each morning in silence;
> the moon disappears, but nobody sees.
>
> Flowers dance by the roadside unnoticed;
> birds twitter sweetly, but nobody hears.
>
> People don't stop to consider what matters.
> People work hard all their lives to achieve
>
> a dream of success that will make them happy:
> position or power, fortune or fame —
>
> until they are old and they realize too late
> that the beauty of living has passed them by
>
> while the river travels alone to the ocean,
> the wind sings alone in the tops of the trees.

When the priest heard that Ken and I would be in Amakusa, he asked Ken if we could give a talk about the war — its history and our experiences — to the supporters of his temple, most of whom know nothing about the war. Beneath a huge banner written almost entirely in Japanese, of course, except for "Bill Ehrhart" and "Kazunori Takenaga," we spoke for about an hour to an attentive audience of 50 or 60 people, after which we all sat down to a multi-course feast washed down with beer, *sake*, and another Japanese specialty called *shochu*.

Part 3: Vietnam

XII. Motorscooter Madness

And then it was off to Vietnam via high-speed ferry to Kumamoto City, bullet train to Fukuoka, and airplane via Taipei to Ho Chi Minh City (which most folks, even the Vietnamese, still routinely call Saigon; indeed, the airport code for Tan Son Nhut is SGN).

The ride from the airport to our hotel in the heart of the business district can only be described as "Motorscooter Madness." Though cars are no longer

Motorscooter Madness on the streets of Ho Chi Minh City (photograph by Sachiko Akama).

rare, including the 8-passenger van we were in, the overwhelming majority of Vietnamese travel by motorscooter. And while this is true throughout Vietnam, nowhere is it more evident — and harrowing — than in Saigon. The roads and streets and avenues and alleys are clogged with motorscooters. Thousands of them. Tens of thousands of them. Defying death. Defying logic. Defying imagination.

Many of the major intersections and roundabouts are without traffic signals, and traffic cops are equally rare. Traffic signs and street markings seem to be considered suggestions only, scooters blithely driving down the wrong side of a street, on the wrong side of a median strip, or up on the sidewalks, weaving in and out and around each other and the cars and trucks and bicycles, using no signals, avoiding collisions by heart-stopping fractions of an inch, flowing like water or mercury or lemmings, all without apparent concern, let alone anything even remotely resembling Road Rage.

And aboard the motorscooters are young women in business attire or, less often, traditional Vietnamese dresses called *ao dais*, or simple blouses and trousers (we used to call them pajamas, but they're not), men in business suits or blue jeans, flip-flops, and Jimi Hendrix t-shirts, two to a bike, three to a bike, sometimes whole families, dad driving while holding an infant, mom behind with a small child standing between the parents. Or maybe a crate of chickens strapped to the seat behind the driver. Or behind the driver and a passenger. Or a couple of pigs. One man had a refrigerator, lying horizontal, balanced on the back of his scooter. Others had baskets of produce stacked on either side like fat saddlebags piled so high you couldn't see the driver. Or cases of beer. Or bags of cement mix.

We arrived during rush hour, but motorscooters fill the streets late into the evening. Cruising on one's motorscooter is apparently a major social activity. After checking into our hotel, I wanted to show Anne the nearby Saigon River. But when we got to the boulevard that runs along the waterfront, the scooter traffic was so constant, so dense, so relentless, that we were afraid to attempt to cross. I couldn't get beyond the potential irony of surviving 13 months in combat only to be run down and killed by a 20-something Vietnamese yuppie on a Kawasaki Slingshot. We walked around the block instead, passing the Majestic Hotel Graham Greene wrote about in *The Quiet American*. When I had stayed there in 1985, the elevators sometimes worked, the air conditioning didn't, and the restaurant's menu offered fewer choices than a Soviet-style election ballot. Now it's a five-star hotel and casino.

XIII. FORMERLY I CORPS

But we weren't much interested in Ho Chi Minh City, neither Ken nor I ever having been there during the war, so the next day we flew to Hue-Phu Bai Airport aboard a nifty modern Vietnam Airlines A321. (The last time I'd flown Vietnam Airlines, 21 years ago, the airline had boasted a fleet of aging Soviet aircraft that did not inspire confidence.) This was the area Ken and I had come to see, the coastal region of central Vietnam between Hoi An and the old Demilitarized Zone at the 17th parallel, the area in which Ken and I and the 1st Battalion, 1st Marine Regiment had spent our time in the war.

Phu Bai had been a huge Marine base during the war, but all evidence of that was gone. Indeed, aside from the ubiquitous soldiers' cemeteries, the occasional monument or statue, a fleeting glimpse of old revetments at Tan Son Nhut and Da Nang, evidence of the American War is hard to find. Even the concrete bunkers atop Hai Van Pass and at either end of the railroad bridge over Song Cai (the Cai River) were built by the French, not the Americans. Ken and I spent more than an hour trying to find our old battalion command post near Hoi An, but when our van ended up on a road no wider than our own wheel base, and it seemed for all the world that we were going to topple over at any moment and end up in a rice field, we gave up looking. Where had all these people and houses and roads come from? When I was 18, I would have sworn nothing would ever again thrive in this place.

Of course, I've since learned, I would have been wrong. Rutted, crumbling Highway 1, made famous by Bernard Fall's *Street Without Joy*, is now four lanes between Phu Bai and Hue with a median strip sporting palm trees and flowering plants, the road lined with houses, noodle shops, sundry stores, repair shops, dress shops (western-style dresses seem to have largely replaced traditional *ao dais* except for jobs like hotel receptionists, restaurant hostesses, and airline employees), and billboards advertising cellphones, banks, cars, gasoline, scooters, resorts, insurance companies, clothing, restaurants.

As we approached Hue, we crossed the bridge over the An Cuu Canal, just as Ken and I had done on the morning of January 31st, 1968, but the war was nowhere to be seen and there were no ghosts awaiting us, just a vibrant, throbbing city that was almost unrecognizable except for major landmarks like the Truong Tien Bridge spanning Song Huong — the River of Perfumes — Hue University, and of course the famous Citadel.

Ken and I and a handful of other Marines had crossed Truong Tien Bridge during that first day of fighting, though we couldn't have told you its name. We had tried to reach the Citadel, but had taken terrible casualties at the hands of hundreds of well-entrenched North Vietnamese firing down at us from windows and walls, and we'd had to fall back to the south side of the river, where most of the fighting took place during the first few weeks of the battle. Now the bridge is lit up nightly by an array of ever-changing colored lights that make the lights illuminating Philadelphia's Ben Franklin Bridge look anemic.

XIV. Towers, Tombs & Tunnels

And this time, we were able to reach the Citadel without a shot being fired. The Imperial City of the Nguyen Dynasty, the last emperors of Vietnam, it shows both the ravages of the savage fighting and the deterioration from decades of neglect. Designated a World Heritage Site, only slowly is it being rebuilt by the Vietnamese with help from UNESCO, but the portions that have been restored suggest a magnificent opulence to rival anything Europe's crowned heads could boast of.

We also visited the tombs of Tu Duc, 4th Nguyen emperor (1848–1883), and Khai Dinh, 12th Nguyen emperor (1916–1925). Tu Duc, known as the "poet-emperor," placed his tomb on the grounds of the summer palace he built for himself, his wife, and his concubines. The history of his reign, which he wrote himself, is carved into a marble tablet weighing 20,000 kilograms, and is unique in that Tu Duc was the first Vietnamese emperor to criticize himself in his own history.

The tomb of Khai Dinh is by far the most expensive of the twelve Nguyen tombs, and was built entirely of materials imported from Europe. By the time of his reign, Vietnam was firmly in France's colonial grip, and Khai Dinh was little more than a figurehead doing the bidding of the French. The pomposity of his tomb reflects the emptiness of his reign. Only one more Nguyen emperor would follow him, the laughably pathetic Bao Dai, who took the throne as a child in 1925, spent most of his reign womanizing on the French Riviera, abdicated in favor of Ho Chi Minh in 1945, rescinded his abdication and returned to the French fold in 1948, got voted out in favor of Ngo Dinh Diem in a 1955 election

Seven-tiered pagoda at the entrance to the Holy Lady Buddhist Monastery on the western outskirts of Hue (photograph by Sachiko Akama).

rigged by Diem with the support of the Americans, and died in 1997 in France, where he is buried.

One morning we took a boat ride up the River of Perfumes to visit the Holy Lady Pagoda and Monastery, built in 1603, where young boys of six and seven still begin training to be monks, choosing after high school whether to remain or go out into the world. On display is the Austin automobile that carried Thich Quang Duc to Saigon in 1963, where he burned himself to death in protest of Diem's persecution of Buddhists. The car is here because Thich Quang Duc was the monastery's head monk.

On another day, we drove from Hue to the old Demilitarized Zone marked by the Song Ben Hai. We walked — stoop-shouldered most of the way — through the tunnels of Vinh Moc just north of the DMZ, where an entire village of 70 families lived underground for six years to escape U.S. bombardment. We walked across the river, from north to south, on the Hien Luong Bridge, destroyed by U.S. bombing in 1967, but rebuilt post-war for pedestrian traffic. Several miles to the west of the bridge is Con Thien ("the place of angels" in Vietnamese), where Ken and I had spent a month living

The Austin automobile in which Thich Quang Duc rode to Saigon to immolate himself in protest of Ngo Dinh Diem's repression of Buddhists in 1963. Holy Lady Monastery, Hue. Malcolm Browne's famous photograph is visible on the wall behind the car (photograph by Sachiko Akama).

in a mud-infested, barbed wire-encircled collection of sandbagged bunkers, besieged by North Vietnamese artillery from the north side of the DMZ, but we could not go there because the area, still sewn with American mines, is too dangerous.

XV. VIBRANT VIETNAM

Rice farming remains the primary economic activity of many Vietnamese, and on the drive to and from the DMZ, we could see farmers busily preparing their fields for the second of three annual crops the climate of the region allows. While we saw water buffalo grazing here and there, those lumbering beasts that inhabit the memories of almost any American who ever served in Vietnam during the war, we saw only one being used to plow a field. Most farmers now have motorized — if primitive — tractors, some that allow the driver to sit, others that the driver walks behind like a powered lawn mower. The planting itself, however, still seems to be done by hand, the very paradigm of backbreaking labor. (In Japan, machines are used to plant the rice, and one wonders how long it will be before that technology reaches Vietnam.)

Everywhere you go, there is building, building, building. The construction industry is booming. In the cities. In the country. In the ever-expanding suburbs. Roads. Bridges. Houses. High-rise offices. Hotels. The ramshackle tin-and-cardboard hovels so many Vietnamese cobbled together during the war are gone. Even the thatched-roof rural houses are mostly gone, replaced by brick homes with ceramic tile roofs. A new hospital is going up north of Hue. An industrial park is going in south of Dong Ha.

And the beaches all up and down the coast of Vietnam are sprouting resorts like mushrooms after a hard rain. Where there isn't a resort, one is under construction, or soon to be built according to the billboard posted on the site. In Hoi An, we stayed in the Hoi An Beach Resort, just

A cubicle housing one of the 70 families who lived in the Vinh Moc tunnels during the American War. The figures make it clear how cramped the quarters were (photograph by Anne Ehrhart).

across Phuoc Trac Bridge, where in 1967 there had been a small fishing village and a mangrove forest, the scene of some sharp engagements with the local Viet Cong. In Nha Trang, we stayed at the Sunrise Beach Hotel & Spa. If you hurry, you can buy a condominium along one of the fairways of the Greg Norman Golf Course at China Beach, Da Nang.

XVI. POTPOURRI

Back in Hue, Anne and I visited the old market across the street from the Huda Beer factory (the beer factory is new since I was last there in 1990; the market is probably older than the Citadel). Partly sheltered, partly open, the market is a vast and bewildering array of baskets, shoes, watches, grain bags, spices, t-shirts, hog ribs, dried fish, chinaware, trinkets and baubles, candy, blue jeans, hats, bananas, onions, lichees, think of something, anything, you will find it here if you wander long enough.

Truong Tien Bridge spanning the River of Perfumes in Hue City. In 1968, on the first day of the Tet Offensive, we fought our way across this bridge only to be driven back again by North Vietnamese soldiers entrenched on the north side of the river. In 2011, Anne and I took a leisurely stroll, hand in hand, across the same bridge (photograph by Sachiko Akama).

Next door to the market, on the way to the Truong Tien Bridge, is a far-less-interesting modern grocery store and mall, complete with KFC. Anne and I passed up that attraction in favor of a leisurely stroll across the bridge. Four decades ago, Ken and I had fought our way over that bridge only to have to fight our way back again, losing friends in both directions. Now here I was, hand in hand with my wife, enjoying the river and the motorscooter traffic (no cars allowed on this bridge), enjoying the other pedestrians, many hand in hand as we were, enjoying the moment.

There was much to enjoy. We traveled by motorboat to a fish farm in Nha Trang Bay, toured the Cham-built Hindu temples of Po Nagar (the oldest dating back to the 8th century), listened to a young woman playing a stone xylophone (called a lithophone) at Hoi Quan Vinh, climbed Marble Mountain, where during the war the Viet Cong had hidden a military hospital right under the noses of the Americans at Da Nang, went swimming in the turquoise waters of the South China Sea, and then ate a cooked-on-the-beach barbeque of fresh prawns, squid, beef, pork, tomatoes, and cucumber on Hon Mun (Ebony Island).

XVII. THE HOUSE IN HUE, 2011

But the most amazing experience of the entire trip was finding the building Ken and I had been in when we'd been wounded. It took some work to find the building — as we'd already seen, a lot changes in 43 years — but we found it. I wasn't sure, at first. But the positioning of the house relative to the street, and to the river several blocks away, and the configuration of the windows: this had to be the house. We had been in the room behind that second-floor window. The NVA gunner had fired from one of the buildings across the street.

Ken and me standing in front of the house we had been in when we were both wounded by the same B-40 rocket-propelled grenade 43 years earlier. The building now houses the business offices of the four-star Duy Tan Hotel (photograph by Anne Ehrhart).

The house, which in 1968 had stood by itself in the middle of a large grass yard with a cinderblock wall around it, has since been entirely refurbished. Looking fresh, crisp, and bright, it appears to be no older than the six-story four-star hotel built in two sections behind it, the two wings of the hotel forming an L into which the house nestles. The grass lawn has been replaced by a tiled driveway and parking area with a motorscooter rental operation and an outdoor coffee shop. The house itself is now the business and administrative offices for the hotel, the Duy Tan (named for yet another emperor). A young woman inside who spoke English told us that the hotel had been built in 2004, but the house dated to 1920. That was the clincher. This was the place. We were so amazed to be here, alive and happy and 62 years old (well, Ken is 63), that we did not have the presence of mind to ask if we could go up to the very room itself. No matter. This was close enough.

That evening, Anne, Ken, and I, accompanied by Sachiko Akama, the photographer who traveled with us, went for an evening cruise on the River of Perfumes. On board with us were eight Vietnamese singers and musicians in traditional garb who performed traditional Vietnamese folk music for us. When they were finished, they gave us each two paper bags with candles inside. The tradition is to light the candles, make a wish, and set the bags

Vietnamese singers and musicians who entertained us during an evening cruise on the River of Perfumes (photograph by Sachiko Akama).

afloat on the river. I cannot begin to tell you how magical that evening was, how profoundly satisfying, especially for two ex–Marines who had nearly died only blocks from that river so many years ago.

Later, standing on a balcony of the Mercure Hue Gerbera Hotel, Ken and I looked out over the city and the river bisecting it. We could see the huge red and yellow Vietnamese national flag flying above the Citadel, illuminated by floodlights, the university that had been used as a refugee center during the battle, the park that had been our helicopter landing zone, the roofs of what had been the MACV compound (Military Assistance Command, Vietnam), even a corner of that building we'd been in when we'd been wounded, now dwarfed by the hotel built around it. But the streets were crowded with noisy, jostling, energetic people on foot, on bicycles, in cars, in buses, and of course on scooters, scooters, and more scooters. Vendors hawked postcards and fresh bread and river tours. The river flowed with colorful tour boats. The bridge, with an unbroken stream of motorscooters going in both directions, blazed yellow to green to blue to purple to red and back to yellow. The Huda beer sign cast a neon ribbon across the water. We did not speak. There was nothing to say. This is what we had come to see. A country. Not a war.

Military History of W. D. Ehrhart

W. D. Ehrhart enlisted in the United States Marine Corps on 11 April 1966, while still in high school, beginning active duty on 17 June. He graduated from basic recruit training at the Marine Corps Recruit Depot, Parris Island, South Carolina, on 12 August, receiving a meritorious promotion to private first class, and completed basic infantry training at Camp Lejeune, North Carolina, on 12 September 1966. (While at Parris Island, he qualified as a rifle sharpshooter on 18 July 1966, subsequently qualifying as a rifle expert on 11 April 1968 and as a pistol sharpshooter on 24 April 1969.)

Assigned to the field of combat intelligence, Ehrhart spent 10 October to 15 December 1966 with Marine Air Group 26, a helicopter unit based at New River Marine Corps Air Facility, North Carolina, meanwhile completing a clerk typist course at Camp Lejeune in November 1966 and graduating first in his class from the Enlisted Basic Amphibious Intelligence School at Little Creek Amphibious Base, Norfolk, Virginia, in December 1966. He also completed a Marine Corps Institute combat intelligence correspondence course in December while at New River.

Before leaving for Vietnam on 9 February 1967, Ehrhart received additional combat training with the 3rd Replacement Company, Staging Battalion, Camp Pendleton, California, in January and February. Upon arrival in Vietnam, he was assigned to the 1st Battalion, 1st Marine Regiment, first as an intelligence assistant, later as assistant intelligence chief. In March 1967, he was temporarily assigned to the Sukiran Army Education Center, Okinawa, where he graduated first in his class from a course in basic Vietnamese terminology before returning to permanent assignment.

While in Vietnam, Ehrhart participated in the following combat operations: Stone, Lafayette, Early, Canyon, Calhoun, Pike, Medina, Lancaster, Kentucky I, Kentucky II, Kentucky III, Con Thien, Newton, Osceola II, and Hue City. He was promoted to lance corporal on 1 April 1967 and meritoriously promoted to corporal on 1 July 1967.

Ehrhart was awarded the Purple Heart Medal for wounds received in action in Hue City during the Tet Offensive, a commendation from Major General Donn J. Robertson commanding the 1st Marine Division, two Presidential Unit Citations, the Navy Combat Action Ribbon, the Vietnam Service Medal with three stars, the Vietnamese Campaign Medal, a Cross of Gallantry Meritorious Unit Citation, and a Civil Action Meritorious Unit Citation.

Ehrhart was next assigned to the 2nd Marine Air Wing Headquarters Group at Cherry Point Marine Corps Air Station, North Carolina, from 30 March to 10 June 1968, where he was promoted to sergeant on 1 April. After a brief assignment with the Headquarters Squadron of Marine Air Group 15 based at Iwakuni Marine Corps Air Station, Japan, he was then reassigned to Marine Aerial Refueler Transport Squadron 152, Futema Marine Corps Air Facility, Okinawa, from 20 July to 30 October 1968, where he received a commanding officer's Meritorious Mast.

Ehrhart completed his active duty with Marine Fighter Attack Squadron 122, based alternately at Iwakuni and Cubi Point Naval Air Station, Philippines, from 31 October 1968 to 30 May 1969. While in the Philippines, he completed a field course on jungle environmental survival in February 1969.

On 10 June 1969, Ehrhart was separated from active duty, receiving the Good Conduct Medal. While on inactive reserve, he was promoted to staff sergeant on 1 July 1971. He received an honorable discharge on 10 April 1972.

About the Author

W. D. Ehrhart was born in 1948 in Roaring Spring, Pennsylvania, and grew up in Lewisburg and Perkasie, also in Pennsylvania. His first published poetry appeared in the 1972 anthology *Winning Hearts and Minds: War Poems by Vietnam Veterans*. Since then, his prose and poetry have appeared in hundreds of publications ranging from the *Los Angeles Times* and the *Cleveland Plain Dealer* to the *Utne Reader* and *Reader's Digest* to *American Poetry Review* and the *Virginia Quarterly Review*. He has spoken before hundreds of audiences including all three of the U.S. service academies, the Dwight D. Eisenhower Library, the Asia Society, the Maureen and Mike Mansfield Center, Oxford University, Karl Franzens Universitat, and Universidad de Sevilla. The recipient of the President's Medal from Veterans for Peace, an Excellence in the Arts Award from Vietnam Veterans of America, a Pew Fellowship in the Arts, and two Pennsylvania Council on the Arts Fellowships, he teaches English and history at the Haverford School in suburban Philadelphia, where he also coaches winter track and sponsors the student arts and literature magazine. Ehrhart and his wife Anne, married since 1981, are the parents of a grown daughter, Leela. *Dead on a High Hill* is Ehrhart's 20th book.

Index

Aeschylus 20
Akama, Sachiko 184
Alburger, David 89
Amin, Idi 8
Anderson, Doug 73
Annesley, Billy 93
Apple, Jeff 95
Appleman, Philip 26
Arden, Bill 91
Aristotle 82
Arnold, Matthew 21

Baky, John 87
Balaban, John 4, 26, 73, 87, 98–106, 108, 147
Balaban, Tally 105
Bao Dai 179
Barleycorn, John 24
Barnett, Colin 91, 92
Barry, Jan 4, 67–69, 84, 87, 100, 160
Becker, Joe 89
Bennett, Alden 89
Berrettini, Jack 93
bin Laden, Osama 131
Bishop, Elizabeth 26
Bishop, John Peale 147
Blake, William 19
Blunden, Edmund 137, 139, 147
Bly, Robert 30
Borges, Jorge Luis 45
Bourke, Billy 135
Brady, James 148
Brokaw, Tom 148
Brooke, Rupert 139
Brown, Dee 121
Browne, Malcolm 180
Browning, Elizabeth 21
Browning, Robert 21
Burns, Robert 30
Bush, George W. 13, 88

Butler, Smedley 78, 121
Bylinoski, Mike 164

Calica, Lovella 111
Caputo, Philip 147
Carruth, Hayden 33, 57, 109–110, 149–151
Cassidy, Don 26, 89, 91, 92
Castro, Fidel 78
Catina, Ray 73–74; see also Catlin, Alan
Catlin, Alan 73–74
Catullus 20
Chaucer, Geoffrey 19
Childress, William 32, 42, 49, 54, 74, 110, 149, 152–156, 161
Ciardi, John 107, 147, 160
Clark, Petula 144
Clark, Ramsey 78
Coffman, Lisa 26, 27
Cole, Charles F. 148
Coleridge, Samuel Taylor 30
Conein, Lucien 85
Connolly, David V. 73, 87, 147
Conrad, Joseph 30
Corn, Alfred 57
Cotter, J.F. 57
Cowley, Malcolm 147
Cox, Joseph T. 3
Crandell, Bill 87
Crane, Stephen 17, 18, 22, 23, 28, 29, 96
Creeley, Robert 25
Crumb, Jan B. 67; see also Barry, Jan
cummings, e.e. 147

Dean, John 113
Deck, John 148
Depew, Donald 148
Dickey, James 26, 53
Dickinson, Emily 21, 32, 43
Diehl, John B. 28, 29
Dionysus 24

Donne, John 3, 19, 20, 27, 28
Douglass, Scott 53
Dryden, John 20
Dutton, Garrett 17, 28; *see also* G. Love

Eberhart, Richard 43, 107, 147, 160
Edwards, Craig 92
Ehrhart, Anne 2, 168, 182, 184, 189
Ehrhart, Leela 2, 84, 189
Eisenstadt, Alfred 107, 108
Elia 74
Eliot, T.S. 19, 20, 21
Elliott, James 143
Elliott, Mary 143
Elliott, Robert 143
Elliott, Robert James 139–143
Emerson, Gloria 4, 83–87, 148
Euripides 20
Exler, Samuel 4, 125–131

Fall, Bernard 121, 178
Fast, Howard 33
Faulkner, William 20
Fitzgerald, Frances 121
Flint, R.W. 57
Floyd, Bryan Alec 74, 160
Flynn, Sean 102
Fonda, Jane 77
Forche, Carolyn 149
Fossey, Dian 8, 10
Frank, Pat 148
Franklin, Benjamin 77, 112
Franklin, Robert 1, 3
Frazier, Joe 84, 100
Frederick, Thomas E. 170
Freneau, Philip 147
Frost, Robert 21, 73
Fugard, Athol 20
Fussell, Paul 125, 149

G. Love 16, 17, 18; *see also* Dutton, Garrett
Gaffney, Gerry 164
Gallagher, T.C. 94
Galvin, B. 57
Gamble, Kathy 26
Gibson, Mel 19
Ginsburg, Allen 18, 26, 68
Grant, Cary 19
Graves, Robert 139
Greco, Blobby 94
Green, Graham 123, 177
Griffin, Jamie 170
Gustafson, Richard 56

Halberstam, David 121
Hall, Donald 106

Hallowell, Edward R. 106
Hammond, Mac 3, 23
Hardy, Thomas 21
Hassett, Steve 160
Heaney, Seamus 26
Heller, Joseph 147
Hendrix, Jimi 32
Hinojosa, Rolando 32, 42, 111, 152, 161
Hirsch, Edward 106
Hitler, Adolf 118
Ho Chi Minh 98, 115, 116, 117, 120, 131, 179
Ho Xuan Huong 18, 105
Hoffman, Barbara 96
Hollenbach, Robert F. 30
Holmes, Regina 126
Homer 147
Hurley, Kevin 44
Hussein, Saddam 131
Huston, John 155

Jacquette, Pete 92
James, Henry 50
Jarrell, Randall 107, 147, 160
Jason, Philip K. 148
Jeffers, Robinson 32, 45
Jefferson, Thomas 79, 115
Jenkins, Stover 92
Jesus of Nazareth 22
Johnson, Lyndon 79, 118, 119, 131
Jones, James 147

Karlin, Wayne 87
Keats, John 21, 32
Kennedy, John F. 118
Ketwig, John 87
Khai Dinh 178–179
Khrushchev, Nikita 119
Kim, Richard 148
Kim Jong Il 77
Kinzie, Mary 57
Kipling, Rudyard 147
Knight, Etheridge 149
Komunyakaa, Yusef 26, 147
Kovic, Ron 147
Kubrik, Stanley 127

Lamb, Charles *see* Elia
Landis, Kendall 89, 90
Larteguy, Jean 121
Laurence, Jack 87
Lazarus, Emma 77
Leaf, Eric W. 36
Leepson, Marc 87
LeGuin, Ursula 57
Lembcke, Jerry 124

Lemke, Brad 89
Lerner, Linda 73
Levertov, Denise 20
Lewis, C. Day 137
Lichty, Lawrence 124
Liebler, Shelby 17
Longfellow, Henry Wadsworth 23
Loving, Travis 94

Maas, Roland 165
MacArthur, Douglas 35, 37
MacLeish, Archibald 51, 53
Magner, James, Jr. 33, 42–51, 54, 152
Mailer, Norman 106, 147
Mansfield, Mike 79
Martz, Louis 56
Marvell, Andrew 20, 27
Marx, Karl 22
McAdoo, James H. 90–93
McAdoo, James J., Jr. 4, 89–93
McAuliff, John 87
McCarthy, Gerald 2, 109, 160
McCarthy, Joseph 153
McClatchy, J.D. 56
McDonald, Walt 147
McGrath, Thomas 33, 149, 151–152, 161
McKinstry, Bobby 92
McKuen, Rod 18
McNamara, Robert 79, 113, 122
McPherson, Myra 148
McRae, John 58
Melville, Herman 30, 45
Meredith, James 51–54, 55
Miller, Jerome 33–40
Milton, John 19, 20
Moffat, Abbot Low 116
Mooney, William 142–143
Moore, Randy 88
Morrison, Toni 20
Mozart, Wolfgang Amadeus 32
Myers, William L. 165

Nemerov, Howard 107–108, 147, 160
Ngo Dinh Diem 85, 117, 118, 179
Nguyen Ai Quoc 115; *see also* Ho Chi Minh
Nguyen Cao Ky 118
Nixon, Richard 113

Obama, Barack 132
O'Brien, Tim 106, 147
Okabe, Morinobu 175
O'Neill, Eugene 20, 30
Ovid 20, 103
Owen, Wilfred 4, 137–138, 139, 147

Page, Tim 102

Pargeter, Edith *see* Peters, Ellis
Patti, Archimedes 116
Peters, Ellis 74
Pfannestiel, Todd 75
Piaff, Edith 32
Pierce, Paula Kay 68–69
Pinzur, Ellen 87
Plath, Sylvia 23, 27
Plato 82
Pope, Alexander 19, 20
Pound, Ezra 21, 28
Prados, John 87

Rabe, David 147
Ramberg, Paal 33–39
Ramsdell, Sheldon 68
Reagan, Ronald 76, 78
Redding, Otis 146
Ricks, Thomas 132
Ritter, Scott 78, 132
Ritterbusch, Dale 73, 147
Robinson, Fred 93
Rooney, Gerard 139, 142, 143
Roosevelt, Franklin D. 119
Rosenberg, Isaac 139, 147
Rosenthal, Joe 107
Ross, Bob 164, 166
Ross, Diana 145
Rostow, Walt 118
Rottmann, Larry 84
Rush, Larry 94, 96
Rusk, Dean 123
Russ, Martin 148

Saint Marie, Buffy 144
Sakamura, Shinmin 175
Sandburg, Carl 22, 27, 28
Saner, Reg 32, 51, 54–63, 108–109, 149, 152, 161
Sassoon, Siegfried 60, 139, 147, 155
Seeger, Alan 147
Serling, Rod 148
Shakespeare, William 21
Shelley, Percy 21
Sherkow, Mark 89
Sherman, William T. 112
Sickle, Stephen 89
Silkin, Jon 25
Simpson, Louis 111
Slack, Dan 19
Smith, Bob 91, 92
Socrates 114
Soldati, Joseph 110
Sorley, Charles Hamilton 139, 147
Spencer, Edmund 19
Stalin, Joseph 116

Stallworthy, Jon 149
Stevens, Wallace 21, 32
Stith, Peter 56
Styron, William 148
Summers, Harry, Jr.

Takenaga, Kazunori "Ken" 163–185
Tennyson, Alfred 32, 147
Terkel, Studs 106, 148
Thich Quang Duc 118, 179, 180
Thoreau, Henry David 8
Tokisada, Shiro 173
Trosky, Susan 52
Troy, Jeff 91,92
Truman, Harry 116
Tu Duc 178
Turner, Brian 111, 147
Twain, Mark 74, 147

Van Devanter, Lynda 73
Van Gogh, Vincent 105
Van Winkle, Clint 132, 147
Vedder, Amy 8–16
Vedder, Ethan 11, 12, 14, 15
Villalba, Cindy 68

Virgil 147
Vo Nguyen Giap 168
Voegtlen, Barney 91, 92

Walcott, Derek 55, 106
Wantling, William 33, 42, 43
Washington, George 77
Weber, Bill 8–16
Weber, Noah 11, 13, 14, 15
Weigl, Bruce 99, 147
Whalen, Richard 48
White, Robert 78
Whitman, Walt 43, 112, 147
Williams, D.H. 57
Williams, William Carlos 25
Williamson, Michael 57
Wilson, Keith 32, 42, 49, 54, 109, 149, 152,
    153, 156–160, 161
Wilson, Woodrow 115
Wordsworth, William 19
Worman, Ken 88

Yeats, William Butler 20, 21

Zedong, Mao 116